SIMON VERSUS SIMON

SIMON
versus
SIMON

The Story of Lucius &
the Magician's Duel

A NOVEL

PHILIP E. SEARS

OVERHILL PRESS | MANHATTAN

Published by Overhill Press
Manhattan, Kansas
OverhillPress@gmail.com

ISBN 978-0-578-54490-8 (paperback edition)
ISBN 978-0-578-54492-2 (ebook edition)

First Edition

Book design by Ashley Muehlbauer

Printed in the United States of America

For Melissa

Who reminded me I was no longer creating things

CONTENTS

SIMON VERSUS SIMON

PROLOGUE

This is a first-hand account of the birth of Christianity in the first century Anno Domini. The Roman Empire reigned over the Mediterranean, from Mesopotamia to Lusitania, from Arabia to Germania and as far in the northwest as Britannia. A tyrant named Nero ruled the Roman Empire. This is the story of my adventures as a young man as I journey through the empire. This is a tale of biblical proportions. This is also the story of a magician's duel.

Now, looking down from the kingdom of heaven, having watched the centuries pass from the dark ages through the Renaissance, on to the industrial revolution, and now through the modern era towards outer space exploration and cyberspace information. The current year is 1998 and the second Millennium approaches quickly. I've held my tongue for the last two thousand years—and now I think it is time to tell my story.

My dear 20th century reader, as I tell you this story, please keep in mind that this is my own story as an eyewitness.

You may ask yourself what is more reliable, an eyewitness or written history? Eyewitness accounts are notoriously unreliable. History is famously written by the winners. Also, two thousand years of history have unfolded, and that could have warped my memory before I've even written a page. This account may not be complete accuracy from a personal or historical perspective. Nevertheless, as I take you through this autobiographical journey, I trust that the larger truth will reveal itself.

Allow me to introduce myself. My name is Lucius Octavius Aurelius. I was born a Roman citizen, in what you would call the first century Anno Domini, in the glorious city of Rome. Rome was the capital of the Roman Empire and the center of western civilization, boasting more than a million permanent citizens. My early years were typical of a Roman citizen of the higher class and wealth. My father, a patrician, was very much connected through business and politics. Through family wealth and the status of my class, I had been privileged with nutrition, safety, education, land, the right to run for office, and other benefits that were not afforded to many people in the empire. (In the spirit of a 20th century style retelling, I use Anno Domini rather than Roman years, even though the Anno Domini reckoning are not adopted for another five centuries.) My life story only starts to get interesting in 54 Anno Domini at the age of seventeen when my preceding sheltered life changed drastically.

Yes, I was a wealthy Roman citizen and a resident of Rome during the finest days of Pax Romana. My father, Decimus Octavius Aurelius, had done quite well for himself as a politician and landowner. He had always wanted me to walk in his footsteps and become a politician. I had other ideas.

Why is it that the son of a wealthy father would want to seek a higher purpose in life and the son of a poor father would want to seek wealth? Father and I were always at odds with each other. If we found common ground, we would toil to find opposing views. Our real differences were philosophical, but they often manifested in trivial disagreements.

Arguments were fought out at the dinner table or during family activities, my mother watching over, indifferent, hoping more that the spat would be over with than it would be resolved. My father was extremely proud to be Roman. He had worked tirelessly to build his reputation and his political capital. I was entirely indifferent to both. The Roman Empire had advanced achievements in military, architecture, and technology. On the other side, the Romans had committed war crimes and countless cruelties such as crucifixions, gladiatorial sacrifices, and mass murder. But, at that stage in my life, I can assure you those concerns did not weigh heavily on my mind. Why should I be so proud of an identity that I was simply born into rather than something of my own design? Why would I give my life to an empire that could not reciprocate any interest in my welfare or fulfillment?

I wanted to feel the warmth of the earth, embrace my fellow citizens, and discover new cultures and new ways of thinking. Looking back two thousand years, this had much more to do with teenage idealism. But, nevertheless, I wanted to experience life and see the world, not just be part of a class that ruled over it.

Life takes on man more than man takes on life. I claim no divinity. Nor do I claim any talents for evangelism or any special skills in theology. As a matter of circumstance or fate, I held witness to the crucible of Christianity. I met sinners and saints, apostles and profits. I also encountered soothsayers, pagans, druids, and magicians along the way. Often, I met many ordinary people trying to understand the purpose of life beyond survival and fortune. I have discovered that inherent in mankind is a desire to look up to some higher power. Or to bring order to the cosmos. Or to seek out mysticism or symbolism from the banality of life.

PART I

BEGINS IN ROME

1

ROMANS WILL BE ROMANS

One beautiful afternoon I took a deliberate stroll through the streets of Rome. I had plans to meet up with some of my friends. I traversed the exhilarating streets from my domicile heading down towards Subura, pushing through the crowds of shoppers and people of all kinds. I absorbed the cacophony of travelers, shopkeepers, and soothsayers. As I shoved through the pungent crowd the bare skin of the plebeians dampened my fresh toga with sweat. As I escaped one cramped alleyway, and left that stench of human waste behind me, the bright afternoon sun warmed my bare neck. Buzzing with youthful excitement, I stopped at a wine shop and purchased two jugs of white wine. Then I headed through lower Subura, towards the Viminalis Hill.

Subura, Rome's original suburb, was a frequent meeting place for our usual gang. It was a seedy place, crawling with the kind of fascinating taverns and characters that attracted young men like us. The dirty, narrow alleys seethed with the poor, lower-class, and criminal elements. Taverns, red-light districts, and shops for money changers, barbers, ironmongers, blacksmiths, and other tradesmen lined the crowded streets. For my parents and other high-class citizens, these filthy shops were a place to avoid. The higher classes loathed the area so much that the massive Servian Wall was built around it to partition the whole district from the Forum.

Subura was also a bustling place of commerce and trade. In those narrow alleys you could purchase leather, wool, wheat, bread, beef, chicken, vegetables, spices, jewelry and about anything else you desire. These shops, called tabernae, were public stores on the first floor of multistory apartment houses, or insulae, where many of the lower-class Romans lived. My father would often send servants to do his bidding when he wanted to trade with shops in Subura, which were often run by foreigners.

Heading towards our regular meeting place, I relaxed near a fountain on the Viminalis Hill. This spot was a nicer, cleaner area for a meeting than the low areas in Subura that we would prowl in the evening. I made myself comfortable and began to imbibe wine, starting with the first jug from an Etruscan vineyard. Enjoying the warming sensation of the wine and the hot sunlight on my face, I gazed out from the hilltop view and was overwhelmed with a fiery sense of optimism. Staring out at the horizon, I made out all the broccoli-shaped pine trees and tall cone-shaped Cyprus trees that glistened in the sun. That solitary moment allowed my mind to wonder and for I to ponder. I thought about my future and those limitless possibilities that are both vague and grandiose. Perhaps owning a grand villa with finely dressed servants, or giving a moving oration to a crowd of loyal followers.

After looking out at the view for a long while, I sat down against the fountain and stretched out my legs.

"Lucius!" My old friend Rufus arrived and cheerfully greeted me, waking me from my contemplation.

"Oh, hello. I beat you here for a change," I said. Rufus approached. I offered him some wine, which he readily took.

Of course, at that time, I did not literally say "oh" nor would I greet someone with a "hello." If I wrote this narrative in the native languages of Vulgar Latin, Aramaic, or ancient Greek, my readers would not be able to follow. Have you ever noticed that most adaptations of ancient stories in modern English use proper English? They write and deliver the dialog in such a dramatic and theatrical way that is so unnatural. Trust me when I say that this adaptation holds more to the spirit and tone of the conversation than a blockbuster film or even Shakespeare. *The Tragedy of Julius Caesar*, for instance, was written in Old English and contained many anachronisms. I'm certain nobody in ancient Rome spoke like a character in a Shakespeare play. William Shakespeare himself would not have a real conversation in the style of the dialogue in a Shakespeare play. So, I will attempt to hold to the spirit of the language rather than the literal translation.

I had known Rufus for most of my life, and he was a very loyal friend. We didn't always agree, but our past bonds

9

created a common ground. We were childhood friends, class-
mates, and my father had known his father. His father was
greatly admired as a political architect, but as a parent, he
had been mostly absent from Rufus's life. His father had
an affair with a plebeian woman that had a scandalous reputation. The family tried to keep the affair a secret and took
Rufus in as a bastard son to be raised among his legitimate
half-brothers. But this relationship was an open secret known
by all but spoken about only privately. Although his father
was initially sentimental about Rufus as a baby, he became an
unwanted child. Rufus was raised among patrician citizens
and afforded superficial luxuries. On the other hand, as a
bastard, he was mistreated at home by his half-brothers. He
was only a spiteful memory for his stepmother.

"Muntimer and I are going to go down to the Caput Porcus
tonight. You should come with us," Rufus suggested. Caput
Porcus was a dark and dingy tavern in Subura.

Muntimer was even more of a troublemaker than Rufus.
Walking the streets at night in Subura was not only a rebellious teenage adventure, but it was also quite dangerous.
A visible criminal element prowled the streets unhindered
since the police mostly avoided that section of Rome. One
minor comfort was that Muntimer and his friends were part
of that criminal element. And Rufus, due to his rebellious
nature, was friends with Muntimer.

"Now you know I can't go with you. My parents would
never permit that." Rufus knew that I was not allowed to
go with him as my mother was more protective than his
absentee parents. I was willing to rebel against my parents
occasionally when it served me, but I was still somewhat
apprehensive about his plans for the Caput Porcus.

Just then a nice-looking young couple approached us. Felix and Octavia were arm in arm, leaning against each other in a laughing embrace. Quintus Felix Dardanus was a gifted, attractive, and all-around good person. He is one of those guys that you try to find a negative angle on but never come up with anything. His mellow and affable personality made him popular and likable. Octavia was tall, thin, and modestly attractive. Her wholesome good looks and friendliness made her even more popular than Felix.

Rufus greeted Felix warmly, but was not as welcoming to Octavia. Was this envy?

"Felix, we're going now, you should come with us," Rufus said, coaxing aggressively.

Felix didn't acknowledge the question and gave Octavia a peck on the cheek. Rufus made a subtle, jealous glance towards Octavia.

"I'm not sure if I can make it either," I said.

"Yea right, you know you're coming. I won't tell your mother on you," Rufus said.

I forced an awkward laugh to brush it away.

I shared some of the wine with Felix, and the couple sat down properly on the fountain rather than the street. Octavia and Felix were arranged to be married. Octavia, as a young woman betrothed to a patrician, was not at liberty to drink in public and carouse with us men later in the evening. Felix would have to decide whether to spend the evening with Octavia or to accompany the men to the taverns.

Rufus and Felix struck up a conversation, and I let my mind wander, feeling the wine flow through me. I was weighing the decision to go out with Rufus, conflicted between the right decision and teenage rebellion.

". . . pound for pound, the Syrian was one of the best gladiators in our lifetime."

If I followed everything my parents told me to do, I would just turn into another version of them. That would be a shame, I thought.

". . . yes, unfortunately, you don't retire of old age . . ."

I knew I was not allowed by my parents but, on the other hand, I knew that in order to experience life I had to take more risks. Carpe diem. Carpe noctem!

"Did you hear how he was slain, finally, after winning over twenty times? That was brutal and disgusting . . ."

A small cloud moved swiftly across the sky and briefly shaded the sun. Looking at Felix and Octavia, I found it frustrating that they were so happy together. What made it so easy for them?

"He was slashed across the abdomen with a short sword while he was . . ."

What in Hades made them so fortunate to have each other? Did they ever have conflicts, or how did they manage to avoid conflict? Where was the turbulence that comes with the relationship between a man and woman? Were they just simple and dull, or were they truly stable and mature at this age?

I thought of Daphne. Daphne was my summer love from last year. We hit it off very quickly. And for the rest of the summer, our relationship was magnetic. Sadly, at the end of summer, she'd moved away with her father, as had always been planned. And that had ended our relationship. She was only sixteen, but to me she wasn't a teenage girl. She was a real woman.

I thought of Daphne's long dark hair, her deeply tan skin, and her tall, striking figure. She had a prominent nose, dark beautiful eyes, and black eyebrows. Her distinguished features—her nose; her thin upper lip with slight overbite; her lanky but graceful figure—all made her more attractive to me. She was my Cleopatra.

"I agree with that. He was brave and fearless to the very end . . ."

Daphne was a free spirit with a penchant for the arts. She had benefited from a privileged education, studying history, philosophy, and poetry. She was particularly educated in philosophy, fluent in Greek and several other languages, having studied extensively while living in Greece. In those long summer days when we started courting, I would come by her home to see her sitting in her yard, studying philosophy or reading poetry.

"I have to meet up with Muntimer pretty soon. Who is with me?" Rufus said, nudging Felix on the knee with his sandal.

My nostalgia was turning to anxious excitement as I came to realize I was being talked into going with him. I was becoming intoxicated by the wine, but also by the rebellious energy that Rufus projected onto us. Although he was a bad influence, he was good at influencing people.

"Octavia and I have plans. We are going to have dinner with her cousins," Felix said. "Sorry, you guys. You have fun without us."

Octavia bid us farewell and they walked off towards home.

"Are you coming?" Rufus asked.

Rufus began to walk towards the usual place where he would meet Muntimer.

"Sure, I'm in," I replied hesitantly. I felt a mix of doubt and fear, but also the thrill of anticipation.

"Alright!" He slapped me on the back.

The sun was beginning to set behind the trees and their elongated shadows crossed our path. We set off down the wide street of Vicus Longus for a stroll through Subura. As the swaths of rough-looking plebeians walked by, we pulled our hoods up and looked down so as to not make eye contact.

2

RUFUS

You are probably familiar with those common, tasteless insults that people throw at each other. Those cliché phrases, such as, "Your mother is a —." Rufus had to deal with a greater share of those insults than most of us. Although he made sure others did not notice, he really took those insults to heart. His mother was a plebian who had a child as the result of an affair with a patrician named Gallus Plinius Macro. Gallus Plinius was a very noble citizen, highly educated, and extremely successful as a politician. But he was not a popular figure or household name. He was, however, a man of the shadows. A man who knew how to get things done, how to navigate the Roman political sphere through influence. He was a puppet master, a true artist in designing campaign strategies. He was skillful at spreading propaganda and false stories to manipulate popular opinion. Plinius had provided for Rufus and had given him a roof over his head. By misguided obligation, he allowed Rufus to grow up in his family with his other children. Rufus was never treated as a first-class member of the family, and since he was a bastard son, Rufus could never think to inherit any of his father's wealth.

When I was a boy my family had a villa in the Roman countryside. I have only childhood memories of that villa since my father sold it, for some forgotten reason, when I was eight or nine years old. I remember its tranquil beauty and expansive size. I did go back and revisit it once when I was an adult and it seemed much smaller. But as a child, it was larger than life. I would often play in the atrium where the sun shone brightly through the garden of roses, lilies, poppies, and hyacinths. Rainwater was captured in pool in the middle of the courtyard that was tiled with tiny yellow, brown, red, and blue tiles. I would sit for hours around the pool creating my own imaginary worlds with rocks, sticks, bowls, or whatever else I could find.

The villa grounds included terraced vineyards and an orchard. The entrance to the orchard was through a gated archway overgrown with vines. As a child, passing through that archway was like entering an enchanted world.

One morning, I was playing in the back of the orchard. That area of the orchard was bordered by a waist-high rock wall. I was swinging my wooden sword, fighting imaginary foes by fencing with the fruit trees. I heard something hit one of the trees and the noise startled me, so I stopped to look around. Again, I heard something hit a tree. This time I went to peer over the stone wall. On the other side, I noticed a boy, around my own age, indiscriminately throwing sticks and rocks.

"Who are you?" I asked. I attempted a tone of condescension, but the words came out in such a timid and childish voice.

"Who's asking?" the boy asked. He sounded like an adult. Fearless.

"Oh, uh," I muttered, stunned. "I'm Lucius Octavius. This is my family villa."

"I'm Rufus," the boy said, carrying on with his haphazard rock throwing. Some of the rocks were flying dangerously close to my head. "I'm a good thrower," Rufus said.

"Are you from here?" I asked.

"I am staying with my father over there," Rufus said. He pointed through the trees towards a villa on the hill. I knew from my father that was the estate of Plinius, who was a politician.

"Do you have a sword? My uncle helped me make this from leftover wood," I said. I was trying to be friendly.

"I don't need one," Rufus said.

"I can have one made for you," I said.

"No need," Rufus said, and he continued throwing dirty rocks towards my orchard. Then he quickly climbed over the stone wall and into my orchard.

He seemed intrigued by the sword. So, I approached him and handed it to him, handle first, both of us avoiding eye contact.

Then I heard a shout. Our gardener was swiftly running through the orchard towards us.

"Rufus!" The gardener shouted. "You know you are not allowed in here."

Casually, Rufus turned his back to the gardener and walked away. He climbed back over the stone wall, and then turned around to face us.

"Now go away! And stay out of our orchard," the gardener commanded. "Do you hear me?"

"Fuck you," Rufus said to the gardener.

I was in shock. Disbelief. Hardly familiar with those obscene words, I would have never imagined they could be said by a child. To an adult. I was also trying to make sense out of the expression. The first word hit home as offensive and aggressive, but I could not pair it with the other word. As a sentence, I could not understand it or tell where it was going or what it was suggesting.

Of course, this was all said in Vulgar Latin. I am now translating them into modern English in terms of equivalent obscenity, brevity, and impact.

"You little brat! You go home right now, or we will report this to your father," the gardener told Rufus.

"I am not on your side of the wa—all," Rufus taunted the gardener in a sing-song. "So, there's really not anything you can do—ooo about it."

The gardener put up his hands and groaned with the futility of it all. Then he walked away, heading back in the direction he came.

I was shocked. I was still trying to process the behavior that I had just witnessed from this new boy. He said those words so fearlessly, and so casually.

"I should probably go," I said lamely. I wanted to tell him I would make a sword for him so that we could play together. Instead, fear took over. Fear that I was going to be in trouble. That I was probably already in trouble for the both of us. Or just for him—since technically I did not do anything wrong. So, I ran back out of the orchard, through the gates, and to our villa.

Later that spring, Rufus and I did learn to sword fight. Our loyal servants created new wooden swords for us. In our own little world, we created our imaginary legions in the orchard. We quickly became friends.

Rufus and I were educated by the same tutor. We learned to read Greek, mathematics, mythology, and astrology. We were both highly educated and literate at a young age. And our education did not limit itself to academics, but encompassed the mind, body, and the spirit as well.

Rufus was emotionally close to his mother, who loved him very much, after her own fashion. It is possible that at one point in time she was beautiful, and perhaps kind. Maybe when she had been young. But by the time I met her, she was haggard, and crude and abrasive in demeanor. Sometimes I would go on outings with Rufus and his mother. These were the rare clandestine meetings that his father would arrange so that Rufus could spend time with her. Plinius also helped the woman through discrete financial arrangements. When Rufus was with his mother they would go on wild and irresponsible shopping sprees. Short adventures. I have only fond memories of these activities. When I was with them on these secret outings, I was able to do things that were fun for young boys, but were considered far beneath my parents' taste or class.

Rufus would bounce back and forth between his parents. His mother would poorly attempt to provide the emotional support while his father provided the not altogether healthy structure, and discipline. His father clearly favored his legitimate heirs. Rufus had three half-brothers, all legitimate, and one was close to Rufus in age. To his father's legal wife, Rufus was little more than an annoyance.

I RECALL ONE TRIP Rufus and I took with his father and half-brothers. We were about thirteen or fourteen years old. His father had planned a treat. He was taking his boys to the chariot races. My parents permitted me to join them. I had stayed at his father's domus in Rome with Rufus for several days leading up to the event. The competitive jealousy and favoritism of the races were palpable as race day approached.

On the morning of the event, Plinius shouted across the house at us, "Rufus, Lucius, hurry up! It is time to head out. We're walking to Circus Maximus, all of us, together."

"Come on Rufus, let's get going," I said. I shook Rufus as he seemed to be falling back asleep in his bed. As Rufus covered his head and turned away, I realized that he was not looking forward to the trip. Rufus groaned and rolled further away to avoid me.

"We do not want to miss the first race," his father shouted.

Eventually I convinced Rufus to get out of bed, we got dressed, and began the walk to where the races would be held. The walk was something that his father had intended as bonding time for the group of boys. No women or girls were welcomed. This was a man's outing.

We went strolling together through the streets towards the Circus Maximus. Plinius was in the lead, with his eldest son Tycho by his side. Tycho had a large and sturdy build, strong shoulders, but his round face housed a drab and dull countenance. Never one to miss a meal, Tycho was getting a little soft, but was still strong and athletic. Tycho was clearly the favorite son, and Plinius had great expectations for his golden boy. He was a young soldier on the path to become an officer. Duty, bravery, and honor were highly valued in Roman culture. As a political mastermind,

Plinius knew how to pull the strings to get Tycho into an important military position. It was clear that he had placed his bet on Tycho as the son most likely to succeed. Tycho showed all the signs of a brave warrior and a dedicated soldier. His unwavering loyalty to the Roman Empire was in stark contrast to the insolence and flagrant laziness that Rufus shamelessly demonstrated. As we walked that morning Plinius and Tycho marched ahead with dignified posture. Rufus and I, dragging our feet, leaned towards each other to share sarcastic comments followed by occasional laughter.

Plinius said to Tycho, "As an equestrian in the military, you will first become praefecti of an infantry. I have spoken to a senator, for whom I have done many favors, so expect a few favors in return. I know there will be a place for you, but you must keep up with your studies and training."

"Father, I am one of the strongest soldiers in my—"

"It is not just the strength of the body," Plinius said, patting his chest, "but mental strength and fortitude." He then tapped his fingertip between his eyes. "The successful general is not only brave, but also performs intelligent decision making on the battlefield in the heat of the moment. As an officer, you will have many lives in your hands. It will not only be your hands that protect those lives, but your mind as well."

"Yes, I know, I know," Tycho said.

I'm sure Tycho had heard this speech dozens of times.

"Well, just work a little harder with your lessons. If you are not happy with your tutor, I can find you a better one," Plinius said.

"Father, thank you. I promise that I will make you proud someday," Tycho said.

Plinius smiled and clapped his arm firmly around Tycho's large shoulder, a manly demonstration of affection.

Rufus acted distracted and aloof, but I could tell that he was disgusted by their rapport.

"Did you see that?" Plinius asked, nudging Tycho. He pointed out, not very discretely, at a woman that had just passed by. "It's only mid-morning — and I see a full moon. There's a Venus between us."

The brothers all reddened. Adolescent admiration. This woman was beautiful indeed and had a very full figure. But it struck me as embarrassing to share this moment with the father of a friend. I considered that my own father would never make a crude comment towards a woman in public.

The brothers kept on ahead of us. They argued about chariot race predictions. As each one was a supposed expert, they would prove their manliness through their racing savvy. This conversation evolved into a more self-congratulatory discussion about their own competitive abilities. It transitioned from chariot racing, to horse racing, to military strategy, to hand-to-hand combat. Tycho, a confident and formidable wrestler, told of his latest victory.

"I'm sure you'd be as good at chariot racing as you are at wrestling," said one of the other brothers, piling on to Tycho's ego. As if he really needed it.

"Just don't wet yourself," Rufus said from the back of the group.

"What did you just say?" Plinius asked, a hint of cold danger in his words. I was confused since I was certain he had heard Rufus.

"Nothing." Rufus said flatly.

"What! Did you say?!" Plinius shouted. He spun around and stormed towards Rufus.

Apparently, Rufus' comment was a reference to the alleged bed-wetting that Tycho had outgrown many years ago. I knew this side of Rufus. He would misbehave, to act out for attention.

"I said," Rufus said, pausing to laugh unnaturally, with a smirk on his face. "Just don't let yourself." This was not at all a clever cover-up, but what do you expect from a thirteen-year-old brat?

"I want you to apologize to your brother," Plinius said.

"Why? I didn't say anything." Rufus changed his pitch to sound like the victim.

"Apologize to your brother," Plinius said.

Rufus didn't budge.

Plinius slapped Rufus on the right cheek, on the left cheek, and on the right cheek again. Each slap increased in intensity until the last one almost knocked him off his feet. Rufus started to whimper. His lip trembled and his eyes watered.

"Don't you ever, ever disrespect your brother," Plinius said. His tone was pure ice. "He is an honorable young man. Something you know nothing about."

I watched Rufus, emasculated and humiliated, break and begin to cry. I felt powerless and disgusted. I felt the strong desire to flee, to find a place to hide from the world. Why was this happening?!

Tycho stood next to Plinius. He put his hands on his hips and his large chest heaved with silent laughter.

"No! Let him cry," Plinius said. "Let us all see who is wetting themselves today."

Rufus turned and walked away. I followed Rufus, although I wasn't sure what to do.

I silently walked with Rufus as he swore under his breath about his father. Then we sat by the side of the road for some time. As children growing up together, we had often sat by the road, talking about what we would do when we were older. Now Rufus put his head on his arms, hiding his face. He was no longer crying, but his nose was running heavily. He was taking large snotty inhalations followed by long shaky exhalations.

"My father doesn't care about anyone," Rufus said, and spit into the dirt. "He doesn't even care about Tycho. He only wants to see him do well, so he can boast to his friends. He just wants to make himself look better. He would turn on Tycho just like he has turned on me if Tycho is not successful."

As we sat there longer, it became more certain that the boys had continued on to the chariot races without us, and that our day was ruined. I was confused and conflicted. On one hand, I could not understand why Rufus would have acted out like that. The entire situation could have been avoided if he would have kept his mouth shut. It was like he had gone out of his way to get that negative attention. Rufus should have known that his father was going to react that way. That was the moment when I determined that, subconsciously, that was what Rufus had wanted. He wanted to force his father's hand, so to speak, in his abusive behavior towards himself. In hindsight, I don't believe Rufus had planned this incident consciously. It was part of his nature. He made trouble because he was troubled. It was an equal and opposite reaction.

I don't remember much more about that day, but we never did make it to the races. When we made it back to his house and Rufus's stepmother asked us what happened, we gave her a vague story, but did not tell her what really happened. Although this incident stands out in my mind, there are many other similar events between Rufus and his father.

PLEASE ALLOW ME TO give credit where credit is due. Rufus had always shown resilience through his younger years. Through emotional trauma, family dysfunction, or just bad luck, I cannot recall many times where he expressed self-pity or shared any negative emotions. As angry as he was about his father on a bad day, he'd be extremely proud of his father on good days. Rufus would brag about Plinius' wealth, power, and influence. He also loved his mother deeply and expressed his gratitude for her loyalty, regardless of her absenteeism and moral depravity.

As you can see by the words on these pages, I don't have a problem sharing my struggles and emotions. But then these are not nearly so severe. I've also had almost twenty centuries of recovery time and therapy. The soldier who has a minor taste of battle tends to brag and share glorious war stories. But the soldier who has been on a bloody field of battle, has killed men or seen close friends slaughtered, will rarely speak about it. Rufus had suffered much more than I had psychologically, to use a modern term, but his emotional shell was impenetrable. Although he had been neglected and abused by his parents and was treated like an outcast by many people, I had never seen him share his pain. Rather than shed the tears of a victim and open his heavy heart, Rufus would make self-deprecating comments about his family with a light sense of humor. I always waited for him to share his pain, or even call for help, but he never once did.

3

TROUBLE IN SUBURA

The streets of Rome at night in Subura were very treacherous in those times. My parents forbade me from staying out with Rufus and his friends. For good reasons. My mother frequently shared stories she heard from her friends, often anecdotes about assault, theft, or other violent crimes.

However, the blood that flows through the young male is rebellious and incorrigible. I recall distinctly our potent desire to prowl the streets, like a pack of wolves, looking for trouble. We seemed so focused on whatever nonsense we were getting into. Drinking and gambling were often in the cards. We always engaged in calculated discussions about meeting women, where we might find them, and what we might do. It was laughable, considering the low odds of actual encounters with women. Also, we postured as chest-pounding tough guys who should not be messed with, each of us was eager for someone to knock a chip off our shoulder, so we looked absolutely ridiculous.

"This way," Rufus said in a comically loud whisper as we turned down a dark alleyway.

Clack! A loud noise caused me to jump and clench my chest, as Rufus slammed the empty wine jug against a wall. The shock and disfavor showed on my face. Rufus responded with a mischievous grin.

We stepped into a small popina, or wine bar, called the Caput Porcus. The Caput Porcus was dimly lit. Numerous patrons stood at the bar drinking and talking. The place was very lively. I was enveloped by the sound of dice being thrown down on table tops. Rough characters shouting over drinks. We approached Muntimer at his table. He saw us coming and he knocked over his stool as he stood. Rufus and Muntimer shared a masculine embrace.

We all settled in and called for a round of wine. Across the table was Soteris, intimidatingly tall, with a dark completion and long dark hair. Despite his looks, Soteris was usually docile and taciturn. On my right sat Muntimer, shorter than average and densely built, thin bearded with lighter cropped hair and wild piercing eyes. Muntimer was known to be aggressive towards both sexes.

"You want to play some dice?" Muntimer asked, skipping the small talk. His was the type that looked for activity and misadventure, and never craved thoughtful discussion.

"Want to play?" Soteris asked. I had strained to hear over the noise around us. Rufus immediately nodded in affirmation. Soteris placed his coins on the table, and Rufus picked up the dice. Soon their dice game was in midflight.

"How about you?" Soteris asked between rolls.

"No thanks. I don't usually gamble," I said. This incited mocking laughter and grunts from Muntimer.

I had met these young men before several times, but they weren't people I would spend time with unless I was with Rufus.

"You just going to sit there?" Muntimer asked, taunting with his gravelly voice. He glared at me from his short hunched over posture.

"No thanks. I don't play. Don't worry, I'll be fine." I'm not sure why this would bother him. I was not interfering with his game or getting in his way. But I knew Muntimer was the type that would be angered by this, so I tried act disinterested in the game.

I tended to observe these group activities without participating. I seemed somewhat aloof. I was content to watch people engaged in these trivial activities.

"Lucius is going to be just fine," Rufus said, drawling in a sing-songy voice. He was defusing the situation. Soteris shrugged indifferently, focusing only on the game. Due to short attention spans and the consumption of wine, they left me alone and resumed playing.

"Ahhh!" Muntimer shouted. "That's mine! Pay up."

He reached out across the table to gather his winnings. Angered and irritated at losing, the others placed more silver coins on the table. Looking at the Denarius coins, I caught a glimpse of Nero's profile, with his flat nose and wearing the wreath of laurels on his head. Winning would be nice, I thought.

The table jumped and coins clattered to the ground. The sudden movement and noise shook me from my rumination. The scene escalated quickly to aggressive shouting and confrontation between Muntimer and some other people who had been sitting at the next table. Muntimer was chest to chest with a much larger stranger.

"Say that again to my face. Say it to my face, *right now*," Muntimer said. His fists were already clenched, and his jaw was locked.

Punches started flying. I froze.

And then, in a shock of pain and lights, I felt several blows land on the side of my skull. The fight between the two of them had spilled over into an all-out tavern brawl. There was swinging and kicking coming from every direction. Hard blows landed on my body, crushing my ribs, and knocking the air from my lungs. I hunched over to try to protect myself, but I kept my hands up and I made sure not to fall to the ground. Occasionally I would try to retaliate and hit back, but there were more of them than me, so I was dangerously outnumbered.

Suddenly I noticed that the fighting had calmed down and there was some clear space for me to get my bearings. I looked out the tavern's front door towards the alley and discovered what had caused the momentary lull in the action. Soteris was charging through the tavern's front door with his spatha, a long sword, lifted above his head by his massive arms. Everyone scattered. Soteris slammed his spatha down on a table, shattering it to pieces with a crash.

I looked around and didn't see anyone in the popina that I knew besides Soteris. From the door I heard Rufus yell, "Let's get out of here!"

We ran.

As we fled down the alleyway, we looked for our allies. I took inventory of my wounds. I was bleeding from my left elbow, but what I noticed most were the lumps on my head, which were throbbing painfully. I tasted blood in my mouth and it was hard to move my jaw. My clothing was torn, and I had lost my sandals.

We eventually found Muntimer. He was grinning manically. He started laughing, and we continued to run through the dark alleys, hearing the light chatter of people and the barking of stray dogs. Eventually we made it to the home of Soteris. Out of necessity, we used his domicile as a safe house.

Subura didn't have a strong police presence, but we still expected the Roman cohorts to arrive and enforce the order of the law. They would be coming after Soteris. He was a plebeian, was not connected, he had used deadly force, and had damaged property. When Soteris arrived at his domicile he was breathing heavily, sweaty, and he no longer brandished the massive spatha.

The adrenaline was still flowing strongly through us. With our hearts still pumping heavily, we sat on the floor in a circle. Soteris poured wine into bowls that we passed around.

"Lucius, look at you. You sure know how to take a beating," Muntimer said. He smirked, noticeably intoxicated and invigorated by combat. "Are you well?"

"Yes, I am going to be fine, but I took a beating," I said. "My jaw might be broken. Where did you go, Soteris?"

"Your jaw is not broken if you are speaking that easily," Muntimer interjected, as a matter of fact. I assumed he was knowledgeable about these things.

"Yes, where did you go?" Rufus pressed on, asking Soteris.

"I had that filthy son of a bitch from the other table by the neck," Muntimer stood and demonstrated, "and I popped him good a couple times in the skull." He reenacted the fight, performing jabbing and grappling moves, veins popping out in his arms and forehead. I noticed that his right eyebrow was disfigured from an injury he had sustained during the fight, and his nose was bent and crusty with blood.

As the excitement of the evening tapered down and I drank more wine, a slight pang of fear crept into my mind. The reality of physical danger had started to set in, especially after observing the serious wounds on Muntimer's face. And I was increasingly worried about having to face my parents. What family trouble might I get into?

"I swear the cohorts were coming after us. Did you hear them, or did you see them coming?" Muntimer asked.

"There were soldiers," Soteris said in his deep monotone voice. He wore a contemplative scowl staring down at his drink. His brow was tense, and he sighed, "There were many soldiers."

The room got quiet and we all looked at Soteris. The firelight cast dark shadows across his large cheekbones and the deep angles of his face.

Soteris held out his large, calloused hands towards the flickering light. We could see dried blood on his palms. Suddenly, I could hear myself breathing and could feel the pulse in my temple. Muntimer stared back at Soteris with his mouth open. Rufus lifted his wine bowl, but I noticed his hands were shaking.

We continued to drink. In the quiet somberness, I could hear the fire crackle. We got comfortable and I covered up, moving closer to the fire. I don't remember falling asleep.

AS I RECALL MY *tumultuous past, I cannot help but think of these fortuitous circumstances of mine. If I had not gotten into trouble that night, I would not have ended up meeting some of the most influential people in the world — apostles, saints, and holy figures. Many of the events that I witnessed still influence what is now called western civilization in a way that cannot be fully understated by mortals.*

In this present year of 1998, I look down now from the clouds of heaven. Actually, none of that statement is entirely true in the full literal sense. I'm not really looking down and I'm not actually even looking. Heaven is not up or down, per se, but more beyond. C.S. Lewis was not even remotely close to getting this right. And neither was John of Patmos with Revelations. Actually, Einstein was the closest person to describing this state of being with his theory of relativity. Since time is relative and not absolute, there is no absolute now. It is not exactly now or the 20th century, which is a very earthcentric view. People have intuited that time is absolute and linear, but this is not the case. We think of the absolute time that is now and that now is the 20th century. Yet that is an earthcentric measurement. It is cosmically relative.

From heaven you can experience multiple nows depending on which world you are coming from. But overall, trying to describe the metaphysical is very difficult to those who haven't experienced it yet. It is like trying to describe colors to someone who has never seen them. I'm not sitting on fluffy clouds, and there are no pearly gates. I can best describe heaven as a very bright and glorious place that is in the great beyond. And I can best describe my present state of being as omniscient. Broadly speaking, I am all-knowing and all-seeing in world events that have unfolded during my afterlife. Thankfully I don't catch every conversation from the billions of people that have lived since my time on Earth. But I can willfully witness events in a way that I can best describe to a modern reader as having 24-hour news coverage. It's like selective listening, if that helps you relate.

History repeats itself. There are no truer words than that. As a fan of the world, I look down from above, only to see the same re-runs, season after season. I watch these seasons with my peers in the afterlife—angels, archangels, and all the heavenly hosts. These viewers from heaven are cynics and fans. We watch the idealistic young couples go forth to forge new lives and then trudge their way inevitably towards divorce and depression. We watch each generation start their own wars and afflict horrible cruelty on their fellow man. For each new generation, willing or otherwise, to wage war and die for their country, often for no worthy cause. The dictators who take over empires, destroy the people closest to them, and who usually end up dying violently themselves.

People commonly try to differentiate themselves from animals, but the animals in truth are far less greedy and violent. The farmer who prays for the sanctity of life on Sunday after treating his fields with pesticides on Saturday. Animals communicate, sing, dance, and experience true suffering. Animals also have families that love one another.

Sorry, that was the cynic in me talking. What about the innocent children that have no designs beyond the simple pleasures of life and imagination? What about the activists and other heroes that stand up for what is right and risk their own well-being? And the millions of exploited victims of power, some that never giving up hope?

Humanity, the show that goes on. What is not to love?

THAT LAST NIGHT OUT in Subura turned out to be big trouble for me. Getting into a public brawl. My acquaintances sought after by soldiers. Father was already frustrated with my insolent, prodigal ways. I was the family ne'er-do-well. This news had pushed Father over the edge. Rufus told me that his father had been contacted by my parents. Rufus overheard his father talking to his stepmother about us. I was going to be forbidden from seeing him again. He heard that my father was ashamed of me and was determined to get rid of me. I knew that the trouble was coming, and soon.

Our family was sitting down together for a large dinner the following night. The servants began to pass around the dishes starting with fruits and nuts. The olive oil, bread, and cheese were my favorite dishes served during our family meals.

"He's going to do a great many things for Rome," my father said, referring to Nero. Nero had just become emperor that October, after the death of his adopted father, Claudius. "Do you remember what the baths and gymnasiums were like before him?"

I kept to myself as usual, chewing on some goat cheese and hoping that they would not bring up the events of the other night.

"I liked Claudius better," Mother said, ignoring Father's question. "He was such a clever and calculated man."

"Claudius was an intelligent man, but ugly as a barbarian from the north, and ever too fond of the Gauls for my liking. I'm not a xenophobe," my father said, starting to profusely expound on his point, "I've traveled the northern kingdoms and have learned to respect many of the Germanic chieftains. I've encountered the most brave and clever warriors.

But outside influence is the beginning of the end for Rome. And you can quote me on that."

"Agrippina is the real mind and power. Behind a great man is almost always a great woman," Mother said. Agrippina, the iron-fisted mother of Nero. My mother always admired Agrippina's fierceness.

"We'll all agree that without her ambition, Nero would have never become emperor. However, Nero is young and ambitious himself," Father said.

Speaking of young and ambitious, Nero was very close to my age, having become emperor at the age of 17. In contrast, at 17 I had no idea what I wanted to become, and I could not relate to ruling an empire. When I thought about what it would mean to be an emperor myself, I could not wrap my head around it. It was also jarring that Nero's forename at birth was also Lucius, the same as mine. But I won't put too fine a point on it. I didn't often think about other people's perspectives in terms of my own life. Empathy and point of view would develop later in life. My challenges and ambitions at that time were living in the moment. Concerns like friends, relationships, and very short-term plans.

"Nero has brought a lot of culture to Rome. His passion for arts and music. I just hope that he doesn't get too caught up in his own personal pursuits and lose sight the import business of running the empire," Father said.

Then turned to me and gave me a look of distaste.

"Lucius, would you care to comment on the discussion?" Father asked.

"Not really," I said, trying to sound indifferent.

"Lucius, when I was your age, I was in Gaul fighting back barbarians. Those brave men fighting by my side never got things handed to them like you. Look at you! You're so pampered. How are you going to grow up to be a man like me? It's a shame."

"Like Hades," I mumbled.

"How little appreciation you have for what we do for you! I've paid for your servants. I've hired the best tutor, who's very expensive, by the way. Your mother just bought you a new chariot and horses. When was the last time you went to the stables? And in return, look how immature you are behaving. Did you know your mother was up all night worrying about you?"

He only thinks about himself too, I thought. He wasn't worried about me. He was angry about how I would make him look. He was never concerned for my safety like mother was.

"Father, you know I never asked for any of that." I was getting flustered. "All I've ever wanted was to find my own way. See the world, meet new people, discover some beauty or the meaning of life," I said. It was an idealistic statement that angered my father.

"Meet new people? Meaning of life? Ugh! What utter nonsense!" His face reddened. "What a naïve and insolent brat we've raised! Have you ever been out in the world, been to Britannia? Do you think those pale bearded bastards have this beauty that you seek?"

"No, I suppose not," I said, trying to disengage. This only increased his rage.

"I know what would be good for you! I'm going to find you some real work, where you can meet all sorts of different people with wonderful ideas!"

Mother glanced at Father. There was something in her eyes. I'm not sure if it was shared anger, or worry, or both? I left the dinner table, and fled my house to stay with Felix that night.

4

SENT TO JUDEA

So, my father marched off, determined to do something about me. He went to the Forum and with his political friends and business associates discussed various plans. My comments about seeing the world had inspired him. He wanted to turn those words back on me. In a few days, he finalized a plan to send me to Judea. There I would learn the trade of carpentry. Hard labor would offer me some new perspective on life. It would teach me to appreciate the privileges that he had afforded me.

Father had initially planned to place me with a Roman construction firm in Judea, but then he came up with a more spiteful scheme. He would make me live with one of the locals. A Jewish man named John, or Yohanan as he was called in his native language. Yohanan would be my landlord and employer, and I was to serve Yohanan as his apprentice. Father informed me that in one week's time I was scheduled to board a merchant ship headed on a route towards Judea. I was apprehensive about the trip, but I was also anxious to get away from my parents. I was also pulled away from Rome by a strong sense of wanderlust and desire for independence.

Although my scheduled departure gave me little time to prepare for my trip, my father gave me a generous allowance. I needed to purchase a few items and attend to a couple errands before leaving Rome. On my way to the market, I wandered down the familiar road towards the Circus Maximus. Nostalgically, I recalled when Rufus, Felix and I had frequently spent summer nights at that very place. We would go to the chariot races, even though we rarely watched the event. We were mostly attracted to the excitement and bustle of the crowds, especially our youthful peers. Occasionally we would get into some verbal altercation with teenagers that we did not know. We taunted and postured, but rarely did it escalate into physical fights.

I continued past Circus Maximus towards the Tiber River. I watched the merchant ships coming up the river into the heart of Rome. They would be carrying grains, wine, fish, and sometimes they even transported exotic animals from foreign lands. Some of those animals would fight the gladiators. Walking down to the river's edge, I threw a couple rocks into the river, watching the splashes and ripples. I tossed a stick onto river and watched the current take it away.

Leaning over the surface of the water, I peered at my reflection. I ran my hands through my hair a couple times. I wiped something off my cheek, revealing a bruise from the tavern brawl. During this time of self-reflection, I drifted into an introspective spiral, recalling all those haunting memories of events that were embarrassing or humiliating. I remembered the last time I had tried to approach a girl that I did not know. How I could barely get a word out. I thought about how afterwards she had laughed at me.

I was being abused by my own inescapable memories in my reflection. I took a last look at myself rippling in the tide, almost becoming unrecognizable and distorted. I felt a rage swelling inside me. I made a fist, and shaking with fury, I started hitting myself. My strikes landed mostly on the right cheek bone and forehead. The last blow hit the wound near my jaw, and I jerked back as sharp pain coursed through my body.

I could feel that my cheek was swelling, and my nose was starting to drip. I looked across the river and up towards the Palatine Hill. This was a grand place, but it made me feel small and defeated. At that moment I decided that it was fortunate that I was getting away from Rome. I had nothing to lose. On my journey to Judea, I would leave these troubled waters, and start with a clean slate.

Although, I was to become a carpenter's apprentice, I had done nothing in preparation for my journey to learn that trade. My education had been rigorous, but I had never done any physical labor. That was for servants and slaves. I considered myself one of the least handy people I'd ever met.

LOOKING BACK, THIS WAS *also going to be my first time living in a land with a culture that wasn't overtly Roman. Up to that time, in my younger years, I had only traveled through Italia with my parents. I had never traveled to distant lands. In hindsight, I've discovered it is much easier to travel to distant lands for a short period of time. While there may be moments of culture shock, one is still in the honeymoon period during short trips, so everything is new and exciting.*

I had a vague idea about the land of Judea from my studies, and I was slightly aware of Jewish culture growing up in Rome. The Jews had been living in parts of Rome for around two centuries. Several decades ago, Julius Caesar had formed a policy that gave Jewish citizens the status of religio licita, permitting them to legally practice their religion throughout the Empire. I had occasionally observed the distinct presence of the Jewish communities in Rome while I was growing up.

In the decades following the rule of Julius Caesar, the coexistence of Roman citizens and Jewish citizens was still civil in Rome. Although the seeds of the Jewish revolt were being sowed across the Empire, particularly in Judea.

THE MERCHANT SHIP THAT my father had arranged passage for me on would leave port in Ostia and then sail to Alexandria. In Alexandria the captain of the merchant ship was to hand me off to another captain, and that captain would take me on another ship to Caesarea where I would meet Yohanan. Naturally, I was naively optimistic about this plan.

That first morning I boarded a clean and sturdy ship, captained by a man named Martinus. Martinus was a strong, distinguished Roman of few words. He was a natural leader and was respected by his crew, never needing to raise his voice. He had known my father and owed him a small favor. This was not a Roman war ship with rows of oars and a threatening face painted on the bow. Instead this was a common merchant vessel. The ship had a small sail at the bow and the large sail at the mid-ship and a swan's head at the stern post. Painted on that larger sail, the only distinguishing feature of the ship, was a large hippopotamus, meaning "water horse" in Greek.

"Welcome aboard the Hippopotamus," Martinus said, greeting me stoically. "You will be treated as a passenger rather than as a crew member. But you will follow the same rules of conduct that I expect from all my crew. We will be at sea for about twenty days, including some time docked in Messana and Cyrene. Make sure you are back on time to the ship after each port call, or we will leave without you."

I nodded in the affirmative. Before I found my place on the ship, Martinus startled me with a question.

"Did you get into an accident, or a fight?" he asked casually.

Martinus noticed some of the bruising on my face. How the bruising had occurred, the tavern brawl and my own self beating, was embarrassing to bring up so I just told him I had an accident. Onward and upward, I thought.

I faced my first day at sea with optimistic excitement. I fashioned myself a real explorer. Our first destination was to be the city of Messana on the island of Sicilia. The crew was pleased that a strong current would take us there swiftly. I breathed in the smell that was a conflation of fresh salty sea and the pungency of dead fish. The cool mist of the sea from earlier that morning had faded with the piercing sunlight. And now with that hot sun on my face, I faced the seagoing journey confident and with the utmost fascination. The sun sparkled brilliantly off the teal blue colors that pushed out and bordered against the dark blue sea water. The waves crested into frothy white splashes against the rocks near the harbor. I marveled at the sea. I smiled and told myself this will be a true adventure.

By the next day I had become extremely seasick. There was a very strong gale and the waves were tossing the boat about like a child's toy in a bath house. The sickness was inescapable, and the feeling of nausea overwhelmed me. That horrible day was endless. I could split those miserable moments into smaller moments, into infinitely smaller moments of suffering. I held to the deck, trying to focus on the horizon, unable to stop the dizzy spinning sensation. I clung and vomited until I lulled myself into a tired calm.

By the time we were past halfway to Messana, I finally got my sea legs. And I realized how hungry I was, having evacuated everything from my stomach into the Tyrrhenian Sea. I was offered fish but refused it with a visceral reaction of disgust. I was then offered some bread, which I consumed slowly. I was tired and chewed laboriously, my jaw nearly cramping. Thankfully, the bread settled into my gut without incident.

Our first stop was Messana, a coastal city in Sicilia, and a common port of visit. Nestled on the foothills of the Peloritan Mountains, Messana's sickle-shaped harbor jutted out into the narrow straight. As we approached the harbor, the mountains took shape, cutting into the horizon, with faint, fluffy clouds skirting around them. I began to make out the pharos, or lighthouse, sticking up from the points of the peninsulas.

After the crew secured the ship to the wharf I immediately disembarked. I was given only hours to explore the city as our crew loaded additional provisions for the trip. I walked through the port area towards the nearest market. On my way, I navigated some narrow pathways, inspecting the numerous stalls for wares that may catch my eye. There was a cacophony of haggling, wheeling and dealing, the clanging of pots, the counting of money. As I walked through the gauntlet of shops, I was continuously accosted. Sweaty, greasy men approached me, one after another, with their aggressive and dubious sales pitches. I saw a plethora of dirty fingernails and ratty hair that day. This aggressive selling tactic was something that I was not accustomed to and it took me by surprise. I made eye contact with an oily little man wearing what seemed like hundreds of bead necklaces.

"You are such a handsome young man," he said with a menacing grin. "I bet you have a nice sweetheart at home."

"Well, yes," I paused, not sure why I had told him the truth, or why I was allowing myself to engage with him at all, "sort of, but not exactly anymore—"

"I'm sure," he said, cutting me off. He held up a necklace, "I'm sure she would look even more beautiful with these jewels."

"I'm just browsing. Just looking around, thank you," I said. Probably my first mistake.

Quickly, he threw a couple necklaces over my head. They got stuck for a minute around my forehead, but then fell and settled onto my neck. A trick, I thought. I was caught in his trap.

Fortunately, I was able to pull off the necklaces and hand them back to him. "I have to meet someone," I said. "Let me think about it and, uh, and I will, uh, I will probably be back for them." Whatever it took to get away.

"OK, I understand," he said. He wanted to bargain. "I will give you two for the price of one."

"Sorry, thank you, but I've got to go." I was getting frustrated. I turned my back on him and quickly walked.

But I feared that he was following me. Stealthily, I sneaked a look over my shoulder. I noticed that he was coming towards me with a handful of jewelry. I immediately picked up my pace.

I was experienced with the busy markets of Rome, practiced in the art of haggling with the local vendors back home. But this was aggressive selling on a whole new level. Until that day I also didn't realize how conspicuous I was as a visitor. I was an easy target. A wealthy, pampered, young man who was obviously not a local.

So, I kept on walking straight ahead, not making eye contact with anyone. Look busy, confident and purposeful, without being too rude. Instead of saying "no thanks" or explaining myself to each person that shouted out to me. I must simply ignore them.

I walked for what seemed like a while, zig zagging through the maze of the market. I was amused each time I saw those same necklaces that the oily man had tried to ambush with me earlier. I bet I could get four for the price of one. I also found lamps, pots, jewels, rugs, and more lamps. As I headed deeper into the market, I found vendors selling street foods and smells filled my senses. I watched someone stirring a huge pot of stew over wood coals, the hot steam floating into the alleyway. The smoky smell of cooked pork made me hungry.

As I perused my options to eat, I heard an abrupt and shaky exclamation.

"Young man, beware!"

I turned and saw an old man beneath the shadow of a nearby tent awning. He had one crooked finger pointed ominously at me, but his face was obscured by a large hood.

I broke form and walked towards him to engage with him. This was a mistake, but he had struck my interest.

"Beware, young man, of the Ides of Julius." He must be a soothsayer, I thought.

As I came closer, I could make out his face from under the cover of his hood. The old man's skin was weathered, wrinkled, and splotchy. He stared obliquely out of foggy eyes.

"You are going on a dangerous journey to faraway lands. You will meet with people who have stood before many gods and kings of men," he said.

Then he paused for dramatic effect.

"On this journey, you will meet many more soothsayers, wizards, and magicians. Beware of the dark magic that you will encounter."

I blinked, at a loss for words.

On his face, I could see the wheels of his mind turning, trying to spin out more yarn.

Then, his features rearranged into a look of casual frustration and he gave up.

"OK, that's all I got, kid." He coughed weakly then stuck out his hand. "Pay up. I gave you some gems there."

I felt conned. But at the same time, I didn't have the guts to argue with him.

"Thanks, this is all I can afford." I gave him a few coins, approaching uncomfortably close to him to drop them into his hand. I could smell his deathlike breath coming from his toothless mouth.

"Is that it?" he asked.

As I walked away from the old soothsayer, I heard him start in on the next young man who innocently fell for his con. I decided to skip lunch and ran back towards the harbor.

5

CYRENE

We sailed across the rough sea to the coast of Africa, docking in at the port in Apollonia. Cyrene, our destination, stood grandly above us on the hillside. I overheard that Martinus was trading for silphium, a popular plant that was used in medicine and seasoning, but has been lost to history. The plant was so valued that it was pictured on Cyrene coins. Martinus flipped one of those coins to me and said, "Why don't you take a look around the city and meet us at the port at sunset." They were clearly asking me to get lost.

I trekked up the hill to Cyrene. The dry African weather mixed with the milder Mediterranean climate which resulted in an abundance of agriculture in the hills around the city. The buildings in the city were a mix of classic Greek and Roman architecture. Many buildings, such as the Fountain of Apollo and the baths, were distinctly Greek with stout Doric columns. The people in the crowded agora looked like they were a mix of Semitic Phoenicians and Romans blended with the native Berber people. I strolled towards the Temple of Apollo. I often found sun's light invigorating and magical, warming the skin and radiating positive rays of energy. I casually gave my appreciation to Apollo for this light that brightened my day. On the occasion, I had the habit of honoring Apollo's patronage of music and poetry as well. I had partiality for music and poetry, much like Daphne.

After my tour of Cyrene, I exited the city gates and hiked the hillside. I had a terrific view of the entire countryside as I walked. I saw the rich green bushes and trees popping out of the gray and yellow stones, with the vast sea on the horizon. In the distance, I could see a beautiful villa with a large fountain surrounded by palm trees. Then I hiked downhill towards the sea where I walked past a large herd of goats. The goats called out with mundane goat noises. I was mostly ignored by them, but a few goats looked over with disinterest.

When I arrived back in Apollonia, I had some time left before I needed to be back at the ship. I decided to visit the baths, because I was filthy and exhausted from my trip thus far. Then I saw a theater that was cut out of the rocks and faced the sea. I walked down the theater steps towards the sea. At the edge of the water, I looked out at the turquoise water, brilliant in the bright sunlight.

I felt like getting into the water. I saw a large boulder to sit down on. I sat quietly and listened to the water splash in a hollow under the boulder. The rock was still wet from the high tide. I took off my toga, folded it, and placed it on a dry section of the stone. I put my wet sandals next to my toga and then finally removed my tunic.

I slowly waded into the water until it was above my knees. The surface of the water felt colder on my skin, but the water underneath was warm. Tense from the chilly water, I clenched my fists and walked in deeper until it was up to my waist. I spent a few minutes standing on the soft seabed, feeling the sand pull out from under my feet as I sunk in deeper. As the undertow sucked away the sand, I almost lost my balance and nearly fell backwards.

Then I walked into the water until the gentle waves were splashing against my chest. I had a love-hate relationship with water. On the one hand, I often had flashbacks to a scary incident in the ocean when I was a child. I had been taken under by a strong current. I recalled the panicked fear of losing my breath, the cold dark water all around me, and the sensation of choking up disgustingly salty ocean water. Even though I was able to swim by young adulthood, I still hated everything about my head being under water. I felt like a fish out of water, or, I suppose it would be the opposite of that.

On the other hand, I was fascinated by the water. I truly enjoyed being by a lake or by the sea. And despite the occasional sea sickness, I loved the adventure of traveling the sea. The voyage to Africa had been unforgettable. I started to relax and tread water. I leaned back to wet my hair. As I was splashing the water, I looked down the coast towards the west.

North Africa had recently held a significance in my heart. Daphne had shared her story about her family's lineage with me. She claimed that her father's people had been Phoenicians, several generations ago, who had then traveled to

Carthage. The Phoenicians where Semitic people from near modern-day Lebanon. They had traveled to North Africa and Carthage many centuries ago. At the height of their power Phoenicians were known as world travelers and traders.

Daphne's father, carrying on the Phoenician tradition, was a successful trader in metals. Her family had traveled all over the coasts and even inland to barbaric lands. Daphne was connected to her family history and proudly felt the Phoenician blood coursing through her veins. But she was proud of her itinerant history, moving around as a child had become stressful. Daphne had confided in me about how she had lived in Carthage as a child and the difficulties she encountered every time her father would uproot the family. In addition to an itinerant father, she faced more tragedy in her family.

When Daphne was younger and living in Greece, her father had an affair with a neighbor's wife. This shamed her family, especially since the other woman was the wife of a close friend. Daphne's family left Greece in shame and moved to Rome where they could start fresh.

I tried to estimate how far up the African coast it was to Carthage from here. It turned out that it was quite a far distance. Since distance makes the heart grow fonder, the vast African coast was having that effect on me. I was drawn to Daphne's memory like a sailor to a siren's song.

I RECALLED THE DAY she was sitting in her emerald green stola, reading poetry, with her long black hair hanging loose down her back. She was reading poetry from a scroll, her lips moving silently. I watched her hand move delicately as she acted out the words to the cool summer breeze. There was a white shawl draped across her right shoulder, but it had slipped off her left shoulder, leaving it bare. I could see a golden bracelet on her arm as it danced in the summer air.

I climbed up the slope to her garden to be closer, within speaking distance, and took a seat on a bench nearby. She smiled, showing her prominent white teeth. She didn't make eye contact, but kept reading her poetry, motioning with her left hand and moving her lips.

I sat back, smiling to myself, happy, and at peace with the world.

When she finally put down her scroll, she ran her hand through her hair, and then looked up at me as if she had just noticed me.

"Hello Lucy," she said. Lucy? I guess this was my new pet name. We had probably only known each other for five or six weeks, but were already advancing to pet names. I enjoyed the familiar intimacy.

"What are you reading?" I asked.

"I am practicing some new poems," she said, killing me with her smile.

"Poems, eh?" Two could play this game. "Yesterday it was Greek philosophy, now it's poems. You are a voracious reader. Which author are you reading now?"

"Me," she said coyly, leaning forward playfully.

"What? You write too?" I asked.

I had been spying on her since the beginning of the summer and had seen her reading before. Her father had moved next to Felix that spring, so every time I visited him I would ty to watch for her from across the garden wall.

"Please, perform one for me," I said. I stood up as an audience of one.

"No, Lucy. You don't get to hear them yet. I don't think you're ready." She was being modest, but I was sure she was a natural performer. She was probably waiting for someone to ask.

"Please Daphne, I promise I won't make fun of you," I said.

"Why would you make fun of me?" she asked. She stood and walked so that we were standing face to face.

"No, that's not what I meant," I argued, playfully.

She put her hand up as if to push me away. I took her hand, lacing our fingers together.

"Seriously, are you going to sing me one of your poems? Will you, please?" I asked. I leaned in, losing myself in her dark eyes.

"There's nothing to make fun of," she said.

"I know, I know," I said, smiling at her.

"OK," she said. "Now, sit down and be quiet, so I can concentrate."

This was not going to be just a reading, but a performance. I watched in silent appreciation as Daphne sung her poem.

> With the love and beauty of Venus
> Our kind breathes new life
> Into the children of the earth
> As a mother and a wife
>
> As the summer sun warms my skin
> Then Boreas blows down the cool north wind
> With the bittersweet twinge of an early fall
> The joyful mother nature must quiet her call
>
> And there is nothing in the stars
> That will defend those hardy threats

When the long spears from Mars
Will pierce your fair flesh

All of my heart
All of my soul
Tangled
Yet proud and whole
Is much more than this figure
That you admire from afar

I was love struck at the time. I was so enamored with Daphne, so distracted by her physical beauty that her words were lost on me. I applauded her but looking back on that moment I feel like a fool for not truly listening to her meaning. The irony is not lost on me. Daphne was indeed a unique and mystifying figure.

That evening we sat holding hands and talking under the light of the crescent moon. I didn't want the night to end, but eventually I was overcome with that sinking feeling of knowing that all good things must end. The entire affair had to end soon. Literally. Her father was now safe to return to Greece, the other family having moved away, and Daphne was going to leave when her family moved back. So, our relationship was destined to have a sad ending. But, in our favor, it had heightened these moments and had given us a sense of passionate urgency.

"Daphne!" I heard her father shout from inside their house. That meant that our evening was over.

"I'm coming, I'm coming!" Daphne called back in frustration.

"Don't go," I said, desperately, under my breath.

"I have to go now. I will meet you tomorrow," she said.

"No, I mean . . . I mean don't go back to Greece," I said.

"I have to," she said.

"Why? Why do you have to?" I asked, pleading with her.

"Lucy," she said, drawling my name out, then she sighed. "You know that would not work out. My father must return to Greece to keep his business going. And I have my own life, too. We've talked about this before and nothing has changed."

She was going back to complete her education in Corinth. She had a great tutor that would help her with philosophy, poetry, and rhetoric. But her father returning to Greece was more of the deciding factor. Young women at that time could not be independent and on their own in the world. Daphne did not really have a choice.

"Find me before dinner tomorrow. Call for me outside the garden. I will be waiting for you." Daphne said, thankfully able to change the subject. There was no argument and now as I anticipated our meeting the next evening with only joy. Daphne was so gifted.

I did not go straight home that night. Instead, I sat down on the hillside and leaned back to look at the stars in the sky. I let the sound of Daphne's poem repeat in my head.

WHILE FLOATING IN THE sea near Cyrene, I remembered that last summer with Daphne fondly. Then I sighed, and I looking at the sky knew I had to get back to the Hippopotamus before nightfall. I swam clumsily in the shallows towards the beach until I was able to stand up. I walked to the boulder where I had left my clothes. I was shivering when I got out of the water, but the sun was still warm enough to dry my skin until I could dress again.

6

ALEXANDRIA

And then I was sailing at sea for our next port of call, the great city of Alexandria in Egypt. The journey was tranquil and relaxing, and the morale was high aboard the Hippopotamus. Based on the high spirits of the crew, they must have made a profitable trade in Cyrene. For the crew, Alexandria was another port where they could potentially make another good profit on their trade of grain and other merchandise. But for me, I was thrilled about the city itself.

As we came within sight of the harbor, I saw the one of the crew men pointing at something in the distance. So, I moved to the starboard side to get the best view. As our ship approached the harbor, I was awestruck by what I saw rising into the sky. One of the seven wonders of the world, the Pharos of Alexandria!

The lighthouse was built on a small island in the middle of harbor. Our vessel passed by the island on the way into the harbor. A large wall was around the base of the lighthouse. On each corner of the wall were small structures that towered at least twice as tall as our ship's sails were high. The lighthouse itself was a massive tower, comprised of three separate sections. The lower section was as wide as our ship, square shaped, and sloped up a steep pitch. On top of this base section, people could stand on a ledge which was decorated with carved stone statues. The second section, of hexagonal shape, towered high above that ledge at least four more stories. On top of this section, flags waved in the sea breeze. Above that section was the final section, a round structure with open columns and a cone-shaped roof. A shiny metal plate from within those columns reflected the blinding light towards oncoming ships. On the very top of that roof was a statue of Helios the sun god, greeting all visitors to the city.

As we passed by the island, we had to turn the ship towards the harbor. We sailed in the direction of a long causeway that went from the island into the port. The causeway was busy with pedestrians walking in both directions, as well as chariots driving along it. As we made the turn around the island, I got a closer look at the lighthouse tower, and I marveled at its grandeur. I was awestruck, in a dreamlike state. So, I wanted to make it real and touch the tower and feel the stones with my hands. I begged Martinus to drop anchor for just a few moments so that I could walk up the slope of the island and touch the walls of the lighthouse. Martinus refused. He said that I could walk the causeway and take a closer look on my own time.

We headed into the harbor, where ships were busily coming and going. Alexandria, the gateway to the Nile and to Egypt, was one of the busiest ports in the Roman Empire. The harbor was a sight to behold, ships of all shapes and sizes surrounded us. Once we docked the ship, I was instructed that I had only the rest of the day to spend in Alexandria. I needed to return by early evening to meet Martinus. Then he would take me to meet the captain of the next boat that had been arranged to carry me to Caesarea.

I WALKED OFF THE docks seeking out the busy marketplace. This cultural melting pot invited more exploration for my open mind. I passed through some warehouses near the dock, given directions to continue eastward.

I was quickly immersed in a smorgasbord of trade. I passed by a shop selling rugs and tapestries made of the finest silk and the most vibrant colors. One store specialized only in ivory, displaying a wide array of instruments, jewelry, weapons, and ornately detailed sculptures. There were also delicacies such as jewelry, perfumes, and incense. At one point the incense was so thick in the air that it became difficult to breath, causing a fit of sneezing. This was fascination by all senses. I was completely entertained by browsing, but too afraid to touch anything, or engage in negotiation with anyone to buy anything.

After traversing the marketplace, I emerged on a main road. Unlike the narrow alleys in the market, this road was very wide, providing much more visibility. The road was straight as much of the city was planned along a grid.

In the distance I heard the stomping of hundreds of feet and the metallic clatter of armor. The people on the streets began to part step up onto the curbs, so I did the same. I leaned out of the crowd to look down the road towards the thundering sound. In the distance, I saw the front of a Roman legion. A standard bearer proudly held a red fabric banner with "Leg III" in gold insignia, an eagle statue perched on top. Each soldier carried an identical rectangular shield with golden wings and a spear. The metallic armor shone brightly in the afternoon sunlight. It must have been very hot wearing the armor and helmets. I stood by the road with the locals and watched as they loudly stomped by, row by row. The soldiers seemed to go on forever, as if they were one collective organism or a single piece of machinery. I don't recall picking out any individual faces in the entire legion. They were followed by mules carrying supplies, and soldiers leading them.

After the Roman legion had passed, I resumed my walk down the road. I passed by the gymnasium and then I turned down a narrow alley. As I walked a few blocks, I could see by the change in appearance of the neighborhood that I was now in the Jewish quarter. I thought this must have been in a very prosperous area. Several of the women I walked by wore veils, as was the custom of the married women, but many were also not wearing veils. I noticed young women with long hair in braids with hairpins, showing off beautiful earrings. Not only earrings, but rings on their fingers and toes, as well as bracelets and anklets. I saw a Jewish man wearing a mantle with the traditional tassels hanging down on the corners. He was standing alone, so I approached him for directions.

"Good afternoon. Do you know where I would find the synagogue?" I asked. I was told by a man by the docks that

Alexandria was home to the most famous, largest, and ornate synagogue in the empire.

"A Roman? Wants directions to the synagogue?" He looked stern at first, but then chuckled amiably. He politely gave me some directions and soon I had found my way there.

The synagogue was awe-inspiring for both its size and splendor. A man on the street said there were jewel encrusted thrones inside. I was not welcome inside, but I caught a look through the grand doorway, and from what I could see it was splendid indeed. What synagogues would I see when I got to Judea? Would they be grander? I gazed through the door and down the marvelous colonnades for as far as I could see. The oil lamps shined on the columns and my vision blurred.

AS I WAS STARING into the brilliant synagogue I began daydreaming. I remembered that one summer afternoon in Rome. We had spent so many days at Felix's family villa engaged in idyll socializing. Felix lived in an upscale Roman neighborhood right outside of the city. It was a beautiful villa with a large garden, fountains, pools, and enclosed yard for recreation.

We would all routinely meet at Felix's family villa for fun and games. His family was most inviting, and his mother was the warmest host. She would always make sure that her servants took good care of us, bringing us food and drinks or anything else we desired. Besides being lonely and enjoying the company, I think she wanted to be young again and enjoyed the youthful drama.

I vividly remember that summer afternoon, Rufus, Felix, and many of our other friends were enjoying our leisure time. We were playing a ball game, and the young women had come to sit and visit, under the ever-watchful eyes of their chaperons, who looked on occasionally with disinterest. Octavia had brought a couple of her friends over and they were sitting and talking on the far side of the lawn.

Rufus and I were competing against Felix and one of his younger brothers. Felix had just scored a goal and was celebrating to both annoy us, and attract attention from Octavia. Octavia gave a distracted cheer without skipping a beat from her conversation with the other girls. Rufus and I had been defeated, and we decided to take a short break from the game to get a drink. Then we would determine the teams for the next match.

As I glanced across the yard and down the hill to the next villa, I saw a tall, thin young lady. She was casually strolling in her garden, smelling and picking flowers for a bouquet. I had been visiting Felix frequently over the last few weeks, so I had noticed her before. My attraction to her had grown subconsciously each time I had seen her. On each visit I always made a point to look for her, but that day was different. That day her figure struck me powerfully and it left an indelible memory. She looked dark and foreign, but at the same time familiar, as if I had known her for a long time.

Though I was fascinated by her, I tried to sound non-chalant when I asked Felix, "Who is that across the way? Does she live there? I haven't noticed her before." That was a lie. Although I had noticed her many times before, I had not shared my interest with anyone. And, since we had not been introduced yet, she probably didn't even know I existed.

"That's Daphne," Felix mentioned casually. "Her father purchased that villa recently. We think the family is Greek. At least, my mother told me that they moved from Greece."

We didn't need to exchange another word. Felix sensed my conspicuous interest in Daphne. Felix had been with Octavia for over a year now. As happy couples often do, Felix and Octavia liked to set others up with potential companions.

Felix nodded in understanding, then said, "My brother is friendly with her brothers. They have visited here before. I can ask them to come join us later this evening,"

Felix made this sound all so easy, so casual, but I was paralyzed. He was already signaling to his brother to come over so that he could arrange an invitation. Part of me wanted to tell him not to bother, and another part of me was already yearning about her obsessively. The longing I held for her was both thrilling and suffocating. Before I could break from my paralysis, Felix had completed his conversation with his brother. His brother smiled at me conspiratorially and then walked away.

I SHOOK MY HEAD to clear those memories of summers past. I had lost track of time. I had wandered a long distance away from the port. I walked quickly through the Jewish quarter towards the harbor, passing between the royal palaces and a Greek theater.

Unfortunately, I did not have time to go to the Pharos. I rushed directly to the port to meet with Martinus. I arrived out of breath, but on time. Martinus was pleased to see me. In his own avuncular fashion, he even showed just a little bit of emotion, which was out of character for him. Maybe he was going to miss me. Martinus escorted me down the dock, past the ships until we arrived at a small, rickety vessel. That ship is no Hippopotamus, I thought when I saw it bobbing weakly in the water. Was it going to make it safely out of the harbor, let alone all the way to Caesarea?

Martinus squared me up and put his hands firmly on my shoulders. "Now Lucius, be careful in Judea."

"Don't worry, I will be well protected, and I'm in great physical shape. My father has secured arrangements with the locals. And, you know, I am a Roman citizen."

"No, I mean be careful of the zealots. There are very dangerous minds in that land."

"I have heard that Nazareth is no more dangerous than Subura," I said. This new information that he was telling me was confusing to me. Was I going to be in physical danger, or endangered by radical ideas? I was starting to think that it was the latter.

"That's not what I mean, young man," he said in a conciliatory tone. "There are many radical extremists in Judea. Do not fall in with those zealots and their dangerous ideas. Do not become a servant to their god." He looked out towards the sea.

That put me off. But I had no other choice but to agree with him. I nodded.

"Well, consider yourself warned," he said. He huffed and folded his arms.

Strange, I thought.

"Let's move on." Martinus stomped his foot on the dock to get the attention of the people on the boat. "Meet the captain who will get you to Judea."

A small and wiry man approached and greeted me kindly. He was probably in his mid-forties but looked much older.

He had a short gray beard and scruffy hair that fell straight down from a bald crown. The tanned surface of his pate reflected the sunlight.

"Boy, you'll like Judea! You will, I do say," the old ship captain encouraged me, having overheard my warnings from Martinus. "Or, at least," he said, "They will love you!" His grin revealed few remaining teeth.

"I look forward to finding out for myself. I appreciate the welcome. I will go ahead and board the ship. My name is Lucius."

After I had spoken, I thought my tone had been too proper and superficial. I was going to need to relax and take it down a few pegs with this sailor.

"I am Abel, the captain of this fine vessel," the diminutive old man said.

Abel grabbed some of my things and was hauling them towards the ship, straining from the weight. I awkwardly followed, looking back at Martinus with uncertainly. He stood up straight and acknowledged my look with a farewell of his own. Then he turned and walked towards his ship. I doubted I would ever see Martinus again.

PART II

THE HOLY LAND

7

CAESAREA

The trip from Alexandria to Caesarea was a short but memorable one that I still hold in my heart with warm nostalgia. The old captain, Abel, made a lasting impression on me. My initial natural pity and condescension towards him quickly switched to admiration. Yes, he was filthy, undignified, and at times a perverted old man. But his basic approach to life was something I afterwards tried to emulate. His life was simple. He had everything that he wanted. Abel was not greedy, or jealous, or ambitious, and he worked hard every day. He lived in the moment like a dog—like a content, old, salty sea dog. He was always smiling and laughing, telling crude jokes and stories, and sharing dubious words of wisdom. His life was limited, but his big heart was expansive.

On the first day of our voyage we did some fishing. The crew literally showed me the ropes as we cast out our nets. At mid-day we sat down and ate the savory fresh fish that Abel had grilled on a small hooded brazier. It was a fine day. The sun was out and the strong winds had calmed. The two of us sat next to each other and shared some wine. We passed the wine jug back and forth, each taking big refreshing pulls.

"I remember being yer age. Boy, like it was just last week," Abel said, laughing. In my teenage eyes he looked rather old.

As we sat and drank in the sun, I told him about my friends, and everything that had led to my trip to Judea. I told him about my family, about how my parents disapproved of me, especially my father.

"Your father probably loves you and wants to see ya do something with yer life," Abel said. "You should not take that for granted. My father, oh, boy, was he something. He was a real seaman. Well, so he said. I only remember his drinking and the fighting," he said. He was still maintaining a smile during this dark reflection. "No, I didn't see him much. Not after I grew up to be a bigger boy."

Abel's story was bleak. But I had just a sliver of envy. He was a free man. His father never provided him any opportunity, but on the other hand, there had been no expectations, no judgment, no crushing sense of family duty. Abel was liberated from the chains of upper-class standards and expectations. I don't want to sound ungrateful or unappreciative, but most Roman citizens did not realize the joys of the lower-classes. Although the upper-class did benefit from proper etiquette and decorum, they were weighed down by the burden of that facade. Abel and his crew were teaching me how to live in the moment, without me worrying about judgment or my reputation, or my family duty. This was incredibly liberating for me.

Abel changed the conversation to his favorite subject, which was women.

"Lucius, look at you. All prim and proper." Abel grinned. "You're a classy young lad from a nice family. I betcha you have a sweet lass."

"No, I don't right now. Not anymore."

"You don't?" Abel asked incredulously, "What is wrong with you? You are keen on the girls, aren't ye?"

"Yes, of course I am. It is just not a good time for me right now," I said, irritated by the implication.

"Not a good time for you? I don't understand ye. When is it not a good time? Yer a young man with your whole life ahead of you," Abel said.

"Well, I had a girlfriend recently," I said. I needed to adapt to the rhythm of telling tales on the sea. There was always plenty of time to share stories while sailing, and I observed that it was customary to take license and exaggerate. There was great appreciation for someone who could spin a good yarn.

"Yes, yes," he said, encouraging me to continue.

"She was quite a catch," I said. My attempt at the fishing metaphor was not lost on the old seaman. I thought I was being clever. I then described Daphne, animating as necessary with my hands, providing as much detail to keep Abel interested but leaving some things to let his filthy imagination fill in the blanks. I shamelessly embellished her beauty and my conquest. Abel was on the edge of his seat.

"Oh, she sounds like a fine lass," he said. He was a real connoisseur.

"How about you? Do you have a family at home? Wife and kids?" I asked. I had exhausted my story telling skills and wanted to shift the focus of the conversation to him.

"Nay, my boy. Ne'er did I have a wife. Kids, oh none that I can say." Abel chuckled, pleased with himself. "But when I was yer age, boy. I was known to be a fox!"

"A fox?" I asked.

"Yea, my boy. I was a *real* fox," he claimed, and made a face that can only be described as fox-like.

"Tell me about it," I said rhetorically, ready to indulge him.

"Many years ago, when I was yer age, I was doing well for myself. I was quite a fox and my satchels were full." I wasn't completely sure what that he meant by that last comment, and what his satchels might have been full of, but I assumed it was a good thing.

Abel went into a fit of coughing. He ended by spitting out something disgusting.

"I had a lady that was going to be my wife," he said.

"Well, what happened to her? You couldn't make a commitment?" I asked.

"She died of a fever. Same as killed me mother," he said.

"I'm so sorry," I said.

"Why are you sorry? There's no reason for you to be sorry," he said.

"Tell him about your Egyptian princess!" another sailor shouted. I indicated my gratitude with a slight nod, thanking him for changing the subject.

"What? No," Abel shook his head dismissively, but he was grinning. "She's not me princess at all."

"Well you have to tell me now," I said to him.

"Oh, alright. So, as you may already know, in Alexandria there are many a fair lady. The fine beauties of the Nile. Well, I used to stay down near those large four-story apartments, uh, around Rhakotis, not so far from the Nile canal—do you know where I mean?"

I did not know the city, so I motioned him to carry on.

"Anyway, my boy, when I had spent time in Alexandria, several years back, I lived down there in those apartments. After a long day's work, I would sit on the rooftop and have me a taste of wine. My boy, those were the days when I didn't have a care in the world. And Alexandria was such a fine city to—"

"Get on with it!" shouted a sailor.

Abel laughed. "Right, so from this rooftop I had a great view of all the other buildings around me, and the neighboring rooftop was what caught me eye. Every evening I would see the same beauty sit out on that roof. And one day she noticed me watching her. We would lock eyes and quickly she would look away and cover up. This went on for weeks."

"This is your princess?" I asked. I was disappointed. I must have sounded disappointed too, because Abel grinned and quickly continued his tale.

"I'm not done yet, boy! After about two weeks or so, she began to uncover herself, and she would lay out and bath herself in . . . in sunshine. In the nude."

"Completely disrobed?" I asked.

Now he had my attention.

"Yes, like the day she was born," he said.

"And she knew you were watching her?" I asked.

"Of course, she knew! It was me she did it for. She was never outside sunbathing until I went to the rooftop. And then, she started coming out and uncovering herself, like she was doing it for me," he said.

Abel showed his nearly toothless grin as he whimsically stared off into the distance. "I swear to you all, she was the love of my life," he said.

"But, did you ever meet her?" I asked.

"No, but she was the one true love of my life," he replied. We all laughed.

"She sounds a lot more like Bathsheba than an Egyptian princess to me," a sailor interrupted.

"Shut your mouth and stay out of my story!" Abel shouted.

"But you never met her, or spoke to her?" I asked, still immersed in Abel's story, "And she was your true love?!"

"Never shared a single word. But, oh boy, her eyes and her, her, her . . . you know, spoke volumes."

A silence fell over the sailors as we imagined wistfully.

"Volumes!" His hands drew a shape in the air of what I can only assume was his Egyptian princess.

As Abel stood up, he pointed crudely at a lump in the groin area of his loincloth. There were several disappointed grumbles from the crew as they walked away. I was more disgusted than disappointed. That was how story time ended that night.

AS I LOOKED OUT on the calm sea on that clear night, I thought back to that fateful day I met Daphne. The day at Felix's family villa. Felix's brother had just walked off with instructions to invite Daphne over. I was vacillating nervously between anxiety and thrill.

Daphne then walked over with her older sister, both women escorted by Felix's brother. As we were up on a hill, the visibility was clear. Her sister was also attractive, but in a different way that had not appealed as much to me. She had a darker complexion, curly hair, and was not as tall as Daphne. They both had their hair styled carefully with hairpins and wore decorative shawls.

As we were resting after the game, Felix and Octavia invited us to sit and refresh ourselves with some food and drinks. So, we proceeded to socialize in the garden on that summer afternoon as we were accustomed to do. Among the social circle were Felix, Octavia, Octavia's girlfriend Portia, Felix's brother, Daphne, her older sister, Rufus, and yours truly. Felix called for a servant who came back with a tray of bread and honey, figs, dates, and carrots of many colors. His mother looked out from the villa to see how we were doing and waved.

"I saw Herminia this morning when I was walking to the temple," Octavia's friend Portia said. "She acted like she didn't even see me, but I know she did."

"She thinks she is a goddess. I think she's ugly," said Octavia.

"Herminia is not ugly. She's not conventionally beautiful but . . ." Felix said. He tried to weigh in, but was also trying to not be unkind.

"Have you seen how hairy her arms are? Her arms look like his," Octavia said, pointing at my arms.

"Herminia looks fi—ine," Rufus said in his sing-song voice. "You girls all don't have to badmouth her because you're jealous."

"Is she still seeing Fabius?" asked Octavia's friend Portia.

"Gross!" Octavia exclaimed, wrinkling her face.

"Fabius? I think he's nice looking," said Portia.

"Ew," said Octavia.

"Didn't you hook up with him before?" I asked Portia, finally able to join in the conversation.

"That was a *long* time ago. It wasn't really anything," Portia answered, defensively. "He was really sweet to me, so I was just being nice. I felt sorry for him. It was a pity date."

"Likely story!" Rufus jabbed.

Daphne's sister laughed at the story. Rufus parlayed the lighthearted moment of humor, sidling up to her with as much suaveness as he could muster.

"I thought you guys were together for several months," I asked, innocently.

"Yeah, didn't your parents walk in on you two?" Octavia asked.

"Was that out of pity?" Felix's brother prodded.

"You guys are so mean," Portia said as her face flushed.

Meanwhile, I gazed at Daphne. She was unique, like something I had never seen before. She cut a fine figure. Tall, slender, and dark, with long, wavy hair. I noticed her dark eyes and long straight nose that was prominent, but also elegant. She had pink, narrow lips that showed her teeth every time that she smiled. There was something visceral and instinctive about my attraction to her. It was like we were two puzzle pieces that were destined to fit together.

Then I noticed Octavia giving Felix a scolding look.

"Anyway, have you all met yet?" Felix tried to change the subject.

"I'm Daphne," she waved at everyone, "and this is my older sister, Cornelia." Cornelia waved too. Rufus took his opportunity to take her hand ingratiatingly.

"We live with our father in the villa that you see on the other hillside." Cornelia pointed.

"Yes, I have been looking forward to meeting you both. Welcome!" Felix said.

We all sat around gossiping and telling stories for quite some time. As the afternoon started to turn into evening, Felix's brother, who had been sitting next to me, stood up and announced that he had to be leaving. He offered Daphne the seat next to me, in order to do me a favor. A favor I had not asked for, by the way.

The blood drained from my head. Do not act effected, I told myself. Be casual. I felt the sweat run down my sides from my armpits. My hands were sweaty too.

We had both spoken up in the group conversation, but we had not spoken to each other directly. Rufus was making a strong pass at Daphne's sister, Cornelia. She was playing hard to get, but in a very easy way.

As the sun set and the stars came out, Daphne sat on the cushion next to me. I could smell her perfume. There was no wind. I could feel my own heart beating.

"I'm Lucius," I said to her quietly.

"I know," she answered, nonchalantly, with her tooth-filled smile.

"How do you know?" I asked, again quietly, smiling back. Both of us were smiling, but avoiding eye contact.

"Felix told me about you. So, did Felix's brother," She answered in a playful tone that said it should have been obvious. "And we've been sitting around the same circle having a conversation the entire afternoon. I did get every-one's names during that time you know."

Then we both made eye contact and smiled.

Octavia and Felix walked up to the house and her friend followed her. Across from us, Rufus and Cornelia began to occupy themselves physically.

I built up the courage to reach across her lap for her hand, which received my hand quickly.

"You remind me of someone," she said, playfully.

"Who do I remind you of?"

"A boy I used to know."

"I doubt it. There is only one Lucius," I stood up, pulled her boldly up with me, our hands still embraced. I trembled.

"Who do you think you are, Lucius?" she asked in the twilight, her eyes glowing. This was my moment. So, I went in for the kiss, her lips parting and eyes closing.

Our hearts were now beating next to one another. As I kissed her, I glanced towards the villa. I thought I saw Felix's mother at a window.

"I think we are being watched. Follow me." I mustered up all sorts of confidence that I did not really possess. I took her arm and we walked further into the garden. We walked under a vine covered arbor and entered a maze of night blooming flowers. There was moonlight shining down on us. I pulled her towards me again in passionate embrace. That night in the garden was like a dream.

"Daphne!" I heard a yell that woke us from that dream. My swollen heart nearly exploded.

"Oh, no. That is my father," Daphne sighed in frustration. "I need to go home."

That voice would become more familiar to me over time.

"No, don't go yet," I said, greedily. Pulling her back to me.

She gave me one last long kiss and then before I could say another thing, she left to go back to her father's villa.

And then I was lovesick. A feverish, consuming, visceral love sickness. A love that was infatuation. The first crush of infantile, fanciful yearning. This obsessive love grew by nurturing it with imaginative development throughout the following days and weeks. This was the childish, and ideal-istic first love that you hear in clichéd love songs.

MY SEA JOURNEY WAS coming to an end as we approached Caesarea and my reflection on it so far was bittersweet. I was drawn by its adventure and how it allowed me to escape from home. But the same time, I was too proud to admit that I also had occasional pangs of homesickness and lingering fears of the unknown despite my optimism about my travels. A poem that Daphne had written for me was apropos. She wrote it while reflecting on her own itinerant life.

When I try to hold on
And make a new home
I have to let go
I must move on

In fate I trust
I try to adjust
No wanderlust
Just loneliness

My heart is heavy
I am at sea again
These days go by
Looking up at the stars

As I go
From one place to the next
Salt from my tears
Falls into salt of the sea

And as the day breaks
A glimmer of hope
Opens my heart
And I make a new home

CAESAREA WAS ONE OF the largest man-made harbors in the world. It was an engineering marvel. When I arrived at the port, I was surprised to discover that Yohanan was not there to meet me in person. Instead, he had sent guides to meet me in Caesarea, and they would then escort me from Caesarea to Yohanan's home in Nazareth.

The guides took me safely down the roads from the coast and inland through Samaria, into Galilee, and on to Nazareth. They were local men and they knew the land well. I did not know if they were formally educated in the manner I had been, but they spoke fluent Greek. Each wore a cloak over their tunics and carried tall walking staffs. Their tunics and cloaks were the inconsistent natural colors of sheep. They did not cover their heads, revealing cropped hair and beards. They were taciturn, humorless, but at the same time agreeable and easy going. In hindsight, I believe that they were radical Jews from Samaria.

The rolling hills were covered with grass as well as green and yellow bushes. Grey stones popped out between the bushes. Many of the hills were sprinkled with red and white wildflowers. The land was quite beautiful and green, unlike the deserts in the south of Judea that are often pictured by the modern reader. Two thousand years have caused much more desertification of this area that was once a land flowing with milk and honey.

8

NAZARETH

I arrived at Yohanan's home without any issues due to the efficiency of my guides. I thanked them and paid them a gratuity after Yohanan paid them, and they went on their way. I wouldn't miss those dull people. Yohanan was a short, shrewd man, with squinty eyes, thick peppered hair, and a long gray beard. His eyebrows pointed out faintly on the ends, giving him a look of both wisdom and experience.

When I met Yohanan, I handed him the papers written by my father's associate, explaining more details of my employment. Yohanan grabbed the papers, looking at them sideways and then upside-down. Then he said, "Welcome to our home, Lucius! Shalom! I trust that your trip was safe and that you did not catch the sickness that's going around."

"Yes, thank you," I said.

"Come in." he waived enthusiastically, "This is my wife, Miriam. My eldest son, Jeremiah. And, my other son, Jedidiah," he mentioned with slightly less pride.

"Let us not forget my daughter, Sarah." She sat in the darker corner of the room with her head and much of her face covered. His face quickly turned from a friendly smile to an overprotective scowl. "She has just turned thirteen this week. That means keep your Roman hands off her!"

Is that how he scolds me, a Roman citizen and the son of a Roman politician? An awkward silence. Yohanan smoothed out his beard nervously, running both hands the entire length from his cheeks down his chest.

"Well, eh—it is nice to meet you all," I said. I was uncomfortable, but decided to be polite. Don't bite the hand that feeds you.

"You will share meals and observe feasts with us—but from the children's table. Maybe you will learn something. As this is Friday, we will begin shortly before dusk." He gave me the frustrated expression of someone who had never had to explain this before. This village did not have many visitors like me. He thought these rituals were self-evident. "Tonight, we will usher in the Shabbat by lighting our candles and reciting our blessings."

As the sun was setting, they gave the blessings. During the ritual, I became restless at the children's table. I excused myself and went outside for some fresh air, looking up at the stars. I made out the constellation of the Great Bear in the sky. While I was looking up at the shape of the stars, they were focusing inwardly on something I did not yet understand.

When I returned to the house and sat down, Miriam was lighting the oil and saying a blessing. Then Yohanan blessed the children and said a prayer.

"Amen," the family said in unison. Feeling left out, I moved my lips without making a sound. I was mesmerized by the lamps as the flames danced in the dark, the smell and thickness of the smoke adding to the ambiance.

There was no real celebration or anything that night. At least, not how my Roman friends would do a celebration ritual. A cup of wine was blessed, but it didn't look like there was much of that to pass around, much to my disappointment.

Yohanan was the first person to get any wine. I wasn't sure if that was part of the ritual, or just Yohanan's way of doing things. I was bored with the ceremony and was getting hungrier and thirstier by the minute.

Following the wine, each of the family members washed their hands. Miriam went first, then Jeremiah, then Jedidiah, and finally Sarah. Then each of them gave a blessing, but I could not catch what they were saying. Miriam's was very stern sounding, Jeremiah was canonical, and Jedidiah awkwardly stuttered in his guttural voice. Finally, Sarah delivered her soft blessing from beneath her shawl. She was gentle and perhaps made bashful by a stranger from Rome watching her. Yohanan gave me another one of his looks and I averted my eyes.

Then it was time for dinner. They passed around a braided loaf of bread called a challah. I was finally able to get a small pour of wine. I was given enough bread to satisfy my hunger, but not my appetite. As I ate, I was told that there would be two more festive meals the next day to honor the Shabbat.

After the meal I was still hungry. "Let me show you to your bed. To the shed!" Yohanan said, regaining his initial humor.

"Shed?" I asked.

I'm not sure if the shed was specifically in my father's plan to teach me humility and to appreciate my station in life but, either way, I don't think he would have been disappointed. After I had displaced some hens and various other poultry, I laid out my personal effects on the hard dirt floor. Then piling up some straw, I made myself at home. Laying on my back and looking up through the cracked roof, I saw the stars in the clear sky. I saw the Great Bear again, and I felt a wave of hope wash through me, as if I knew that the gods had wanted me to be here.

AS I LOOK DOWN *from heaven now, I recall that fateful time that I was staring up into the cosmos. Humans have held a ubiquitous obsession with the cosmos. Modern Christians are familiar with the Star of Bethlehem. The star leads the Zoroastrian Magi, or three wise men, from the east to Bethlehem, where they find the Christ child.*

Human obsession with astrology is found across the ancient world from Meso-America to India. Astrology can be traced back four thousand years to the Babylonians. The Babylonian priests looked to the stars for the will of the gods. The Romans, like the Babylonians, associated their gods with the planets, such as Mercury, Venus, and Mars.

Presently, humans focus on the conquest of space in the name of scientific progress. The NASA space missions landed man on the moon. By the time you read this, Voyager 2 space probe will have left our solar system and entered interstellar space. The SETI institute monitors the cosmos for transmissions from intelligent extra-terrestrial life. And, yet, with all this scientific progress, we're losing the spiritual wonder for the cosmos that has been universally held by mankind for millennia.

THAT NEXT MORNING, I was up bright and early. To get on the good side of my worthy bearded host, I gathered some of the tools that I found in his shop. I grabbed what looked like a hammer, and a marvelous cylinder with handles on opposite ends. I rolled the cylinder over a piece of wood, tiredly wondering about the purpose of such an instrument.

"Shabbat Shalom!" Yohanan greeted me, sticking his face and beard out of the door of the house. He had observed me in the shop, and was now looking at me with a mixture of confusion and frustration.

"It's Shabbat. The holy day of rest. There is no work! Get cleaned up and get your ass inside," Yohanan shouted.

"Yes sir," I said. I was confused.

"And, bring the rolling pin with you!" he said.

"Of course," I responded, embarrassed. Honestly, I hadn't the faintest idea what he was talking about. Holy rolling pins and Shabbat? I put the other tools back and walked into the house with the rolling pin.

Yohanan and his family were seated around the table. I took my seat at the children's table.

"Lucius, as you know, we are Jews," Yohanan explained. "We are the chosen people of the God of Abraham and Isaac and Jacob . . ." He explained, extending beyond my attention span.

I was starting to feel fortunate that I was not part of the chosen people myself.

"And that means that on shabbat, we do not work. Which means, as our guest, you do not work," Yohanan continued.

On the other hand, being part of chosen people didn't sound so bad. As far as I was concern, I'd rather be chosen to not work every day of the week.

SIMON VERSUS SIMON

"On the seventh day of creation, Yahweh rested, and so will we."

"Who?" I asked bluntly, still confused on several points.

"Young man, you have a lot to learn. Oh, but it is such a shame, you are a Roman citizen and would not be interested in the creator of all things, now would you?" he asked.

"I'm sorry, sir, but I've never heard of Yahweh." I was trying to learn about the world, so I did not want to discourage him from explaining. "Would you explain please?"

"Yahweh is the one true God," Yohanan said solemnly. "The God of Abraham, and Isaac, and Jacob."

I returned a blank stare.

"Yahweh, is the creator of everything," he stated proudly.

"Everything?" I asked.

"Yes! Everything," he said.

"You mean, he created this rolling pin?" I asked.

"No, jackass! My brother made that," Yohanan became frustrated and took the pin away from me. He took a calming breath, then said, "Yahweh created all the heavens and the earth. We were created in his image."

"Why?" I asked profoundly, but by complete accident.

"Well, because," Yohanan said, and then he glanced at Miriam for help. Miriam shrugged and busied herself with meal preparation. Then Yohanan looked at Jeremiah, who shook his head with disinterest. The family disapproved of having a theological discussion with a foreigner. I was a Roman citizen, and a gentile, with no hope of understanding.

Yohanan sighed and continued, "Because, after Yahweh created all of the heavens and the earth, *He* rested. And, so, on the Shabbat, we rest. This was a commandment given to the people by Moses."

I was getting the impression that Yohanan was reaching his limits as a teacher of theology, and so I stopped asking questions about his god.

The Shabbat consisted of two meals that day, saying the prayers again with each meal. As I sat with the family around the large table, Yohanan asked, "Lucius, did you enjoy your travels through Galilee?"

"Yes, I did. But I was confused when I was traveling with the guides whether I was in Judea or Samaria. Eventually they told me we were in Galilee," I said.

"They are all parts of Judea," Sarah jumped in, eager to teach me a lesson. "Judea is made up of Galilee, Samaria, and Judea."

Judea is a part of Judea? No wonder I was confused.

"We are in Galilee which is the most righteous of the three. Judea is where Jerusalem is," Sarah continued. "The people from Judea are self-righteous hypocrites that believe they are superior to us because the Temple is in Jerusalem. They think we are dumb because of our country accents. But we know they are just jealous of our good country living and bountiful farms. Right, aba?"

Yohanan wore a stern look but did not disagree.

Sarah continued, "Samaria is to the south of us on the way to Jerusalem. Many Samaritans are not Jews, but gentiles like you. The Samaritan Jews are what aba calls 'radicals.' We say in Galilee that the best part of Samaria is the road that takes you through it to Jerusalem. Have you been to Jerusalem?"

"Jerusalem? No, I haven't, but I have studied it," I answered.

"You are a Roman," Sarah said, "Maybe you don't want to go there. Our rabbi said that gentiles like you would not be welcome in the Temple."

"Sarah, mind your manners," Yohanan said. He pulled his beard repeatedly.

"But, aba," Sarah said. She opened her mouth to continue, but her father gave her another stern look. That was her signal that she wasn't allowed to talk about this topic anymore.

"The fruit is very tasty here. Is this local?" I asked. There was no answer, no more conversation. After Sarah's lesson, I knew I was never going fit into this culture. I was welcome here with Yohanan, but only as a paying guest and nothing more.

I went to bed with satisfied stomach, but with a restless mind. I turned uncomfortably on the hard dirt floor in the shed. As I suffered from insomnia, I held a conversation with my father in my head, as I had a habit of doing. This time I updated my father on my apprenticeship with snide pleasure. Father, you spitefully sent me to this squalor to teach me a hard lesson, and my first day on the job is resting. Yea, no work the first day. And, three square meals. Not so bad. I guess you taught me a tough lesson. I continued this mental conversation for a while. And then my mind wandered from one thing to the next, tossing and turning, until I finally fell asleep.

Shabbat ended at sunset that day and the next morning work was to begin. Someone gave a knock and that woke me up. I felt like I had just fallen asleep. I pretended not to hear it. Finally, I rolled out of the hay and walked towards the house to join Yohanan at work.

YOHANAN TOOK ME UNDER his wing. He was not only a carpenter, but did masonry, furniture making, and other kinds of home repairs. Since Jedidiah was already his right-hand man, I was not typically needed for actual skilled work. For the most part I was a manual laborer and errand boy, but I did pick up a few skills. I learned to work with my hands, day in and day out. We were building new homes in Nazareth. It turns out I was capable of hard work and enjoyed the cathartic toil of manual labor. They assigned me mostly mindless tasks and this afforded me ample time to imagine my future or simply to day dream.

At the end of one day of hard work at a job site, I was cleaning up and thinking about my family back home, happy to prove them wrong with my contentment. I imagined my father's reaction if I told him that I wanted to be a carpenter for the rest of my life in Judea. That I had found my true calling.

I was picking up my tools when a local man approached me. He was middle aged, stocky, with a short beard and cropped, black hair. He had a dark complexion, tanned darker from working in the sun.

"Hello. Are you one of Yohanan's people? Yohanan, the master carpenter," he asked. He stepped in front of me, coming very close, invading my personal space. He then looked at the house, and with an exaggerated expression of awe on his face he asked, "Is this one of his works of art? His latest crowning achievement, his magnum opus?"

"Yes," I said. Agreeing with the part about being one of Yohanan's people.

"I'm some degree of a master carpenter myself," he said, introducing himself with both thumbs pointed towards his chest and a wide smile, "I'm James."

"I'm Lucius Octavius Aurelius," I said. "You can call me Lucius."

"Where are you from, kid? You don't look like a local," James said with a chuckle. My name and accent would have indicated that right away. "And you don't sound like a Jew. No, surely, you are not from Judea."

I was going to answer, but he interrupted me. "Wait, let me guess. I am good at this. I can place people easily by observing their features and mannerisms. You must be a Roman. You have that countenance, in regards to your facial expressions and mannerisms, of a genuine Roman."

"Yes, I am Roman, but," James interrupted me before I could get another word out.

"Yes, you are a veritable Julius Caesar. The very image of a Caesar. I would even say you are statuesque. Like a statue of a Roman emperor, you are the spitting image of Augustus."

"I am from Rome, born and raised, as was my father, and his father before him," I answered proudly.

"I knew it!" James said.

"Well, to be fair, I kind of gave it away," I said.

"Allow me, my good man," James said, and he offered me his hand. As I happened to be holding a large hammer in my hand, he was gesturing for me to let him have it. I hesitated, and he smiled.

"No, relax. I won't touch the domicile. This is just for your edification. Allow me. I'm going to impart some of my wisdom and experience."

I gave him the hammer. He turned, and then he walked up to the face the side of the home.

"Observe carefully," James said. He held the large hammer in his left hand. "Observe how I am holding the hammer, not

86

as *such*." He choked up on the handle. "But as such." Then
he slid the hammer so that his left hand was holding it at the
very end, down the handle so that his smallest finger was
wrapped around the knobby end. "Doing this will provide
the most leverage. Observe, that the hammer makes an angle
thusly, and there is, uh, the most mechanical advantage, in
regards to the physics of the, uh, swing, thereby increasing
the velocity and hence the power of the hammer swing . . .
down on its target." He seemed pleased with himself after
this explanation. I thought I already knew how to hold a
hammer. It did not really need to be explained.

James seemed satisfied with this lesson in hammering
and continued onward. "OK. Now let me canvas the house.
Did you do this masonry work yourself, Lucius?"

That was when James started walking around the house,
rubbing his hands on the building. What a strange character,
I thought. And what an exhausting personality.

I followed, watching him carefully. "No, not really. I mean,
I helped, but Jedidiah did most of the work."

For a while he was crawling around in the back of the
house. Then he was standing on top of a small ladder. He
made several noises that indicated he was thinking critically.
Some of the noises sounded like disappointment and some
of them indicated a job well done. I observed his posture,
searching for what was peculiar about his shape. Not only
was he short and stocky, but since his chin and jaw were
so near his body, he did not really have a neck. He was not
exceptionally strong looking, nor obese. His chest protruded
outward and was at least twice as big around as mine.

"That is a shame," James said. "Jedidiah is nothing compared to his father. Yohanan, the master carpenter. The
reputable. The incomparable."

James came down the ladder, then squared me up and grabbed my arms firmly. "You have the hands to be a true tekton."

"A what?" I asked.

"A tekton. It is the Greek word for an artisan, a craftsman. What a carpenter does, as opposed to what to a stone or iron worker does. Skilled work as opposed to brute force."

"Well, yes, but I am only doing carpentry because my father wanted to teach me a lesson." I said. "I am Yohanan's apprentice. Only for the rest of this season."

"May I ask, then what are you doing after that?" James asked.

"After that? I'm not sure. I'll probably go back to Rome."

"You don't want to do that, Lucius." He shook his head and tightened the belt on his robe. "I will mentor you. Lucius, you will be my new protégé."

He held out his hands to present the offer dramatically.

"I appreciate that, but I am already being trained by Yohanan, but only temporarily." I said.

"Not as a tekton. Wait, allow me to amend that statement. Not only shall I mentor you in carpentry," and then he paused dramatically, "but in *life*."

I wasn't sure how to respond to this offer. Nothing had prepared me for this. I had just met him.

"Oh, let's finish up here. I am running late," James said, putting up his hands. "My mother is probably waiting for me. So, where do I find you?"

"This job is almost done, probably like next week or so, but I'm not sure after that," I said.

"No, I mean, where is your lodging? Your residency? Do you have accommodations in Nazareth?" He asked.

"I'm living with Yohanan and his family during my apprenticeship," I said.

"Tremendous! Then I know where to find you," he said.

And then James walked off shuffling his sandals down the dusty road with his stout legs.

I resumed gathering my tools. Yohanan and Jedidiah arrived as I was packing my bag to leave the work site.

"Was that James, son of Joseph?" Jedidiah asked.

"He said he was James." I answered.

"Yes, that looked like him," Yohanan said.

"That guy is weird," Jedidiah said.

"He seems pretty nice to me," I said. Although he was exhausting to talk to, I found him interesting and harmless.

"Well, his family has been through a lot. He is the younger brother of Jesus of Nazareth." Yohanan said, and then a darkness came over his face. "That poor mother of his."

"Jesus of Nazareth?" I asked, "I've never heard of him."

"You've never heard of Jesus of Nazareth?! The messiah? The king of the Jews?" Jedidiah exclaimed with dramatic sarcasm.

Yohanan cut him off, and he turned to me. His face became serious as he said, "Jesus was a radical. A troublemaker with a lot of wild ideas. Sure, many of his teachings helped a lot of poor people. His message was uplifting to many downtrodden souls. He was a carpenter, just like us. I knew his father, Joseph. He used to sell me his old tools that he didn't need anymore. Jesus was a solid carpenter, a hard worker too, quiet and modest. But then his wild ideas went to his head. He thought he was speaking for God. He upset some of the wrong people. The pharisees, and other people in power that do not like radicals like him. He ended up being crucified." Yohanan sighed heavily.

On the walk home that night, Jedidiah told me more about Jesus and his downfall. Not only did this make me want to learn more about him but it also elevated my interest in James. If James was his brother, he would know more about this man, his life, and his teachings.

9

JAMES

I wiped at my sleepy eyes and swore at the new day, awakened by the sunlight that shone through the cracks in the shed. It was time to get to work. I grabbed my tools and started the daily routine of walking up the hill towards Yohanan's shop. To my surprise, James was already there, chattering away with Yohanan. Jedidiah was also hanging around, in the background as usual.

"Good morning Lucius," James said. He patted me firmly on the back. My tiredness only seemed to add to his enthusiasm. "What a fortuitous occasion that I would meet you here. I was just talking to Yohanan about you. My Roman friend, this is serendipity."

Yohanan looked askance at James and me with a puzzled look.

"Hello, what are you doing here?" I asked, rubbing my sleepy eyes. I was still waking up, but I made a better effort to be polite. "How are you doing? What brings you to these parts?"

"Yohanan and I are associates as part of the larger tekton community. We were just transacting a business arrangement. As you approached us, we were just commencing some negotiations, concerning some hardware, regarding some of Yohanan's surplus inventory of which in recent days has become superfluous," James said.

"I sold him some nails," Yohanan said. His voice reverberated in the large pot he was digging through. He spit some dust and straw out of his mouth. Some of it got caught in his beard.

"I have an opportunity for you," James said to me. "Let us discuss it over dinner. My mother is a great cook. Come join us tonight and we can sort things out."

"I'm kind of busy with this house job Yohanan has me doing, so I'm not sure if tonight will work," I said. Even though I had nothing better planned, the prospect of having dinner with an older man and his mother was not very enticing.

"Lucius, you go on ahead. Jedidiah can finish up with the job, don't you worry," Yohanan said. He knew he was setting me up. I could tell it amused his odd sense of humor since he was struggling to hide his grin.

"Then that settles it!" James was so pleased. He grabbed my arm aggressively, shaking at the wrists, so that my hand shook his furry forearm.

I was ambivalent about James. As tiresome and weird as he was, I also enjoyed his company. And James seemed genuinely interested in me. I'd had enough conflict with authority figures in my young adulthood that it was refreshing to have someone that seemed interested in me.

Yohanan was a good employer but performed out of duty rather than interest.

On the day of the dinner I had toiled in the hot sun from sunrise to sunset, so I was sweaty, sore, and depleted. I started to walk home alone since Yohanan and Jedidiah had other errands to take care of. Then it struck me that I had almost forgotten about my dinner plans with James and his mother. I rushed back to my residency to rinse myself off quickly with some cold well water. I put on a different robe to make myself a little more presentable, and then rushed across the village to James's house. Soon I was at their door.

James welcomed me emphatically with a smile and his hairy-arm wrist shake. "Please come in. Mother is making one of her delicious meals for us. Mm-hmm, can't you smell that home cooking? Come this way. We have a table set out back."

Their house was small and cluttered, and I instantly felt claustrophobic. So, the prospect of sitting outdoors caused a wave of relief to flow through me. A small wooden table in the back courtyard was set with a delicate tablecloth and lamp. Solid gray stone walls enclosed the yard on three sides with the house behind us. Small stones outlined the paths in the dirt yard. It was a humble abode, but the surroundings provide a private comfort. There were a few palm trees that provided shade. As the sun was setting, the heat would abate into a cool evening.

"Please, sit down. Relax, take off your sandals," James said. "Help yourself to some wine." He motioned towards my feet as if he was going to help me with the sandals. Instead, he went back in to check on his mother.

I took in the surroundings past the stone wall. I could see past the neighboring Nazareth to a shepherd with his flock on the hillside beyond the village. I leaned back comfortable, spreading my legs out to relax. I looked at the wine jug on the table about three or four times before finally deciding to help myself. The wine was surprisingly tasteful. I felt a tranquil numbing warmth fill me instantly.

I heard clattering and banging noises from the back of the house, indicating where dinner was being prepared. Then I heard a few unintelligible words in an argumentative tone spoken between mother and son. The son retaliated in frustrated resistance and tired explanation.

As bizarre as it was to be with two strangers in this strange land, I felt an odd welcome in their home. The awkwardness that swirls in the abdomen. I had been homesick, although I was stubbornly proud of my independence. I believed James truly wanted to make me feel at home.

I took another healthy sip of wine, feeling more casual, watching the sunset, listening to the birds and the sheep.

"My deepest apologies for taking so long. Mother can be a bit of a perfectionist." James had brought out some earthenware plates and bowls for the three of us as well as some bread, oil, and dried fruit. He busied himself setting the table, restless and enlivened, giving the impression that having guests over to share a meal was a rare and special occasion. Finally, James relaxed enough to sit down. He turned and smiled at me, but found himself without a word to say, which was rare for James. I cleared my throat and started the dinner conversation.

"Since I started living with Yohanan, I have been learning a lot more about Jewish customs. You do not eat pork, or certain kinds of fish?" I asked.

"That is right, Lucius. We are permitted to eat meat that only comes from animals with cloven hooves that chew their cud, such as the goat and the lamb." James said.

"So, you don't eat any pork?" I asked.

"No. Pigs do not chew their cud," James said.

"And shellfish do not have fins or scales? That is why they are forbidden?" I asked. Yohanan had already educated me on the dietary rules of his people, so I was making small talk.

"Precisely! Lucius, you are knowledgeable in the ways of our people, and our laws regarding food. A rare Roman specimen. You have so much potential," James said.

"Potential for what?" I asked. His comment was intentional, so I really wanted to know what he was getting after.

"The laws of living are mutually of special interest. But let us save that conversation until after we have completed our sumptuous dinner. We can examine that subject in depth when our bellies are not empty. Speaking of eating, I will go check on the cooking." He stood and shuffled back into the house. In a very short while he returned with a large pot of stew that was the main course for dinner. His mother followed him out and sat gingerly at the table.

"B'tayavon," James said, to commence our dinner. "In appetite."

James poured some stew into his mother's bowl.

"Lucius this is my mother Mary. Mary this is Lucius. Now Mother, I must tell you, Lucius is Roman," he warned jovially. "But he is becoming acclimated to our Hebrew customs. He is living with Yohanan, the carpenter, as an apprentice. He is from a wealthy Roman family, very well connected, I should say."

"Yohanan? Doesn't he still owe us money?" Mary asked.

"No Mom, I already told you! We squared that away a long time ago. I've told you that many times and you keep forgetting!" James said, turning to me, "She's losing her memory these days. She can't remember anything I tell her and asks me the same questions over and over."

Mary heard him but dismissed it politely.

"Welcome, Lucius. It is nice to meet you," she said to me. "Please, eat up. We have plenty of food. How long are you staying in Galilee?"

I took several bites of the lentil stew before getting a taste. I was then struck so harshly by its repulsive taste that I gagged. I quickly turned away to hide my reaction and choked it down.

Recovering, eyes watering, I turned back to answer her, "At least until the end of the season. I'm not quite sure yet but I will probably return to Rome."

"Do you like it here?" Mary asked.

"Yes, I do like it quite a bit. It is relaxing and the people I've met have been very welcoming." In fact, many people had not been happy with Yohanan and his family for having a Roman stay with them. They had just been passive about their concerns in front of me, out of fear, discomfort, or for some other reason. Mary and James were warmly inviting and did not show concern for what the village would say.

We continued to have a nice dinner and there was plenty of small talk and local gossip that I could not follow. They offered more stew, that I politely ate as much as I could tolerate. The sun was setting, and the stars were coming out. The lamp and candles were lit and we continued to share the wine. Mary served herself another generous pour.

James scolded her, asking her to slow down, but this did not seem to discourage her.

"Hold on, I need to find something to show you," James said. Then he got up and went into the house.

"Lucius, come here so that I can see you better," Mary said. I moved to the vacated seat next to Mary. "You look like Joseph did when he was younger. Joseph was my husband, but he is dead now."

"I'm so sorry to hear that," I said.

"You don't need to be sorry," Mary said. She looked towards the house for a moment and then said. "I worry about James. He desperately needs a friend like you. He lost his brother Jesus tragically at a difficult time in his life. But what was so hard for James was losing his wife."

"His wife died too?" I asked.

"No, I wish she had," Mary said, shaking her head in sadness and looked away. "She left him and now lives with her family. She never even cared for him. I don't think she ever felt love. I think she had other men, but I don't know for sure. They remain married, both refusing to divorce, so neither are free to remarry. So, he is stuck now with an absentee wife."

"Do you know what happened between them that caused the falling out?" I asked.

"Well, she could not bear him children. All James ever wanted was a family," Mary said.

"He doesn't seem unhappy to me," I said. Maybe he's trying to befriend and mentor me to fill the void.

"He is staying with me for a while and helps me out too. He's a good boy, but he's a little lost, you know. He's searching for his way and sometimes that gives him some

97

wild ideas, like Jesus."

"Mother!" yelled James from inside the house. He was still looking for something.

"Don't yell at me!" Mary yelled in return. She stood up. "Sorry, let me go see what James is looking for."

They were both inside arguing again, but I couldn't make anything out. In a short while James came back out and sat down again next to me.

"My mom really likes you," James said. "She thinks you are a nice young man. She said, in a word, that you are 'sweet.' Not the word I would choose to describe a young Roman rascal, but, nevertheless. She said you remind her of my father Joseph. He was a carpenter too, you know."

"What were you looking for?" I asked.

"Oh, right, so I was looking for something that belonged to Jesus, but I could not find it. You have heard of the Messiah, and his teachings of course."

"Yes, I know of Jesus, but I don't know of this messiah," I said.

"Well, Lucius, they are one in the same. Messiah means the anointed one, as in, anointed with oil. Like a king, or high priest. Now there have been many anointed ones in our ancient tradition. King David, for instance. Many prophecies in the scripture foretell of a messiah, a descendant of David that would usher in an age of peace and perfection. The Messiah is none other than Jesus Christ," James said.

"Your brother? Who was crucified by the Romans?" I asked with unveiled doubt.

"Yes, Jesus is the Messiah. We are direct descendants of King David," James claimed.

I was speechless.

"Jesus fulfilled the prophecies. Allow me to recite from the book of Jeremiah," James said,

> The days are coming, said Yahweh,
> When I will raise up to David a righteous branch,
> a King who will reign wisely,
> and do what is just and right in the land.
>
> In his days Judah will be saved
> and Israel will live in safety.
> This is the name by which he will be called:
> The Lord our Righteousness.

"And you believe this is your brother?" I asked. I went along with James's story to see where it would go but did not mask my skepticism.

"Yes. We were his disciples in Galilee when he walked this earth not so many years ago. And as his disciples, it is our duty to spread the good word of Jesus. Have faith Lucius, you have a good heart and I know you will accept salvation," James said.

"I'll be safe on my travels. Don't worry about me," I said, not understand salvation at the time. "I can take care of myself. But I am a little lost on these relationships. I have been taught of the one true God named Yahweh. Now you are telling me that Jesus is the Messiah, and the son of God? So, that makes Mary the mother of God? And, Joseph is?" I asked. Because of my upbringing as a Roman, I was trained in the pluralistic pantheon of gods and their relationships. So, I was confused and trying to reconcile the monotheism of Yahweh with the family relationships of mother, father, and son.

"Yes, Mary is the mother of Jesus, and Jesus is the son of God," James said. I must have looked disturbed, because James quickly said, "Lucius, you are getting the wrong idea! Allow me to share more scripture from the book of Isaiah with you,

> 'Therefore the Lord himself will give you a sign:
> The virgin will be with child and will give birth to a son,
> and will call him Emmanuel.'"

"What does 'Emmanuel' mean?" I asked.

"Emmanuel means, 'God is with Us'," James said, spreading his arms majestically.

"So, why was he named Jesus and not Emmanuel?" I asked with suspicion.

"He is Christ, Emmanuel, the Lamb of God, he goes by many names," James said. He sighed after, then continued, "According to the prophecies, the name of the Messiah is Jesus. And my mother is the foretold virgin. Lucius, you must understand that Jesus was the first born of Mary. When Mary was pregnant with Jesus, she was still unwed by Joseph."

His explanation was interrupted by Mary calling for James to help her in the house. She sounded aggravated.

"Allow me to provide some assistance to my mother, and we will recommence our discourse on the teachings of Jesus and his life on earth after I return." He hurried back to assist his mother with dinner cleanup.

I tried to reconcile the woman I had met at dinner with the story James just told me. Mary struck me as so down to earth, warm, and casual. She also had shared pity towards James, so it was hard to consider that she had another son that was the Messiah and Son of God.

When James returned, he said, "I can see that this story fascinates you. I can read your dubious expression, but have faith. I will help you find the way. As we digress into genealogy, divinity, and prophecy, we lose sight of the most crucial aspect of the life of Jesus Christ. The teachings of Jesus provide us words to live by."

James never found what he had been looking for in the house. He told me that it was something that Jesus had given him, and that he wanted me to see it.

My contemporary reader, if you are thinking it might have been the Holy Grail, that could not have been possible. The grail myth was invented over a thousand years later, never once mentioned in the time of Christ.

James wanted to share something of the teachings of Jesus. He was very proud, both as a brother and as a disciple. James also told me about the other disciples of Jesus. I was interested. I wanted to meet new people and see the world, so that should include their gods. At the very least, my interest in foreign gods would annoy my parents. The conversation went on late into the evening. Finally, I had to say farewell and walked back to Yohanan's shed.

I HAD DIFFICULTY FALLING asleep that night in the shed. I could not keep my mind from racing from one thing to the next thing and then back. Like a chariot race that would circle round and round, and never finish. My honeymoon period in Nazareth was over. The unwelcoming discomfort of being a foreigner in a foreign land was setting in. I was a Roman and nothing like the Jews that surrounded me. They were civil and at times inclusive but I was not going to be an integral part of their lives. As much as I was ready to flee from Rome when my father sent me away, I now missed the familiar social norms. I was now tired of feeling out of place. I was now tired of trying to adapt to outlandish customs. The excitement of new discoveries diminished and the daily toil was wearing me down.

The wind howled and the roof canvas flapped wildly above me. As I tossed and turned in the shed, I thought of my plush bed back in Rome. I thought about how much in my old life that I had taken for granted. When I visited Felix's villa, I expected my friends to be there socializing. I yearned for those summer nights with my friends. Was that lost forever? Would I never get to see them again? By the time I get back home, would they be married, or have children, or not be around anymore? I was a fool who took that for granted and got sent away. In my straw bed on the hard ground, I kept replaying these worries and regrets for what seemed like hours. Finally, I fell asleep remembering my warm and comfortable bed back at home.

10

MARY

I was walking down a dusty street in Nazareth with high stone walls on both sides. I went around a couple of older women carrying jars on their heads. As I turned the narrow corner, I ran into James again. He was standing next to the wall, talking to a few young women. He was working to impress them in his usual gregarious and animated fashion, making unrealistic, exaggerated expressions on his face. I was tired that day, so I tried to avoid him. But he noticed me so I could not safely walk away.

"Lucius, the Roman Caesar, the noble citizen!" James said loud enough to be embarrassing to me, although it should have been James who was embarrassed. He grabbed my shoulders forcefully and pushed me in towards the group such that James and I faced the three women.

"Ladies, let me introduce you to Lucius. Don't you think he is a good-looking young man? He is a wealthy citizen

from Rome and does not have a wife. Can you believe that?"
James asked.

This introduction was answered with an awkward silence.
Slowly, each woman revealed a coy smile. I assumed these
young women were not yet betrothed.

"Lucius, this is Anna, Matilda, and—my deepest apologies, your name escapes me although your beauty has not."
James poured it on heavily.

"I'm Ruth," said the third woman, followed by gentle
laughter.

"Lucius, this is for your edification," James said to me
not so discretely.

"Ladies, my dear associate, Lucius," James signaled his
hands back and forth between myself and the three young
ladies, "is a scholar and skilled tekton. He has a very bright
future in construction."

I was interested in young women at that time of my
life. Of course, I was. But I was also irritated and taken by
surprise by James's tacky flirtation. He gave the appearance
that he was impressing me with his skills, but I thought it
was affected and pathetic.

I decided to start speaking for myself.

"I have not been in Nazareth for long," I said. "I have
been staying with Yohanan the carpenter and his family."
I pointed towards where he lives.

"So, you know Jeremiah?" one of the women asked. I
think it was Anna. I was flustered, so I might have mixed
up their names. They exchanged some whispering between
them and laughed. I gathered by their amused mannerisms
that they favored Jeremiah.

"Yes, I know Jeremiah, but I know Jedidiah much better.
I work with him frequently," I answered. They wrinkled

their noses about Jedidiah in disapproval. "We are working on the new home across from the orchard."

"Did you travel all the way here from Rome by yourself?" one of the women asked.

"Yes, I did. Yes and no. Well, not exactly," I said, bumbling. "My father, uh, well, he arranged the trip. I had several different guides by sea and by land. It was an amazing trip and I was able to visit Alexandria and Cyrene on the way."

They all listened intently to my worldly exploits with mild fascination.

"None of us have ever left Galilee," possibly-Anna said.

"We have to go now," the quiet one spoke up. They all said their goodbyes, then they walked off together, arm in arm, chattering conspiratorially.

"Lucius, you Roman pig!" James gloated. "You have been getting a lot of attention from the women around here. This will only upset their fathers, so be very cautious. They do not want a gentile getting close to their daughters. You are the proverbial fox in the hen house."

I only answered with a half-smile of relief and amusement.

"Come to my house and we will have dinner with mother," James said. I was ambivalent about another round of Mary's cooking. Still, I found them entertaining and warmly hospitable.

We walked back up the hill and turned the corner towards Mary's house.

I BEGAN TO SPEND more evenings socializing with James and Mary. I spent so much more time with them than I spent with Yohanan's family. Gossip traveled like wildfire, as it did in small villages anywhere. Since Yohanan's family had a Roman citizen living with them, disparaging rumors spread about them and me, and they could not help but channel some of that disapproval in my direction. Now those rumors spilled over in James and Mary's direction as well.

One evening we were relaxing in their tiny yard after dinner, having some wine and talking. James had walked off, as he commonly did, either looking for something or acting busy doing handy work. He liked to look busy and important. At one point in the conversation I did not hear him anymore, so I wasn't sure when he had walked away.

Mary and I sat together looking at the rock garden, taking the occasional bites of bread. Once Mary knew James was safely out of hearing distance, she started speaking about his marriage again.

"James's marriage was arranged between their fathers. Rebekah's father was a merchant from Sepphoris. Sepphoris is a step up from Nazareth. They even have a synagogue." She smiled her wrinkled face at me. "You see, we were just poor peasants from Nazareth, so we were quite pleased with the marriage arrangement and the dowry. James was nervous and scared, but he did not want to admit it. We could all tell that he was not interested in the girl. He and his father would shout and bicker. They were so different they could not understand each other. My dear Joseph, may he rest in peace, never understood James and they did not get along very well."

"Did you and Joseph get along well? What was he like?"

"Yes, eventually. I learned to love Joseph much more over time—but he was a proud and very frustrated man. He had a very bad temper when he was a young man. When I look back now, I realize we were just children when we were married. I was younger than you are now."

"So, were there not more men suitable for you?" I asked.

"Oh, there were so many nice young men that treated me better than he did when I was an unmarried young woman. They wanted to impress my father and they showered me with gifts. But they seemed like dogs that were begging at me and I found them pathetic. Lucius, my boy, I didn't want to be treated like a child, just to be adored and doted on. My parents had done that to me my entire life, so I wanted to be treated like a grown woman. Joseph was different."

"But, do you regret that at all? Would you not ever want a nice guy instead?"

"What difference does it make now?" she answered. I looked at her warm smile that was permanently etched into her wrinkled face, "Besides, I didn't have any choice in the matter. In the end my father was going to arrange my marriage without any input from me. If I had begged my doting father hard enough, I might have influenced him. But it was never my place to select my own husband."

"I am not going to allow my parents to choose a wife for me. My father and I agree on so little that I doubt I will approve of his selection. Besides, I know that I will be free to choose my wife," I said.

"So, you think you are that free? That you are completely independent from your parents?" Mary asked with a raised eyebrow.

There was a pause in the conversation. I got up to pour more wine for us. It was improper for Mary and I to sit and drink wine together, but Mary didn't care. She said at her age and after all that had happened in her life, she was done being pressured by social norms. James would routinely try to talk her out of things and give up. The wind picked up and the clouds uncovered the moon for a moment.

"There was one boy that I really liked a lot when I was a young woman. I had no idea what true love was at the time, and I'm sure now it was nothing but infatuation, but if I could have chosen for myself, I would have had him," she said.

"But you did love him? You still think about him. Do you have any regrets?" I asked.

"No, I have no regrets. I have seen him several times when I have passed through Cana. He has an inn there with his wife and their children. He is old and fat now. Can you imagine me?" She laughed and coughed, her body shaking and her eyes watering. "Can you imagine me as the wife of a fat innkeeper?"

I shook my head and offered her a smile.

"Joseph was a flawed man. But he was good, honest, and hard working. James is nothing at all like his father. He is much more sensitive. That can be a good thing," she said.

"Is it? What about his marriage?" I asked.

"Oh yes, I'll tell you what happened. They were married in Sepphoris and they lived in Nazareth for several years. James worked as a carpenter and several other jobs, but never kept a consistent job. Rebekah . . ." Mary paused, then shook her head in disgust. "She did *not* like me around. They did not seem unhappy, but she was never once friendly to me. They were trying to have children and they had all sorts of problems until she finally became pregnant. She gave birth to a baby girl who they named Deborah."

Mary covered her face with her hands and looked down.

"Deborah died of a fever before she was a year old. We were all saddened, but James was completely devastated. I felt so bad for him. He told me many years later that Rebekah went on to have several more miscarriages. Then they no longer believed she was able to bear any children, so they stopped trying. I always doubted whether James loved Rebekah, but I never doubted that James loved Deborah. He was shattered when she was taken away from him. There's nothing worse than losing a child, especially your first born."

"James never told me any of this," I said. "He has talked about his wife, but never shared any of their problems. He only told me she was visiting some relatives in Samaria."

"James is so sensitive. Rebekah left him and went back to live with her family. I hear she is seeing lots of other men now—that bitch," Mary swore. "She's not coming back to him. James has his way of coping with his storytelling and always running his mouth, but he is in a lot of pain."

I was growing new sympathy for James as Mary shared more of his tragic story.

"After his wife left him, James quit working and came back to live with me. He said he would take care of me since I was a widow by that point. James is a skilled carpenter, like Joseph, but his marital problems interfered with his work. Sometimes he'll tell me he has plans to go and get his wife back. Then I have to talk him out of it and remind him that his wife left him. I wanted him to divorce. He would not do it because he knew that Jesus preached against it."

Even though Mary was not an educated or sophisticated person in the traditional sense, she struck me as wise and morally upright.

"How many children did you have?" I asked, changing the subject slightly.

"There were the five boys—Jesus, James, Joses, Jude, and Simon. Then there were the two girls, Miriam and Martha. And I have fourteen grandchildren!" she said proudly.

SIMON VERSUS SIMON

I was tempted to ask her about her first-born, Jesus. I had heard so much about him from James. There seemed to be radically differing views on his life and teachings. Due to his tragic execution, I was not eager to bring up the subject of him with Mary.

It was at this point that James had returned to the yard and rejoined us for another drink of wine. Mary had grown tired and told us that it was past her bedtime. She stood up and went into the house. James returned after helping her and we had another pour of wine.

"I'm terribly sorry that I left you with my mother for such a long while," James said. "Some days she is lucid and other days she is not so good. I have noticed lately that she is beginning to lose her memory."

"She seems pretty sharp to me," I said. Then, just to give him a hard time, I added, "Maybe you drive her out of her mind."

"I have that effect on people," James said.

"I have to work very early tomorrow, so I better head back. Yohanan has been tolerant of me lately, but I don't want to push my luck. Even though he doesn't pay me," I said.

"Listen, Lucius, I want you to take an expedition with me to meet some of my brethren to become more familiar with the followers of Jesus. There is a tekton symposium in Lydda we can attend. This professional gathering that will provide a perfect cover story for you. I will sponsor you as your mentor, or, if you prefer, in loco parentis. This will ensure that Yohanan doesn't carry any suspicion in regards to clandestine meetings of a theological nature," James said.

I agreed to join him.

"Also, I don't want Mother to find out," James added.

"You don't think your mother will let you go?" I asked, joking with him. "How old are you?!"

"Be very careful, Lucius! These are very serious matters." James said solemnly. "We are going to meet some of the disciples of Jesus Christ, the Messiah, the Son of God."

James had a colorful personality. He liked to tell tales and to inflate himself. But when James spoke about Jesus, his tone of voice changed drastically, and his attitude turned uncharacteristically serious. It was at this moment that I had a clear and sudden epiphany. My life had been rudderless, and I was now feeling the tugs of a larger purpose. I wanted to meet these followers of Christ and open my mind to their teachings about Jesus.

"James, I am enthralled. I will go with you. I just need to get home now—it is very late. We can talk about it later," I said.

"Lucius, we will go next week and stay for the symposium. Please let Yohanan know so I can make travel arrangements. You just have to meet me here Sunday morning," James said.

It was another starlit walk back to the shed at Yohanan's. I had a vivid dream that night in which I finally met these followers of Christ.

I FELT TIRED AND depleted from the late night and struggled through my next day of work. I knew some hard, physical labor would help me work through the hangover and that I would eventually feel better. Around lunch Jedidiah informed me that there was a Roman courier at the build site looking for me. I went out onto the street and found the Roman courier. He had been hired to deliver a message from my father. The courier took out the message, stood up straight and proper, and began reading aloud from the scroll. "This message is from Decimus Octavius Aurelius of Rome."

"I beg your pardon," I interrupted him. "I can read it myself just fine! I've had the best tutors in Rome."

"I'm terribly sorry," the courier apologized.

I took the scroll from him, and read the following message:

> This message is from Decimus Octavius Aurelius of Rome, dictated on the year 56 A.D. on the 18th of Junius, to be delivered to my son, Lucius Octavius Aurelius, in Nazareth, Galilee, in the province of Judea.

> My son there is some news from the state since you have left for your apprenticeship. Be proud of your father as I have been assigned to an official administrative position in the government of Britannia.

> I will be representing that interest in Rome and have already begun to communicate with Aulus Didius Gallus, the general and governor of Britannia. Our strategy is to invest in Roman infrastructure and subdue any further rebellions from the native tribes. My desire is to grow that territory. We are faced with many challenges such as a lack of political support, contention for natural and military resources between Britannia, and a plethora of border conflicts. But I will waste no more words on this subject as you have never concerned yourself in these greater political matters.

> Martinus has sent me a report that you made it safely to Alexandria and embarked on your final trip

to Caesarea. I am pleased to hear that you were on good behavior during that trip. I trust that you are safe in Nazareth and working hard for Yohanan day in and day out. The courier who has sent this message has also been tasked to return with a written report from Yohanan on your conduct and performance during your first term. He has already been compensated to do so. I hope that you have learned something from the daily toil so that you appreciate everything that your mother and I have given you. We hope this experience cures you of your apathetic and insolent ways.

I have the occasion of running into Gallus Plinius Macro when I visit my associates in the Senate. He is a pompous man, but a very shrewd observer. He said that his bastard son Rufus is still up to no good and spending most of his time with his mother. Your mother and I are relieved that you will no longer be influenced by him or connected to him in any way socially. He will only bring you trouble and has already jeopardized your future.

Your mother is well, but you know how she is. She worries about you. She wants me to tell you that she hopes you are doing well in that foreign land. And that you have not had to put up with too much nonsense with the Jews. She finds the gods of the Jews and their practices of worship nonsensical and intolerable. But my advice to you is not to take after her. Don't worry yourself about her. Learn from her example—it is pathetic to worry so much. Worry

without action is weak and pointless. I told her that
your time with the Jews will only make you miss
Rome. This assignment will give you some sort of
perspective on what we have accomplished with this
great empire and all of civilization.

It is imperative that you become a productive member of society for yourself, for posterity, for our family name and reputation. I have abandoned all hope
that you will follow in my footsteps as a politician.
I am putting plans in motion for you when you get
back later this fall. Your uncle, who was a business
owner in construction in Rome for decades, has
given you a good reference for a supervisor position in Rome. You must carry on properly with
your apprenticeship in order to gain the proper job
knowledge. My name and reputation are tied to this
referral. You will not make an embarrassment of me
as you have done many times before.

I noticed the courier was discretely holding out his hand,
hoping for gratuity. My father's tone had put me in a foul
mood.

"Take this message to my father. I'll be brief. I'll pay you
a gratuity that should easily cover the cost to deliver it." I
took a deep breath and then delivered the words for the
courier to scribble down:

I am grateful that you sponsored this journey for
me. I am doing quite well in my apprenticeship.
Yohanan has been a great mentor and I have met
many new associates. Please share with mother that

I have joined the Christians, a religious group that is growing steadily. They are great people and are spreading the good news of Jesus, the son of god. If I decide to honor their gods, it should not preclude me from honoring our pantheon of gods.

You know Rufus as well as I do. He has a good heart, but he has not found his way in life. He does not benefit from the guidance and direction that some of us have. I am sure I will find my own way in life soon and you won't have to worry about me or your reputation much longer.

I was quite proud of the brevity and sharpness of this message. I paid the courier a tip and a fee to deliver the message, then watched him depart to deliver it. I hope it would wound my father's pride. I assumed my mother would be worried that I was taking up with Christians. I imagined she would be asking her friends what that was all about. My father will also be haunted by the disappointment that I was turning out to be. His plan to make me a successful Roman businessman was being foiled. I wasn't going to be scared into going back home by this dirty, low-end job in this backwater. Instead, I was telling my father that I was grateful he had sent me away, and that because of my journey I was joining up with some radicals.

11

THE ROAD TO LYDDA

It was a scalding hot summer day when James and I, and the donkey carrying our tools, began our trip to Lydda. Lydda was hosting the symposium, a gathering of tektons and other skilled workers in the land. These gatherings provided a venue for these specialists to exchange trade secrets and pass their wisdom to the next generation. Lydda was almost directly south from Nazareth, through Samaria, and into the province of Judea. Lydda was an ancient city known as a hub for commerce and skilled labor, making it an ideal place for this symposium. Lydda sat in a valley that was aptly named Gehaharashim, or "valley of the craftsmen."

We traveled on the Roman road that would bring us through Samaria and eventually to Lydda. The countryside was by far the most scenic I had visited thus far in Judea. We walked through fertile hills and valleys, covered with yellow flowers and leafy trees. The climate seemed milder during our trip and the weather was more pleasant than it had been in Nazareth. Since Samaria was not wanting for rainfall, we passed fertile fields of crops and pastures brimming with healthy herds of sheep and cattle along the way.

The summer sun beat down upon us as we walked the road to Antipatris. By late afternoon we were both hot and thirsty, so agreed that we needed to stop to relax and hydrate. The donkey squinted at me and flicked one of his long ears to show his irritation. He was also showing signs of fatigue from the heavy load. I rubbed one of his ears to reassure him. James pointed at a large acacia tree just ahead that would provide us with ample shade to rest in. I gave the donkey a gentle tug and led him from the path towards the tree.

As we sat in the shade, resting our legs and stretching out our sore bodies, James handed me some water. I took a large swig that filled my belly too quickly. Any more water and I would feel sick. I knew it would be hard to get up and move again when we had too. I felt tired and sore. James leaned his stout body back against the tree and closed his eyes for a just a moment. We both enjoyed the quiet relaxation.

After a while, James sat up and said, "Lucius, I have told you some about these great people that we will meet in Lydda, but have I told you the history of Simon Peter and how he met Jesus?"

"No. You told me about Jesus and his twelve disciples, but I am not familiar with them individually," I said.

"There is much to tell you! I shall start with the biography of Simon Peter. First, let me provide some clarification on nomenclature regarding Simon Peter. Simon was his given name at birth. Jesus gave him the surname Peter, or Cephas in Aramaic, or Petros in Greek. All of which mean stone, or rock. Jesus told Simon Peter that he was the rock on which he would build his church. For those that know him well, we call him Rocky, as a friendly nickname."

"Does he like being called that?" I asked.

"Hell no, it bothers him tremendously. Especially if you invoke that name when he is among his followers. But, if he is with close friends and not out teaching or performing healing, he seems to tolerate it well enough," he said.

James shifted his weight, having difficulty breathing, while trying to sit up straight.

"Anyway, where was I? Right, The story of Jesus meeting Simon Peter. Simon Peter had a brother named Andrew. Andrew, and many of the original disciples of Jesus, were fishers on the Sea of Galilee. These men were not educated, or wealthy. They were poor and illiterate, and they stank heavily of old fish. They earned meager wages from their daily catch, so they were not blessed with many worldly possessions. Jesus met Simon and Andrew while they were casting their nets into the sea. He said to them, 'Come with me and I will make you fishers of men.' Lucius, believe me when I tell you that Andrew and Simon dropped their nets that very moment and followed Jesus forthwith."

"Jesus must have really made a great first impression," I said. That was an impressive beginning, but several unanswered questions were still swirling in my head.

"Yes, but remember these were poor men. It is easier to abandon all your worldly possessions and enterprises when there is not much to give up and leave behind," James said.

"Had they heard of Jesus before?" I asked. I wondered what else had led up to their following of Jesus.

"John the Baptist was a key figure of tremendous influence for Jesus and his disciples. Although John the Baptist was born to a family in the priestly class, he was a radical figure that lived on the fringes of society and threatened the priestly establishment. John was a prophet that lived in the wilderness and provided ceremonial cleansing through baptism, hence his name. This was not uncommon at the time. There were many other communes with leaders providing similar purification rituals that had large followings. John the Baptist, however, was the most influential. He had been preaching in the desert of Judea and baptizing a multitude of followers in the Jordan River for a great many years. He was so influential that Herod considered him a serious threat. He imprisoned him and eventually had him executed by cutting off his head."

"That's terrible!" I said. I realized the gravity of these offenses.

"Yes, we were all devastated by that. John was an eccentric man. He lived a primitive life, wore ragged clothing made of camel's hair, and ate only locusts. Still, he never deserved to die. Unfortunately, he made enemies with people in high places. He stood up to the pharisees and called them all out as hypocrites," James explained.

I was fascinated by the story, but also little lost on how it tied into the story of Jesus.

"How does this relate to Jesus and his disciples?" I asked.

"Jesus was also a follower of John the Baptist. Jesus went to meet John. John was so taken by the presence of Jesus that asked to be baptized by Jesus, and not the other way around. Lucius, John was the leader up until that point. After Jesus baptized John, it became clear to many of those followers that Jesus was the new teacher to follow, although many of John's followers would never follow him. Jesus had already been teaching around the lake for some time. So, Jesus had a reputation before he met Andrew and Simon." he said.

"What was Jesus teaching about?" I asked.

"He was telling his disciples and followers to repent, that the kingdom of heaven is near!" he exclaimed.

James went on for quite some time under that tree, imparting to me the teaching of his brother Jesus. Over time I began to absorb more of the history and the details so that I began to piece together the life story of Jesus as well as his teachings. At this point of my life, I was open to meeting new people, discovering new ways of life, and learning about new gods. Yet I had not yet begun to grasp the meaning of the Christian faith.

AS I THINK BACK now from the kingdom of heaven, I recall the significance of that message. The kingdom of heaven that was preached about was supposed to come during our lifetimes. Nothing else mattered by comparison. I remember trying to imagine what it would look like. As a Roman citizen, I thought of the kingdom as a new empire that would take over the Roman Empire. This new kingdom was going to be a direct threat to the empire. I thought about what affect it would have on all those that did not repent. What about all my friends and family in Rome that were not aware of the new kingdom that was coming?

Occasionally, I remember thinking of the kingdom of heaven as not just a place, or an event. The operative word of Kingdom meant there would be a king. The King was the Father Almighty, and his son was Jesus Christ. There would be a coronation ceremony and all men would honor the King.

I WATCHED JAMES NOD off several times while he was leaning against that tree. We both lost track of time.

"Well, I suppose, it is about that time," James eventually said. He re-positioned his middle-aged body using a four-point rotation to stand up. At one point he was on all fours grunting, pushing off and kicking up the dusty ground. We stood there together, dusting the dirt from our clothes. Again, we prepared for the next leg of our journey on the road that led to Antipatris, then on to Lydda. I led the donkey back onto the Roman road.

We could tell that we were getting closer to Antipatris by the increasing number of travelers headed in the same direction. The Sharon plain was expansive. As we traveled through, we could enjoy the scenic vistas across the miles of fertile planes. The hills and pastures were punctuated by small clusters of trees. James pointed towards the west at one point and indicated that the sea was not too far away. This busy Roman road would also take many of our fellow travelers to Jerusalem.

Antipatris held an important place in Hebrew history. This was the battle ground where the ancient Israelites suffered a devastating defeat by the Philistines who then captured the Ark of the Covenant. The city was built on a hill and there were fortress walls visible as we approached it from the road. A nearby river provided the city with cool, fresh water. Near the banks of the river were many tall reeds and large trees that had been missing on the grassy plains. We walked down to the tranquil river and splashed the fresh water on our faces. Our poor donkey took a satisfying drink.

"So, what happened after Simon and Andrew and the other fishermen started following Jesus?" I asked. "As he was already a master rabbi—"

"Lucius, you are a sagacious learner. Jesus was already prolific teacher and healer. During his early ministry his twelve disciples were following him all around the Sea of Galilee. Crowds of people were following him too, coming from all around Judea, and as far away as Jerusalem and Idumea, up the coast in Phoenicia to Tyre and Sidon, and even—"

"Phoenicia?" I asked interrupting him. My youthful mind had taken a detour. Daphne was of Phoenician decent. I was struck by a pang of nostalgia, the kind that is both exhilarating and heart-rending.

"Yes, Lucius, Phoenicia, as well as many other places. Jesus was healing the sick that suffered from diseases and illnesses."

"What did Jesus do in Phoenicia?" I asked. I had a one-track mind.

"I will tell you about the incident with the gentile woman in Phoenicia. All the disciples were cursing these gentile dogs that came to receive Jesus. A Phoenician woman among them came to Jesus and begged him to drive an evil spirit out of her daughter. All his followers were distraught by his generous nature towards this unclean woman. Jesus was struck by her great faith and that very hour healed her daughter and cast out the evil spirits. Jesus had been rejected by his own people in Galilee and even as close to home as Nazareth. On the other hand, when he went to these unclean cities the gentiles had already heard about him and received him warmly. Jesus was clear on his disdain towards the chosen people who were no longer chosen to him."

I was at once impressed by the healing powers of Jesus. The lesson that James was trying to impart was not lost on me. As a gentile I was welcomed among the Christians with open arms to follow Christ and his teachings. The Jews of Nazareth did not follow Christ. Jews across the land and the Hebrew priests rejected his message. But the unclean, idol-worshiping Phoenicians had found salvation through faith. As a gentile of Roman descent, as an idol worshiper myself, this resonated with me to the bone. As a foreigner, as a citizen of the conquering empire, I found the Christians most welcoming.

We walked back from the river towards the city where we looked for a place to stay for the night. I was still thinking about the Phoenicians. Or at least one beautiful Phoenician. As we were eating a modest dinner at an inn that evening, I decided to share more with James. I thought I should be more open with him since he had shared so openly with me that day.

"Did I tell you about Daphne, my Phoenician lover?" I asked.

This got his attention right away. He almost stopped eating.

"No, no, I don't recall that you have. By all means, young man, divulge all germane details of your amorous affair," James said. He took another large bite of food and winked, "You Roman dog."

"Daphne was not herself from Phoenicia. Her family was from Carthage originally, but was of Phoenician descent several generations back. I met her in Rome because her father moved there because of his business. Last I knew, she went with her father to Corinth, Greece to continue her studies," I said.

"Carthaginian Queen, very lovely. Go on, tell me more

about her," he said. My story increased his appetite, for food. He tore into his bread with zest.

"Daphne is a free spirit, smart, and passionate. She is the artistic type. James, I'll tell you something else. When I walked with her arm in arm through Rome, I could tell that the men all looked at her. Then they looked at me with disappointment."

"So, she is a splendid siren of a woman!" he exclaimed.

"Yeah, she is. Well, that's not the point I'm trying to make," I said, gaining my composure. "What I'm trying to say, is that when they saw me, they knew that she did not belong to me, but belonged to someone else. Someone better than me. She was too fine of a woman for someone like me."

"Someone like them, you think?" James asked sarcastically, but I didn't notice his tone.

"Sure, why not?" I replied in earnest.

In a rare turn of events, James was quiet and introspective. A silence took over and we chewed our food.

This was one of the first moments where I allowed myself to look honestly in retrospect at the relationship I had with Daphne. I reflected on some of the negative aspects of her during our time together. I remembered one incident in particular when we had gone to the theater together. It was a special event that I had been looking forward for a romantic evening. Instead, Daphne spent much of the time between acts talking to a young man in the audience that was an acquaintance of hers. She gave him much more attention and admiration than she had given to me. I was so sick with anger and jealousy that I wanted to leave. She had literally turned her back on me to give her time and attention to another man. And she did it right in front of me. Rather than confront the situation, I walked away and left them together. I assumed that Daphne would notice and come after me. Instead, she did not appear to notice me. That was when I knew I was her fall back plan when her better options were not available.

"Long distance relationships are very difficult," James said suddenly.

"Well, I will take your word for it. Honestly, we only had a short relationship before she moved to Greece. So, we are not together now," I said.

"Well, that is good for you then," James said. "You are still young and have your whole life ahead of you. I have been managing a long distant marriage for many years now and it is not easy. But since my wife and I love and care for each other, we still make it work somehow. It takes hard work and dedication."

I was appreciative of James and his kindness, but I didn't believe the part about managing his marriage and his wife loving him. Mary had told me the contrary. Regardless, I was not going to press him further about his wife. I attributed some of his kindness to loneliness and wanted to return the favor.

"I will take your word for it." I said. I decided to change the subject. I asked, "Did Jesus ever have a woman in his life?"

"Yes," James said. "Mary of Magdala was one of his closest followers. I think she understood Jesus better than any other person, and that includes his original disciples. Jesus loved her dearly, and she took great care of him and the disciples."

"So, she was his wife, or a lover, or?" I asked.

"Oh, no. Not in that way. Jesus was never married. He was flesh and blood, but he did not need the love of a woman in the same way that we do. Jesus loved Mary of Magdala in the same way that he loved Simon Peter and his other disciples, but perhaps with an even closer bond. Mary is one special woman. Beautiful, strong, and wealthy. But I will warn you Lucius, she is not without detractors. Jesus loved and doted on her openly, and this caused a fair share of jealousy and envy, especially among his original twelve disciples. As all these disciples were men, and were brought up in a patriarchal tradition, they had difficulty with women being treated as equal partners."

"Is Mary still alive?" I asked.

"Very much so. She's alive and well. There is a good chance we will meet her in Lydda," he said.

"She sounds like a special woman," I said.

James nodded. "She was a wealthy patron of Jesus and his followers. She took over her family fish-salting business and became quite prosperous. The fishermen disciples probably knew about her before they began following Jesus from fish trading. She was like many other women that Jesus met and healed during his ministry. Jesus drove seven demons from her and cured the dreadful illness that she had suffered from for many years." James said.

"Seven demons?" I asked incredulously.

"Yea, seven." James answered with certitude.

12

TEKTON SYMPOSIUM

I loaded up our donkey before sunrise the next morning and we embarked on the road out of town. We arrived in the city of Lydda early the following day. The symposium was set up in an open-air marketplace and comprised of a dozen tents where the tektons had displays. On the first day I walked through the gathering and took an inventory. The market was bustling with carpenters, masons, furniture makers, painters, and even tile-setters. A juggler provided entertainment. Overall, the symposium was not impressive. It was nothing like a Roman symposium, which was more like a glorified drinking party. At that point, I realized that this was a real tekton gathering, not just a cover for James and I to meet with Christians.

I walked back through the market and found James behind a tent with a few men. They were all talking in a huddle. A tall man seemed to be doing most of the talking. He had well-groomed dark hair cut below his ears and a short beard. They all broke apart and the tall dark man walked away swiftly with a confident swagger. James waddled towards me laboriously.

"We meet at sunset at Mary's house in Lydda," he said. Although the symposium was legitimate, the true purpose of our trip was clear. James and I were here to meet with the Christians.

Mary answered the door when we arrived. I was immediately struck by her presence. She had long beautiful silver hair, and lustrous dark, expressive eyebrows above emerald green eyes. She carried herself with a strong and confident grace that was both intimidating and attractive. She embraced James warmly in welcome. When she introduced herself to me, she wrapped her cool hands around mine, and smiled showing her pristine teeth.

We were invited inside and went upstairs to a large room. Several men were in there, lit only by the candles set on the large table. The air was thick with candle smoke and the smell of warm bodies. I found it very stuffy and hard to breath.

The others in the room instantly recognized and greeted James like a celebrity. His welcome was unlike anything that would have happened in Nazareth. I recognized the tall, dark haired man from behind the tent. I tapped James on the shoulder and asked who the dark-haired man was, since he seemed important.

"That is Philip. He's one of the key deacons bringing the new church forward in Samaria. He is part of this prolific community consisting of evangelists, healers, and magicians there," James whispered to me.

"Magic?" I whispered loudly in reply James, "What kind of magic in Samaria?"

"I have an announcement," Philip stood and addressed the room. "I have received a message from Simon Peter." This got everyone's attention and provoked murmurs of interest.

"Simon Peter shares good news from Antioch. The Christian church is thriving there. Membership has grown tremendously in the last year. We have exceeded our annual baptism goal by more than twenty percent this year."

The room was filled with light applause.

"Also," Philip grinned, "Simon Peter will be attending the symposium tomorrow and will also be joining us for dinner." The excitement in the room elevated to another level. People were all talking at the same time.

"Quiet, quiet everyone for one last item," Philip said. He waited for the room to settle down again, and then said in a serious tone, "I need to remind you, that it is critical that the location of Simon Peter needs to be kept the secret for his safety. It is vitally important that the Romans do not know his whereabouts. Now, by all means, carry on with your conversations."

We stayed with them late into the night, talking about Jesus Christ, the kingdom of heaven, and so many other fascinating topics. I met Philip in person, and many of the other Christians. Philip and James shared more stories of Jesus, and the miracles that they had witnessed. When James and I walked back to where we would be sleeping for the night, and I was so excited that I was unsure if I would even be able to sleep.

WHEN JAMES AND I returned to the symposium the next day, a much larger crowd gathered. Many people were standing around the outside edge of the tents, so James and I pushed through them to find out what was the big attraction. The people had circled around to watch one very distinct man. As we approached, the man was walking in front of the crowd in a very theatrical manner, asking them to allow for a little more space. He was tall and gaunt, dressed in a deep purple robe of the finest fabric, and had long black hair that was streaked with gray.

He walked across the front of the crowd to display something in his large bony hands. As he walked, I noticed his fingers with long twisting fingernails, adorned with sparkling rings. He held a large salted fish, the kind you could buy in the market, humming a tune and shuffling his feet rhythmically. After he made a full circle of the crowd the man danced back to the center part of the clearing and started a more energetic shuffling dance and started speaking in strange verses. All at once his motions became more animated, sandals kicking up dust, his arms waving and legs scissoring and kicking. He swiftly spun his body around, and then came to an abrupt stop. He flung his head back, looking towards the sky. Then he spread his arms out wide, throwing out dust from his long fingers, causing a cloud to cover the area. All the people up front, including James and I, coughed and wiped our eyes. As the dust cleared, we saw him holding a large fish that was very much alive and flapping in his long hands. He showed the fish to the crowd, continuing his shuffling dancing, and humming his song under his breath. His strange silver eyes reflected at me like marbles. The crowd erupted. They had just witnessed a miracle!

James grabbed my shoulders forcefully, trying to turn me away, and then I noticed several men shoving their way through the middle of the crowd. Philip was leading the charge. Eventually he and the man who had worked the magic with the fish were face to face in the clearing. The two very tall men stared at one another as the crowd watched the spectacle.

"Simon Magus, you are a sorcerer!" Philip proclaimed. "A man who uses dark magic for his own glory and benefit, rather than for the glory of God."

The man with the fish, Simon Magus, let out a maniacal, high-pitched laugh. That sound seemed to reverberate outward from him and through the masses.

Philip addressed the crowd. "Good men. You have probably heard of Simon Magus. For some time, he has been practicing sorcery in the city and amazing the people in Samaria. But I warn you all about the dangers of following this man. He has tried to obtain the powers of the Holy Spirit for his own benefit. Not long ago, I brought him into our Christian brotherhood and baptized him as a believer. Then he turned his back on us in betrayal, performing dark magic, and pursuing his own selfish and sinful ways. He does not follow the laws of God and has dealings with many pagan cults."

The crowd booed and shouted. Philip continued, "Simon Magus even approached Simon Peter, the rock of our church, and offered to buy from him the powers of the Holy Spirit!"

This caused another outburst in the crowd. Simon Magus chuckled and tossed the fish to the ground. He moved his arms outwards and wavelike, shuffling his feet, taunting Philip even more.

"Oh, Philip, you are a pretty man. I have always liked you," Simon Magus said to Philip. He reached towards Philip's face to pinch him, but Philip slapped him away. "But you are a jealous man that smells like your fishermen friends." Simon Magus withdrew for a moment, then put one hand on his hip and waved his other hand all around Philip as if pointing out a fashion faux pas. "And it's too bad that you dress like a tax collector."

"Leave this symposium at once or I will be forced to box your ears!" Philip threatened.

Simon Magus showed contempt on his gaunt and distinguished face for a few moments, but his expression quickly transformed when he began to realize that he was in danger. The crowd was on Philip's side, and the murmurs around him were turning into angry rumblings. Simon Magus pulled up his highly fashionable robe above his knees and ran away from the crowd. I watched him escape between two tents, his long legs kicking up dust and sand.

James and I were speechless.

Simon Magus was allegedly an evil man, but I was conflicted as I found him quite entertaining in a magical kind of way.

And then I was struck by a falling, dizzying sensation, as a memory hit me like a ton of bricks. The soothsayer in Messana had said, "Beware, young man, of the Ides of Julius." Indeed, today was the Ides of Julius! That old soothsayer had predicted that I would meet soothsayers and magicians. He also warned me of dark magic!

"James, I have been warned by a soothsayer in Messana of this dark magic! We must beware," I shared my memory excitedly with James.

"Young man, you are quite impressionable. That is, I mean to say, you believe in some far-fetched conceptions like soothsayers and fortunes," James said ironically. "But you are right on the nose with that last remark. Simon Magus is an evil sorcerer and his black magic is heinous and ugly. We'll have no dealings with him! Mark my words."

"So, are there soothsayers in our presence as well?" I asked.

"Well, no," James said, pausing to contemplate, "But, our prophets can foretell the future. They are appointed by God to reveal the future through God's will. Jesus and many of his disciples are prophets. Indeed, you are speaking to a prophet now."

"Now what?" I asked. I was exhausted from all the action that morning.

"I'm famished. Shall we break bread?" James asked.

JAMES AND I JOINED the Christians at Mary's home for dinner that evening in that same room. On this night, the assembly was even larger and more rambunctious. I recognized many faces around the table, including Philip. There were several other women present as well that evening, Mary being the most distinguished of them. We were visiting casually for about an hour or so. Then a pale older man with brown wavy hair and a short wavy beard walked in. Many of the people stood up in respect so I followed along.

"That's Rocky, or, I mean, Simon Peter," James whispered to me.

As I watched Simon Peter sit down at the head of the table, I did not observe anything distinguishing about him. In contrast to Philip, Simon Peter did not carry himself as a confident leader, blending in with the others. James had told me that he had his humble beginning as a fisherman, so I was not taken by surprise.

Simon Peter stood and smiled sincerely, and asked rhetorically, "Shall we all say a prayer?" The room all chanted the Lord's Prayer in unison. Since I had not learned that prayer yet, I moved my lips silently and out of sync with the others in the room. Simon Peter closed his eyes, and passionately pounded his fist on his chest as he prayed. There were no pretensions in his behavior or his devoutness.

After the prayer had finished, the table broke out in theological discussion and debate. Rather than a dozen different people talking at once, we were all part of one discussion, primarily focused on asking Simon Peter questions. These queries related to the life of Jesus and Simon Peter's ministries. Simon Peter shared many anecdotes of his evangelical missions and the overall growth of Christianity. The morale was high in the room until someone in the back mentioned the altercation with Simon Magus.

Simon Peter's face went from pale to bright red with furious anger. "How dare that heretic perform his dark sorcery in our presence!"

The air was sucked out of the room.

"I warned him to never set foot anywhere near our congregations. If a man tries to buy or sell spiritual benefits, it will forever be referred to as the sin of simony!"

We fell deeper into silence for a long moment.

"Simon Magus is the only man I know with more than ten pairs of sandals," someone quipped for comic relief. Light laughter ensued.

"His clothing was made of linen, wool, and the finest

silk," a stern critic shouted. "To wear garments made from a combination of these interwoven materials is against the Talmudic law."

"It's not like we follow that anymore," a man behind me mumbled.

The crowd grew restless, and there was more shouting, and more raucous laughter.

"Yes, Simon Magus boasts that he has the magical power of levitation. We already knew he is a little light in his sandals."

Laugher and lively discussion continued. As everyone was talking around me, I noticed Philip leaning in to talk to Simon Peter, who then nodded his head in agreement. I assumed they were catching up on the events of the day.

ON THAT LAST DAY of the symposium, James and I missed most of the day's events. It became more obvious that the Christians were using the symposium as a cover for their congregation to meet. On the final evening, we gathered for dinner at Mary's one last time. Again, we broke out in a theological discussion. I was growing more eager to engage in the conversation and had finally worked up the nerve to ask a purposeful question.

"When the disciples joined Jesus, he said to follow Him, and he would make you 'fishers of men.' What did—" I spoke nervously, choking up and momentarily losing my voice. The entire room turned to wait for my question, "What did Jesus mean by 'fishers of men?'"

Simon Peter cleared his throat to ready himself for oration.

"As we were fishermen of fish," Simon Peter explained, "we abandoned what we were doing so that we could follow

Jesus and become fishers of men rather than fish. Actually, what I mean, is that as disciples . . ." Simon Peter became flustered and was at a loss for words.

Mary came to the rescue. "As with many parables and teaching of Jesus there are multiple levels of meaning, both literal and figurative. Jesus meant to tell the disciples that they were going to be fishing for men in literal sense as far as spreading the word of his ministry in Galilee. As a metaphor, the fishing relates to the spreading of the good news of the coming of the Son of God and the kingdom of heaven. This metaphor was put in a way that these common fishermen could relate to. Please take no offense to this, Simon Peter."

Simon Peter was not able to hide his scowl.

Mary continued, "Let me also remind us of the miraculous catch of fish that occurred shortly afterwards. Simon Peter and his crew were working very hard one day and were not catching any fish. Jesus instructed Simon Peter to steer into the deeper part of the lake and cast out his nets. Simon Peter reminded Jesus that they had not caught any fish, but reluctantly obeyed his instruction. When they cast out into the deeper water, they quickly caught such a huge number of fish that their nets began to tear. As we look in retrospect, it is not the just hard work of the fisherman that pulled in the fish. We find God's grace through our obedience to God and His will and purpose. One can also clarify that rather than netting fish to be killed, the disciples were to catch men so that they would repent and find salvation and eternal life through the coming of Christ."

"I caught an enormous haul of fish that day with Jesus!" Simon Peter exclaimed with his usual passion and plain way of speaking. "I was so afraid of Jesus after I had so openly doubted him. Afterward, Jesus told me, 'Don't be afraid, from now on you will catch men.'"

Everyone in the room was touched by this sermon. The conversation went on for several more hours, but inside my heart of hearts, I had already decided I wanted to follow these evangelicals, but I didn't know exactly what that would mean. I was too afraid to address the room, so I asked James. He took it upon himself to address the room for me.

"Brothers and sisters," James said, "Lucius and I would like to announce that we intend to accompany you all on the next evangelical mission. I can assist Lucius before I go back to Jerusalem, where I plan to serve as deacon. Have we discussed any details in regards to the itinerary and travel plans for the next mission?"

I was a little shocked, but thrilled that the die had been cast. We all looked to Simon Peter.

"Well, I recommend that we go to Cyprus and then back with you to Jerusalem," Simon Peter said. "Hold on, let me see, actually it would be better if we just went to Caesarea, so that we are in a harbor city. But I was just there, so never mind that." Indecision overwhelmed Simon Peter, the rock of the church.

Philip said, "I recommend a mission to Ephesus. They need our vigilant support since Paul's departure. On our way we'll pass through Damascus and then stop in Antioch." Philip lifted his eyebrows and wrinkled his forehead in a manner that works best if you are handsome.

James spoke quietly to me, "Now let us go forth and make plans. I will accompany you to Antioch and Ephesus, but then I must follow my own calling to Jerusalem."

"I will have to talk with Yohanan to make arrangements to release me from my apprenticeship. I guess I should also write to my parents," I said to James.

"Now all of the sudden you are the organized pragmatist." James kidded me, "You told me that you wanted to travel the world and meet new people. My friend, you truly have found your calling."

AFTER THE SYMPOSIUM MOST of the missionary group headed towards Nazareth on the Roman road. Our journey went by quickly and was filled with wonderful story telling. Once we arrived in Nazareth, I was able to stop by Yohanan's shop and talk to him in person.

"I don't understand young people," Yohanan said, shaking his head in frustration. "For as long as I knew him, Jesus was just a carpenter's son from across the village—no different than if we said Jedidiah was the Messiah. You hear what I'm getting at boy?" He was not looking for an answer. "I will grant you leave of your apprenticeship since I don't have much work this late in the summer. I will send a message to your father, communicating the same. But I will not tell him anything about this mission of yours. That is not my responsibility. You hear me? I'm a poor carpenter and I need to protect myself. I need to earn a living and provide for my family."

I thought fondly of Yohanan and his family. I figured I would never see them again.

Yohanan sighed and said, "You should send word to your father too. Someday you'll realize what a foolish thing you are doing. But I know I can't talk any sense into you now— young people—so I'm not even going to try."

I thanked Yohanan once again with a warm embrace.

He smiled at me and bid me farewell. "You are a good worker and a smart young man. Leich l'sshalom. Safe travels."

Then I headed back across town where I found a Roman centurion. I gave him several coins and asked that he find a courier to send a message to my father. At first, he resisted, but then I mentioned that my father was an influential politician and had the power to put in a word about him. I just needed to know whether it was going to be a good word or a bad one. After he capitulated, I gave the centurion the following message, dictated on the year of 56 A.D. on the 5th of October.

> My apprenticeship in Judea is concluding. You will probably hear from Yohanan the Carpenter of the same news. Please pay him promptly and provide him with a generous gratuity. He welcomed me in his home and taught me to be a tekton. He is a good man, a loving father, and needs the money more than us.
>
> Do not hold any position for me back home. I do not plan on returning to Rome any time soon. When I do, I would much more consider a career in construction than in politics. At least then I would be contributing to society and creating something of use.
>
> Right now, my plans are to accompany a Christian mission to Ephesus. These Christians are great philosophers and wield magical powers that can cure

the sick, heal the blind, and destroy the wicked. I
do not know how long it will take to arrive in Ephesus as there are many stops along the way such as
Antioch. If you want to reply send your message to
Ephesus.

I hope Felix is doing well and Rufus is staying out of
trouble. Tell mother that I miss the comfort of our
villa and our nice dinners together. I do not know
what my long-term plans will be. I will know more
after I've seen more of the world and ventured far
outside of the Roman way of life.

The centurion went off to deliver this message. I went
to find James and the rest of the group of travelers to leave
for Antioch.

PART III

EVANGALISM

13

CARAVAN

After discussing our route, packing, and saying our farewells, we began the long journey to Ephesus. The autumn of 56 A.D. brought milder weather. We took a route through Damascus, approaching Antioch in Syria as our first destination. The missionary group included Simon Peter, Mary of Magdala, James, Philip, me, and a dozen more Christians traveling in a small caravan. While we had camels and donkeys to carry our supplies, we walked on foot for most of the journey. As we traveled through deserts, forests, and mountains we faced many trials and tribulations. There were bouts of hunger and thirst. Dry, hot winds and sandstorms eventually gave way to torrential rain that muddied and then flooded the roads. We battled snakes, hostile foreigners, and worst of all, exhaustion.

We spent our nights in large multi-roomed tents that were set up alongside the road to Antioch. Our stay in the tents was comfortable and my fellow travelers were quite ingenious and resourceful. On several nights I stayed up late with James sitting next to the campfire after the others had gone back to the tents to sleep. James had picked up a terrible flea infestation and had spread fleas to many of the travelers, so we all had to crop our hair and beards short in an effort to eradicate the pests. This made James considerably less popular in the caravan. As James was now more desperate for a friend, he slowly let down his facade and I got to know more about his personal life.

We sat together one night on our blankets next to the fire in the dry evening air cooling off after a scorching hot summer day. The flames flickered, and we began chatting casually about the weather, our itinerary, and other things before the conversation slowly shifted to more personal topics.

"I have a confession to make. There are a few things I should tell you." James said in a matter-of-fact manner.

"You can tell me anything. We are friends now, aren't we?" I asked carefully, hoping that our budding friendship would help to coax out his confession.

"Well, that's just it," James said. "I should tell you my original motivations with our connection. Within the church, we had many intense deliberations and arguments about gentiles joining the faith. I was a strong opponent against the gentiles, and was adversarial in regards to opening up the church to them. Please understand that I did not welcome gentiles like you primarily because I was holding on to our Jewish traditions. We've held those traditions for hundreds of generations, since the time of Abraham. I was requested, ordered if you will, to recruit a gentile that could be added to our ranks. I chose you, Lucius, not only because I was instructed to do so, but because I wanted to dissuade the disciples."

"What do you mean by that?" I asked, troubled by this confession.

"What I mean, Lucius, my friend, is that my original intent was to use you as an example. To be precise, a bad example. A clear case against gentiles joining the church."

"What the hell?!" I was half mad, and half confused, and maybe another half indifferent.

"I know, it was terrible. But you must accept my apology, please! Believe me when I tell you that I respect you as a friend and a colleague, and I accept you now with open arms into our congregation. I have even vouched for you to the other disciples. Your character and integrity have changed me." James placed his hand over his heart. He was flattering me. "OK, maybe I'm going too far with that, but please consider me a friend."

"Of course, I do. James, I appreciate your honestly. So, I convinced you otherwise, because of my character?" I asked.

"Yes, after a fashion. And, since we are being honest, I also considered the benefit of having Romans on our side. You are connected, aren't you?" James asked.

"You are also using me for my connections in Rome?" I raised my eyebrows.

"No, not exactly, Lucius," James said, now patting me on the shoulder. "I just see things differently now. I have come around to see that Christianity will prosper more with gentiles joining the faith. Gentiles like you."

I paused to take it all in and then stood up. I faced the fire and the smoke burned my eyes. I wasn't sure what to believe. It certainly made me realize I had been naive.

"In addition," James continued, "we needed someone that is educated and literate like yourself. You may have gathered by my articulate and erudite manner of speaking that I am highly educated, but actually I can't," and there was a pregnant pause, "I can't read. I am illiterate. So is Simon Peter—and most of the original disciples. Out of this entire group only Philip, Matthew, and Mary can read. So, as you can see, an educated, wealthy, connected man like you can contribute so much to our cause."

James found a way to turn insult into flattery, but he still hadn't quite found a way to redeem himself.

"Is this an apology then?" I asked him.

"Yes, I would like to make amends," James said in earnest. I could tell he was very sincere.

"I accept your apology and appreciate your confession," I said.

James rubbed his forehead and let out a deep sigh. I had him in a vulnerable place, so I decided to press into more personal history and ask a personal question.

"Do you miss your brother Jesus?" I asked. I know, it was blunt, tangential, and indiscreet, but he had provoked me. I asked it with warmth, and I was truly curious.

"I miss him terribly," James said with a heavy sigh. "They nailed him to that cross and he suffered so horribly. I was scared and powerless." James began to tear up. "Why did it have to happen that way? Could he not have saved himself—the son of God?"

"You told me that Jesus had risen from the dead—and now sits at the right hand of the Lord," I tried to console him, sitting back down on the large blanket.

"I know, that is true, praise God," James said unconvincingly, "but my mother was there to witness the crucifixion.

She suffered so horribly watching him. I was so afraid and powerless . . . that I could not face it. I could not bear to watch his suffering. I could not watch him die. I abandoned him. Mother watched him die, alone."

"I'm sorry, James, it must have been horrible. I don't know why people are capable of such vile behavior." I thought of the cruelty of nailing someone to a cross, to die slowly in agony. The callousness of mankind. I was feeding some of my own anger. "Do people not feel any empathy towards the suffering of others? Do people think that if some people are different that it is acceptable to kill them so that they don't suffer? Are we not all human?"

"Sometimes I'm haunted by the thoughts," James said with a deep shaky breath, "of his pain and how much he suffered up there."

He rolled his stout heavy body towards me on the blanket, wiping his teary eyes. "I have another confession to make," he said. "The main reason I'm going back to Jerusalem is to try to find my wife, Rebekah. I have heard she is now residing there. I need to win her back and she needs me too. Jesus preached strongly against divorce."

"But do the two of you even care for each other?" I asked. "Wasn't it just an arranged marriage gone bad? What exactly are you expecting to accomplish?"

"I miss my baby. My daughter, Deborah," James wept. "She was such a pure, innocent, and beautiful girl, taken from this earth. Taken from me. Why did God have no mercy? Why did God take her from me?"

This information was moving me quickly outside of my comfort zone. James put his head in his hands, quietly shaking with grief.

"I don't know James," I said, trying to console him. "Perhaps we could search for those answers together on our journey."

I thought about suffering and how ill-equipped people are to cope with the tribulations of life. I thought about how suffering is dealt out unjustly by man. Why are people so cruel to one another? Why did Jesus have to suffer on the cross? Why doesn't God do anything for suffering people? Why do children have to suffer and die?

We sat together by the fire, no longer sharing any words. We were deep in our own thoughts until the early morning. Then I saw James was closing his eyes, so I gently nudged him awake and encouraged him to go into the tent to rest.

THE CARAVAN TRAVELED SLOWLY, walking into the hot wind, laboring our feet over the loose dirt road. The dust blew up and swirled around our caravan. The satchels and goods tossed wildly against the camels and donkeys. We pushed ahead towards a remote little village on a hill. In the distance, we saw a group of children running towards us. As they got closer, I noticed their faces, dirty and sticky, pathetic with ignorant excitement. Eventually the adults approached with the measured stride of tired age. They were coming out to see us from this poor village since apparently our reputation for healing powers had preceded us. The children were tugging on our clothes and chattering unintelligibly.

"We have heard you bring a man known as Simon Peter," one of the elderly villagers said hoarsely, "who possesses the powers of magic and healing."

Simon Peter approached the man and said, "I am Simon Peter. If there are people of faith that need healing, please take me to them, and I will bless them with the Holy Spirit."

A small group of us were led to a house in the village. An honorable man lived there whose entire body had become painfully deformed due to a chronic illness. A large crowd had taken the crippled man out of his house on a makeshift stretcher, and then stayed to bear witness. As Simon Peter approached, the crippled man reached out desperately with his twisted hand and touched Simon Peter's arm.

"God bless you," the crippled man said. He struggled to turn his head that was pressed savagely against his contorted body.

"Heal this man so that he can walk again and release any demons that possess him! In the name of Jesus of Nazareth!" Simon Peter said in a crescendo.

Suddenly the sky darkened with thunderclouds, the ground quaked, and my knees shook. A bright light shone from Simon Peter's hands in all directions. The light was followed by a deep thunderous boom that lasted several moments. I felt that rumbling in my chest so heavily that I could not breathe. As I came back to my senses, I was bumping into the people that stood in stunned silence next to me.

The crippled man slowly unwrapped his bandages, uncurled his body, straightened out his neck and rolled his shoulders, and began to laugh like a tickled child. He sat up in the stretcher, put both his feet on the earth, and wiggled his toes. He raised his arms straight up to the sky.

"A miracle!"

Then all the crowd converged on the healed man in celebration, jumping up and down, their delighted cries mixing with joyous laughter. The cured man tore off the bandages that had covered the sores of his former twisted body until he was wearing only a loin cloth. Then he ran out over a hill and out of sight, followed by a cheering crowd and most of the children.

One of the elders of the village approached Simon Peter and said, "Bless you, Simon Peter. Before you continue on your journey, please forgive me if I ask you to consider one more favor. We have been suffering from a long-lasting famine. We have not had any rains in a very long time, and our fields are bare. When the heavy rain clouds finally appeared, instead of bringing life giving rain, they only poured down hail stones that destroyed our already dry and brittle crops. We have been informed that by invoking the name of your man-king, you can bless us with rain which restore our fields."

Simon Peter looked down and scratched his wavy beard as he pondered.

"Alas, my good people," Simon Peter said, addressing not just the old man but also the villagers that had remained. "It is evident that you have been suffering famine caused by this long drought. Please do not let this weaken your spirits. Instead, let this be a fortuitous event that teaches each of you a lesson in the suffering of Christ. By his love and mercy, we may follow him in his suffering. You are now all blessed to partake in the practice of fasting. Remain steadfast in your hunger so that you come closer to Christ."

"That is pure goat shit!" yelled a rather large villager.

"We are hungry, and you tell us that it's a lesson! Be gone with you!" cried another villager with such anger that veins popped out of his neck.

"Yea, get lost or we will strike you down!"

Simon Peter and James looked at the now angry mob of villagers with open-mouthed alarm.

"We need to get out of here immediately," James said.

We ran back towards the road to Antioch followed by the angry mob. They began to throw stones at us as we fled. I felt a stone hit me in the back of the leg, but it was not a solid strike and deflected sideways. I saw blood running down the forehead and cheek of Simon Peter. We rejoined the larger group of Christians near the road and urged them to pack up and flee immediately. Nobody was seriously injured and we all escaped in one piece. As we headed towards Antioch in silence, a dispirited and somber mood took over us. The stone throwing attack cast a shadow over the miraculous healing. Although Simon Peter was wounded and appeared vulnerable, I did not lose any faith in him. The incident with the villagers only made me feel more cynicism towards mankind.

14

ANTIOCH

After we had traversed many more miles of dusty road, we finally approached Antioch. Antioch was one of the largest cities in the Roman Empire, and it was incredibly culturally diverse. The city was home to Greeks, Jews, Romans, Christians, and Syrians, to name a few. According to Luke, Antioch was the city where they were first called Christians. Fleeing persecution in Jerusalem, the disciples founded churches in non-Jewish cities like Antioch where the good news of Jesus spread quickly. After Barnabas founded the church of Antioch, he and Paul continued to use the city as a launching point for their missions. Just a few years ago, Simon Peter and Paul first met here, resulting in their first arguments over what to eat. By the time we arrived at Antioch with the caravan, the church was well established in the city.

Antioch was magnificently built below gray mountains, with Mount Silpius rising sharply into the sky behind the city. The citadel and city wall wound high up on the mountainside. The city wall enclosed a thriving metropolis of urban structures; Greek temples, Roman baths and forums, gymnasiums, a palace, and large tenant buildings. The Orontes river flowed rich, thick, and calmly around the front of the city. I was immediately taken by the beautiful sight of the evergreen pine trees, stately fir trees, and brick-red roof tiles which contrasted against the dark stone mountains.

Our caravan crossed the Orontes by walking over a beautiful arched bridge made of stone. Then we passed by a palace before entering the main city by way of another smaller stone bridge. We had a quick discussion and decided that our first meeting spot would be the stone houses in a Jewish suburb. We took the main street through the city center in the new city. I was able to see a grand Greek temple in the distance as well as the construction of a new Roman amphitheater. The main street was so loud and busy that it was hard for us to keep together. A series of chariots charged through, causing us to move out of the way and divide into smaller numbers.

We eventually left the busy part of the new city through a large gate. Philip let us know we were approaching the Jewish suburb where we would be staying. There were accommodations there arranged by the church of Antioch and sponsored by Mary of Magdala. I felt a sense of comfort and safety in the company of Simon Peter and Philip. Clearly, they had been to these houses in this Jewish suburb before, I thought. As it had been a long and exhausting trip, I was ready to go directly to sleep. When we arrived at the stone houses, we were greeted, and we quickly unloaded and unpacked. We found our peace and rest in those stone houses and were reinvigorated for the next day.

THE NEXT MORNING MARY of Magdala led the group to our congregational meeting place where we would spend our first full day in Antioch. Simon Peter, James, and Philip had some private business to attend to and did not join us. The large group set out through the suburb, out of the city, and along the steep mountainside. We walked for quite some time on a narrow path covered in bush and trees. Soon the group was hot and sweaty from the long walk, but the shade of the trees made for a pleasant and welcomed respite from the hot morning sun. We took a sharp turn into the deep woods and found a small clearing. The side of the mountain was exposed there, towering high above us and showing the different colored layers of the mountain's face. Slightly hidden by some brush was a carved door, set into the side of the mountain.

Mary opened the door, and led us into the mountain cave. We entered a large room, a cave dwelling that had been craftily renovated into a clandestine church. There were other people waiting for us in the church, but I could barely make out their faces on the other side of the giant underground room even though the space was lit with several large oil lamps. Mary encouraged us to follow her towards the group. A thin old man approached us from the shadows. As his face came into light of one of the oil lamps, his countenance transformed from apprehension to elation.

"Oh, Mary," the old man said as he embraced Mary, "my dear, how are you?" Then he gently greeted several more of the Christians that had arrived with us.

"There is someone I would like you to meet," Mary said to the old man graciously, "This is Lucius of Rome. He is joining us on our mission to Ephesus."

"Lucius, praise God," he said as he shook both of my hands. "It is so wonderful to have you. Welcome!" He was quite old and frail, but he was dignified and upbeat. I recall that he had such sagging friendly eyes. "I am Theodoros of Cyrene. You may call me Theo. I am the caretaker of this church. I cannot tell you how pleased I am to see another gentile. You are a Roman, are you?" He looked up at me and squinted in closer examination. He was still holding my hands.

"That I am," I said. "I was born and raised in Rome. Then I was working in Judea for the last year."

He squeezed my hands genially, then let them go. I continued, "I passed through Cyrene on my way to Judea. Theo, your name, are you originally from there?"

"I am actually Greek, but my family has been in Cyrene for quite some time. And I'm an old man of the world now. So, I consider myself first a Christian, then a Greek, and then an African from Cyrene." He winked somewhat theatrically. "But they call me Theodoros of Cyrene and I cannot change that. Well, no matter. Please sit down and join the group for discussion. We were just having our most popular deliberation on gentiles and Christianity."

Mary smiled at me as I sat, and then she jumped right back into the conversation.

"The problem I have with the Judaizers," Mary explained, "is that they are too bent on Judaizing. They expect the gentiles to follow all of the Laws of Moses, which were given to the Jewish people many ages before the coming of Christ."

"As a gentile myself, I am on Paul's side of this argument," said Theo. "When we evangelize and bring new gentiles into the Christian church, we must focus on the gospels of Jesus rather than the Laws of Moses. We are not converting gentiles to Judaism. We are sharing the good news of Jesus and baptizing new Christians."

"I agree with you," Mary said. She pulled back her hair as she turned towards me, placing her hand gently on my shoulder. "Take my young friend Lucius as an example. As we bring him into Christianity, should his diet be more important than accepting the good news of Christ and being baptized? Must he be circumcised to be a Christian?"

I whispered to the man sitting next to me, asking him what circumcision entailed. Dear God! I cringed. How bizarre and barbaric. I'm not sure why God would require such a painful adjustment after birth. I thought, why did God not factor that into the design up front? Perhaps I had misheard him. As I opened my mouth to ask for clarification, Mary made eye contact with me. She must have read my expression and indicated silently that now was not the time to ask about circumcision. I trembled.

"I do not accept the pejorative term of Judaizer, but I know you call me one behind my back," said a young man I had not met. He had a long beard, long curled sideburns, and was dressed in traditional Jewish clothing.

"We call you a Judaizer to your face," Mary said with a sardonic smile.

"I find your teachings far too radical," the Judaizer went on unfazed. "I do believe the Hebrew laws should be followed in regards to the matters of diet and circumcision. Firstly, because these are some of the laws that Moses brought directly to the people from Yahweh, the one and true God of Abraham. Secondly, if we abandon some of the Hebrew laws arbitrarily, is this not a slippery slope? Will we be debating which of the Ten Commandments to abandon next?"

"That is a ludicrous comparison," said a man behind me. This struck a chord with the group and intensified the tone of the conversation. Arguments started to break out.

"I see your concern," said Mary, silencing the congregation. "We must preserve the laws of God and all be mindful that we are all sinners here. I do not believe the selection of laws is arbitrary. We must now think as Christians reborn."

"What about the laws of circumcision, for instance, as it relates to slaves?" an old man asked. "Genesis states that, 'All the men of his house, born in the house, and bought with money of the stranger, were circumcised with him.' I assume by this same line of thinking that this no longer applies? For that matter, what about all laws for the treatment of slaves as it applies to gentiles? If that gentiles are equal in the eyes of the church, then slaves are all treated with the same law, regardless of whether they are Hebrew or foreigners?"

"After all, did we not escape as slaves from a foreign land?" the Judaizer asked, alluding to the exile from Egypt. He did not get many laughs.

"What do the laws say about the treatment of gentile slaves?" the old man asked again.

"This is a valid point as there is preferential treatment of Hebrew slaves over foreigners," Theo weighed in with a scholarly tone. "We shall refer to the Torah. The emancipation of slaves is clearly defined in the book of Exodus, but only for Hebrew slaves. As chapter twenty-one of Exodus begins,

'If you buy a Hebrew servant, six years he shall serve, and in the seventh he shall go free.'"

"Friends, this is supporting the point that I am trying to make . . ." the Judaizer interjected.

"And then we can also read the words of Deuteronomy, which provide us laws on how conquered foreigners may be enslaved," Theo proceeded calmly with his argument. "In chapter twenty-one, 'When you go to war against your enemies, . . . and you take captives, and if you notice among the captives a beautiful woman that you desire, you may take her as your wife.'"

"Does that really speak to slavery or marriage?" A comedian in the crowd jabbed, and several of the men chuckled and others frowned at the joke.

"Touché," the old man said.

"Back to subject at hand, my brothers and sisters," Theo said. "We shall refer to the previous chapter in Deuteronomy to support the case in point. And may you all be happy in your marriages. I am a confirmed bachelor. In this lifetime I will have only the church as my bride. As I was saying, if we look at Deuteronomy chapter twenty, the verse states, 'As for the women, the children, the livestock, and everything else in the city, you may take these as plunder for yourselves.'"

"Do not the laws of treatment of slaves still apply? Are we going to rewrite those?" the Judaizer asked in frustration. "Theo, I am also able to read from the Torah. Let us again reference chapter twenty-one of Exodus." The Judaizer began receipting the verse from memory, "'If a man beats his male or female slave with a rod and the slave dies as a direct result, he must be punished. But if the slave survives a day or two—'"

"You're off the hook, free and clear," the comedian chimed in again. This time he got some more laughter.

Mary, Theo, the Judaizer, and the others continued deliberating on the subject. I took a chance to get up and talk to another young man who was closer to my age, much younger than most of the other church members. We exchanged greetings and he told me his name was Tiridata and that he was from Persia in the east. I gathered that he was newer to the congregation.

"I've heard this entire conversation before. Several times I have heard it," Tiridata spoke to me quietly. He had a thick accent. "Do you want to leave? Find to do something else to do? You are a man of Rome? You enjoy the bath house?"

"Most definitely!" I said. No hesitation. "That is much more my speed. I sure do miss Roman comforts these days. I should tell Mary."

I shared my plans with Mary, who was not happy with my plans to leave with Tiridata.

"He is very new here. We know that his father is a benefactor of the church of Antioch, but we do not know what sort of character Tiridata is yet. I'm not sure if he has Christ in his heart," Mary said. "I'd rather you stayed here and then went back to the lodging with us. James will be looking forward to spending some time with you."

"Mary, I appreciate it, but I'm not really asking," I replied.

Mary appeared hurt by this, but I could see from her expression that she knew she was not going to change my mind. So, she resigned herself to letting me go.

"Young men, you are leaving already?" Theo asked as he noticed Tiridata and me moving towards the cave entrance. "Please stay longer. It has been such a good discussion. We will have refreshments in the early evening."

"That is a generous and tempting offer," I said politely, completely full of shit, "but we are going back to the city. It was nice to meet you all."

Mary looked worried, and it bothered me to leave, but the prospects of going out on the town with Tiridata easily outweighed my doubts at leaving her and the others behind.

15

TIRIDATA THE PERSIAN

As we walked back to the city, I was able to get a better look at Tiridata. He was about the same build as me, slightly above average height. His facial features were distinct and sharp, especially his thick dark eyebrows that came to subtle points. His complexion was slightly darker than mine, and his skin was clear and smooth. He wore a gold headband around his forehead, so that his thick hair pushed out above and beneath it. His hair was shoulder length and was wavy, black and shiny. He wore a colorful robe that conveyed wealth and status. He was a prototypical young Persian nobleman.

I stopped by the stone house first to see if James and the other Christians had returned from their day's events. We were told by a caretaker that they had not, so we left for the bath houses. As soon as we stepped onto the main street, I was met by a Roman courier. He had a message for me from my father. I was apprehensive about any word from Father, but ordered him to hurry up and read me the message:

> This letter is from Decimus Octavius Aurelius of Rome, dictated on the year 56 A.D. on November 17, to be delivered to my son, Lucius Octavius Aurelius in Antioch of Syria.

> Lucius, my only son, who is still under my care, my sponsorship, and my supervision, and who carries on my family name, take heed and pay close attention to the message forthcoming.

> Firstly, do not tell me where and how to message you. I was not going to wait for you to arrive in Ephesus when I am perfectly capable of messaging you in Antioch. I am a man of great means. I am acutely aware of the operations of the Roman courier system.

> Your mother gives me this warning to impart to you. Do not dishonor our gods by worshiping this new god of these Christians. Do you not think our gods will turn their backs on you if you turn your back to them? Do you not think you will bring shame on your family by worshiping this foreign god? Is this one Christian god the god of war, love, sky, earth, sea, sun, and rain? Can he do the work of Jupiter, Neptune, Apollo, Mercury and all the other Gods at the same time? Lucius, that does not make any sense!

Your mother does worry about the Gods and re-
minds you to pay proper tribute to them. Remember how your mother celebrated all the festivals at
home. How she always set a place for Saturn at our
table during Saturnalia. You must always honor the
gods so that they repay you in favor. Quid pro quo.

The Roman courier took a pause from reading the message. He appeared proud of himself for imitating the voice
of my father. I scowled at him and urged him to continue.

I am a man of the Roman Empire and a man of
the world. I have always kept both my feet on the
ground. I am a practical man. I do not foresee that
Nero's empire will be kind to these Christians. The
more these Christians propagate their religion, or
mention their kingdom, the more oppressed they
will become. This Christian obsession of yours can
be part of your education while you are traveling,
but I am warning you that we will not accept it when
you return home. Expect persecution and harsh
treatment. As your mother said, think about your
family and how you will shame us with your worship of a foreign god.

This can all be water under the bridge. I must lower
my expectations since you no longer show promise
in either politics or business. I can still find you
placement in construction as a supervisor so that
you may not bring as much shame to my name.
However, this requires that you return to Rome as
soon as possible. To that end, I have commissioned

Martinus to bring you back safely. You are advised
to stay where you are in Antioch until he can send
someone to take you to meet his ship in Cyprus. By
the time this message has found you, he will already
be on his way.

"So, you must go home?" Tiridata asked with concern
after I explained the back story of the message.

"Damn, I hate my parents! Why don't they listen to me?"
I clenched my fists in anger and indignation. "I'm not going
home! Let's get out of here."

"Are you sure?" Tiridata asked. "Should you not honor
your father and obey him?" He began to worry. "This sounds
bad. I do not want trouble with the Romans."

"Yes, I'm sure. Don't worry about it." I let out a deep
sigh, mumbled some foul words, and then said, "Put it out
of your mind. Let's go to the bath house."

Tiridata and I resumed our walk towards the baths. How
quickly and easily I could escape my family worries by jumping head first into the hedonism of Antioch.

We entered the opulent bath house. We decided to first
visit the bathing pools first, then get massages. We would
start in the lukewarm bathing pool and move into new pools,
each with progressively hotter water. We walked through the
first grand hall decorated with the most beautiful frescos of
women playing sporting games. We took the first turn to
the enormous pool with the lukewarm water. I was pleased
that it was not busy, and we had it mostly to ourselves so
that we could continue to speak. We slowly entered the pool.

"So, what do you think about this new Christian movement?" I asked. "I bet it is strange compared to what you

grew up with in Persia. Especially with just one God—it is definitely radical compared to the Greek and Roman pantheon of gods."

"No, not so different," Tiridata replied. "I followed a prophet named Zoroaster, who is also from Persia. We have the one supreme god Ahura Mazda, who is the creator of life and all-knowing and powerful. We also believe in both good and evil, much like God and Satan. We have both heaven and hell, same as Christians." Tiridata explained.

"I have heard of those traditions while living in Judea," I replied. "But Christianity changes everything with the coming of Christ. Are you most compelled by this good news of the messiah?"

"Lucius, this messiah is also found in Zoroastrianism. In Persia, there is an ancient prophecy of the coming of Saoshyant. The messiah Saoshyant who will come to end all evil. Maybe Christians take this idea from us, no?"

Although I had just discovered Christianity, I was offended by a Persian telling me that his religion was older than Christianity, and possibly held a link to Jesus. Christianity was not a derivative! Childishly, I wanted this new god that I now followed to be bigger, better, and more original than his god.

Frustrated, I tried to set him straight in a condescending tone. "I seriously doubt that. I have met James, the brother of Jesus Christ. And Mary, the mother of Jesus. Jesus is the promised messiah."

"Do not get angry at me, Lucius." Tiridata laughed confidently. "I'm just telling you what I learn as a boy."

We decided we were ready for a warmer pool, so we got out and headed for the next one. On the other side of the pool was an open area for exercising. We heard some men grunting loudly during their workout. We stepped into the next pool and made ourselves comfortable.

"So, Tiridata, where are you from in Persia exactly?"

"I grew up in a very small village. You would never know it. It is not so far from Persepolis."

"I have heard of that city. I have learned about all of the lands of the Roman Empire."

"In my homeland, we are in the Parthian empire, not part of Roman empire. We have our own empire that borders the Roman Empire." Tiridata drew a map on the surface of the water, which didn't help much. "We also have our own king, Vologases, much like your emperor Nero. Vologases is the king of kings."

Again, we were comparing our gods, our empires, our kings, our prophets, our messiahs. This caused a competitive tension between us. It was imperative that mine be superior to his.

We were ready for the hottest pool now. We got up again and walked to the hot pool, steam rising from its surface. This time we were not alone. There were three older men on the other side of the pool. Their backs and shoulders were covered with thick black hair that was wetly down in a mat as the men bobbed in the water. The hairiest man was completely bald on the top of his head. He ducked under the surface of the water and then jumped up, spitting pool water at his companions.

"Did you know, I was named after the Parthian king," Tiridata said.

The conversations had an adversarial undertone. This had added a small amount of stress to my day, in addition to having heard that my father was sending Martinus after me. I reminded myself that this was an excursion to escape from worries.

"So, Tiridata, do you drink?" I asked, hoping to lighten the mood.

"I drink all the time. Must drink all the time to live." Tiridata answered very seriously.

"No, I mean drinking wine."

"I mean the same!"

We both laughed.

"Do you know a good place to go for wine? We can skip the massages and find some place for a good time."

"Yes, I do. Wine, and, also beautiful women," Tiridata grinned.

"That sounds perfect!" I replied.

"In Antioch there is only one place. One neighborhood. Daphne!"

Of all the names of all the places and people, it had to be Daphne. I was just starting to move on and think about her less.

Now this?

I thought of our last night together. Of what she was doing now in Corinth. Of whether she had moved on and forgotten about me. Of whether she was seeing other men.

Thoughts of Daphne transformed my face from wistfulness to worry. Tiridata read my expression and could tell I was not present. Tiridata's expression changed in tandem with mine.

"This does not appear to your liking? You said our plan 'sounds perfect,'" Tiridata said, imitating me.

"Yes, yes . . . it sounds fine. Let's go now to . . . Daphne.

I was just thinking about something that I forgot to do at home. I can take care of it when we get back."

We headed for Daphne after we dried off and got dressed. The Daphne suburb was several miles from the center of the city, back on the other side of the Orontes River. It was early afternoon, and we both craved a drink and bite to eat as we walked. We stopped at a street vendor and got some wine, bread, and nuts to eat.

"Why won't you get ready to return home to your father?" Tiridata asked.

"What? Oh, don't get me started! My parents are ridiculous. They can be so overbearing and completely out of touch. My father wants me to go back home. He has a job lined up for me but I have absolutely no interest in that. There is no way I'm going home."

"You do not look up to your father? How not? Is he a criminal? Does he beat you?" Tiridata asked.

"No, he has not abused me physically," I replied.

"Has he—how do you say, disinherited you?"

"No. He helps me financially and tries to set me up with jobs. But he's not giving me any choices in my life. My father is obsessed about making me who he wants me to be. Then he can talk about me proudly to his friends in Rome," I explained.

"You should be thankful for your father. He supports you," Tiridata said.

"Wait, what in the hell is wrong with you? Do you always get along with your father?" I said, trying to turn the tables on him.

"Not always, but I look up at my father. He is . . . larger than life. He was the master of my world until I was a grown man," he answered.

"Do you feel close to your father? Like he is a friend that understands you?" I asked.

"My father has six wives. I have twenty-seven brothers and sisters. My father is very noble. Brave. He always provided for us. He is a rich man," he said.

"I cannot imagine having that many siblings, since I was an only child. Twenty-seven children! How did he even keep track! I suppose I can understand the wealthy aspect, just not such a large family and the admiration," I said.

"My father is a very smart man. But at home he was the boss. Our family was his kingdom and he was king," he said.

"Twenty-seven brothers and sisters! Well, so what does he think of you then? Did he even know you that well?" I asked.

"No. He treated all of us with love. I would get jealous of any brother that has the attention that you do from your father."

Tiridata and I had a long conversation as we walked to Daphne, jumping from one subject to the next. As we entered the Daphne suburb, we passed by opulent Greek parks, temples, splendid villas, and extravagant gardens with beautiful bright-colored flowers, and lush groves of bay and cypress trees. Tiridata led me to an estate on a steep hillside garden. After we went through the large gates of the estate, I could clearly see the entire garden and house sprawled atop the hill before me. The stately house had white stone columns and archways that held up a second floor surrounded by a wide balcony and covered by a sprawling tiled roof. There were stone steps that led the way up the hill and through the garden, lion statues and fountains punctuated the grounds. The many tiers of the garden were already lively with party goers.

Tiridata and I worked our way up the steps to the first tier of the garden. There was a circular pool surrounded by people that I thought looked mostly Greek. Gold fish swam in the pool, occasionally biting at the bubbles from the ornate fountain and then darting back under the lotus flowers to hide.

"Tiridates!" a man shouted. "Come on over!"

"Pericles!" Tiridata shouted back.

We approached the man, Pericles, and I was introduced. This was his brother's estate. I noticed a smaller fountain built into the hillside. The fountain was surrounded by scaly fish statues, and from their puckered mouths something frothy and red flowed into a pool shaped like a giant seashell. It was red wine. A young lady walked towards the wine fountain, weaving and wobbling. As she reached for the pool she fell in the grass. Then she sat up, laughing, in no rush to stand up again. The men watched and started laughing along with her. We took some cups and filled them liberally from the fish fountains. We walked to some stone benches by the circular pool filled with the real fish.

"How do you know these people?" I asked Tiridata.

"I've come here many times. Greeks in Daphne know how to party," he replied.

"Apparently!" I said.

A distinguished man overheard us.

"You have not been to Daphne before?" He asked dramatically, talking with his hands, which were bedazzled with rings. "You poor thing. You haven't even *lived*!"

"Do you know the story of Daphne?" The man standing with the many ringed man asked me. He did not wait for my answer. "This is where Apollo, all charged up and randy, chased down the nymph Daphne. But before Apollo could catch her, she was transformed into a laurel tree. My man here can show you the tree!"

The ringed man nodded emphatically and puckered his face.

"Have you been to the Greek temples? Julius Caesar built us a pantheon here," he waved a fabulous finger with a large ruby ring down the hill at a faraway temple. "Say! Look at you. You look Roman."

"No, I haven't seen the temples yet, and yes, I am from Rome," I answered.

"You absolutely *must* visit the temple of Apollo and Diana." He pointed some more flashy fingers at some more faraway buildings.

"Yes, it's a very beautiful tribute," Tiridata said.

When our cups were empty, we had another pour of wine from the fish fountain. And then another. The laughing girl in the grass was still laughing.

Tiridata and I walked up the stone steps and eventually made it to a marble patio where an even larger crowd of party goers had gathered. I looked out at the view of the garden and towards the mountains in the east. I felt like I was on top of the world that day.

Then we stepped inside the grand house and into the main hall, walking over a glorious mosaic floor that depicted a hunting scene. A hunter with a bow and arrow was shooting at lions. One lion was pierced with several arrows and bleeding out in mosaic drops.

People were sitting on cushions along the sides of the hall lounging, eating, drinking, and talking. Servants were decorated in golden clothes, jewelry, and painted in gold from head to toe. They walked by with silver platters of decadent appetizers and drinks. Tiridata and I grabbed some libations from an attractive gold painted servant whose hair was held up in an elaborate style with hairpins. I noticed a small orgy of people in the corner. Two women and two men were writhing together in lustful indulgence, like blind kittens searching for milk.

Needless to say, I was getting more intoxicated by the minute and Tiridata and I were having a blast. The crowd of people increased as the hours went by and I lost track of time. After we had been there for some time, impossible for me to even estimate in my state, I had momentarily lost Tiridata.

The women were all very attractive. I observed that there were more young women than men. The women were dressed ornately and they had laurels and flowers and hairpins in their hair. They were all very attentive and friendly to the men. It was hard to believe my own eyes.

"Want to meet a Daphne woman?" Tiridata asked, surprising the hell out of me. Where had he gone? How had he snuck up on me? He must have known what I was thinking.

"Yes, of course. They are very beautiful and seem very, well, uh, convivial. I am less nervous with help from the wine."

"Do you want one? I will get you one. No worry, I pay." Tiridata said. He reached up to waive someone forward.

"Wait—what?" I asked, confused. It was loud in the room and his thick accent was sometimes hard to follow. Also, the wine drinking.

"Yes, I pay. My treat," he said.

"Do you mean these are prostitutes?!" I asked.

"Yes, of course, Lucius, my new friend. Oldest profession

in the world. Why do you think all these women are here? Young women love old men with money," he said.

"Tiridata, don't get me wrong, I love women, but I don't want it that way," I said.

"You decide," Tiridata stood, and he was laughing at me. "No pressure, nervous boy Roman."

He signaled me to follow him out of the house. And then we were off to the second party. The night was still young, and so were we. As dusk approached, we walked down the stone street to another Greek villa with an even more lively party. People were pouring out of every door and archway of the villa. A harpist and a percussionist danced around in the yard entertaining the crowd. The party was much louder, and the crowd was also younger.

"We now go to the Lotus Eaters club," Tiridata said and he led me into the villa. I was drunk enough at that point and up for about anything so I followed him. The club did not seem too exclusive as we had to push through many happy people to get to the other side of a large room.

"We will find some blue lotus tea. I know the right person." Tiridata spoke in the ear of someone while I stood by waiting. Apparently, we needed to talk to someone else and went through the crowd again. Tiridata spoke again to another young Greek man who was shaking his head emphatically. That first exchange had not been fruitful.

"I know just the place, trust me," Tiridata said, determined.

We walked out the back of the house to smaller building filled with revelers. Tiridata found his friend, who waved us to follow him back into a small kitchen area. He poured us both cups of the blue lotus tea Tiridata had been seeking, and we drank it quickly.

We went back to join the larger party in the main room of the villa. Tiridata and I were discussing something, and I completely forgot about the tea. That is when I felt a slight nausea and disorientation wash through me. This worried me at first, and I voiced my concern, but Tiridata comforted me. He told me that the bad feeling would soon go away. This feeling quickly left me, and it was replaced by a lighter feeling of sedation. I had completely lost track of my surroundings for a moment.

The sedation turned pleasantly into a mild euphoria and all of the sudden my consciousness became astonishingly clear. I noticed the vibrant colors of my clothing, heard the music powerfully in my head, and felt the softness of my hair.

"Did you hear me?" Tiridata asked, pressing my shoulder.

"Did I what?" I asked, trying to regain my normal senses.

"You are feeling the *effects*." Tiridata smiled.

"Yes!" We both laughed.

I looked across the large room and I saw a tall man embracing a stout man that I recognized.

"Is that James?" I think I said that out loud.

The man that I thought was James kissed the other man on the cheek.

"James?" Tiridata asked. "What are you talking about, man?"

"James, the brother of Jesus."

"Jesus? You see Jesus?" Tiridata said, laughing.

"No, the brother of Jesus, James. Seriously! He came with me to Antioch. He is here with another man. Look!" I pointed across the room, but he was no longer there.

Tiridata shook his head. "It is the tea that is talking in your head. You have tea-talking head! No Jesus or James here."

I tried to piece it together but began to have my own doubts.

"No James. No Jesus here. We go," Tiridata said. He pulled me by the arm, and we walked through the throngs, out the front the villa, and into the street. By now it was completely dark and hard to see as we stumbled uphill towards the next party. Tiridata said something about this being the most exclusive club, and the best party.

After wandering through the suburb, feeling completely lost, we strode up a winding path between bushes and trees to a much more modest house. I did not see anybody outside, but I did hear noises from inside the house. Tiridata knocked on the door.

"What is the secret password?" A female voice asked from inside.

"Poppies, herbs, and dreams," Tiridata replied.

"Tiridates!" A girl opened the door, smiling at Tiridates and waving us both in.

The house was divided into several small candlelit rooms with people lounging and talking casually in each room. Tiridata took me to the back of the house to a room that had a table of food and drinks. We helped ourselves to more wine. A young woman with long waist length hair and a bizarrely painted face approached us.

"You have pretty eyes," she said to me. I was speechless.

"You should say thank you," said a young man from behind her. He was wearing a toga with a wreath in his hair.

"Thank you," I said in monotone.

Then she poured something out of a small vial into our wine cups and stirred them. I watched her, incapable of managing any response or reaction, mesmerized and staring at her painted face.

"This is my own secret recipe of magical herbs," she said mystically.

Tiridata patted me on the back. We drank some of the wine and went back to one of the rooms in the front.

"It's not even fair. I have no say; I must rely on everything from my brother. . ." I overheard some people talking. I was not a part of any conversation. I relaxed and listened to others conversing in the room. Overwhelmed by my senses, I felt like talking would be a challenge.

This is when I got tunnel vision and the world closed in around me. The room was a darkened blur, and the sounds around me went in and out. When I turned my head, the candlelight drew long traces of orange, yellow, and white in my vision. As wild patterns formed in my vision, I decided to sit down. Unfortunately, I sat down on a table and nearly fell backwards into some people.

"Are you okay?" someone asked me, most likely trying to comfort me.

"Yes, I just wanted to rest." I heard my voice inside my head.

They seemed only mildly concerned. After a while some people brought me back into the dining area.

"Your stomach is empty," someone said. "Have some bread and water."

"No!" I protested. They were trying to feed me more magical herbs, I was growing paranoid. I thought about how they would bring me into their mystical cult. These are pagans who worship heathen gods, gods who were already grasping control of my mind!

"It won't work on me," I said. Unsteadily, I tried standing up. "I have already learned the good news—of the coming of Christ, the son of God."

"That's beautiful," said the long-haired woman with the painted face. "Find a peaceful place with your god. This will help you find him."

"You can't trick me," I said. "I won't forsake him!"

Then I wobbled out to another room, joining a few conversations that I cannot fully remember. I could not find Tiridata anywhere.

I WOKE UP, OR really, I came to consciousness sitting on the ground in the back yard next to the house. The sun was just rising, and I heard the birds chirping loudly from all directions. I walked back into the house in a haze, still foggy in the head, but feeling light all over the rest of my body. My throat was dry and I had a painful thirst, so I took several large drinks of water from a jug.

I began walking through the suburb of Daphne, recognizing almost nothing from the night before, trying to find my way to the heart of Antioch. I wandered aimlessly and luckily found the road back, recalling it from a relatively sober time during the previous afternoon.

The walk was long, tiring, and my head began to throb. My mouth was dry again and I couldn't even work up enough saliva to spit. It tasted as if something had soiled itself and died in my mouth. I was determined to get back to the stone house and rest safely. After a long hard walk, I made it to the Jewish suburb. I entered the stone house, making sure to avoid any fellow Christians. I gulped down several more cups of water, lay down, and covered myself from head to toe before instantly falling asleep.

SWEATY AND DISORIENTED, I was awoken in the middle of the day by the sound of hymns and prayers being sung by many voices. I got up and went next door to where the Christians had gathered. Simon Peter, Philip, James, Mary and the others had formed together in assembly.

"Lucius, where have you been?" James asked me. "You look like a veritable Lazarus. As if you've just been raised from the dead."

Did I not see James last night in Daphne? I searched my memory for what had really happened, what I had imagined, or what visions had been brought on by the mystical spirits, or the wine and the drugs.

Mary informed the group of my premature departure from the cave church the day before. I divulged a few of the tamer exploits from my escapades in the Daphne suburb. I was still in the process of piecing together what had happened, but I was able to share a few good anecdotes from the first party, such as the laughing girl and the wine fountain.

"The hedonism of the gentiles is evil and sinful," Simon Peter lectured. "Lucius, you may have been living a life of ignorance before learning of Jesus. You followed your gentile friends and did what gentiles choose to do—living in debauchery, drunkenness, participating in orgies, carousing . . ."

My mind was still foggy, but I followed some of those last points.

"Do not conform to the evil desires of your former life— take action and be self-controlled. As it is written, 'Be holy, because I am holy.' Purify yourself, live in truth, be born again, through the living word of God," Simon Peter urged.

My head hurt way too much for a sermon.

"Tiridata?" Philip asked, wrinkling his handsome brow in disdain, "Is he not that wealthy Persian?"

"He said he was from Persia, or the Parthian empire to be more specific. But he is God-fearing." I answered diplomatically, as I didn't have it in me to argue.

"It does not matter," Philip answered, changing the subject. "We have more important topics on the agenda." I later discovered more about Tiridata's wealthy father, a major benefactor in Antioch, so there were financial and political implications to his remaining in the church.

"Come along, one and all, for we sail to Ephesus today!" said James. Some of the disciples who had joined us in Antioch were coming with us to Ephesus, but Philip and Mary would part ways with us here. Philip was going back to Caesarea and Mary planned to return to Samaria for the rest of the business season.

We packed and made our way to the harbor. I broke into a nervous sweat, suddenly remembering that my father had sent Martinus after me. I told James, so he could also be on the lookout. There was no sign of Martinus, or that sturdy ship Hippopotamus, when we reached the harbor. I conveniently avoided thinking about my father, and everything else back home in Rome, as we prepared to sail for Ephesus.

RECALLING THESE EVENTS IN Antioch from heaven in the 20th century, I feel nothing but nostalgia. Antioch was fascinating, beautiful, decadent, and easily the favorite city that I visited in my younger days. In fact, my modern reader, there would not be cities like this in the western world until the modern era.

After watching the centuries go by, I have grown weary of the progression from the horse and buggy to jet airliners, from mail carriage to global communication at the speed of light. During the 20th century, humans advanced at an astonishing rate.

Mankind has not always made forward progress. In fact, western civilization has sometimes backpedaled since Roman times, in terms of both enlightenment and technological advancement.

After the collapse of the Roman Empire, the Dark Ages brought several centuries of regression. The Dark Ages were marked by the plague, barbaric witch hunts, Crusades, and the overall forgetfulness of the advances made in art and science of the cultures that came before. The Renaissance, inspired by Greek and Roman classicism, would not arrive for more than a thousand years. The Pantheon in Rome was the largest dome in the world until the Astrodome was built in the 1960s. The recipe for concrete used during the Roman Empire was forgotten for centuries until it was reinvented in the 18th century.

Frustrated and dejected, I ponder over this history and only believe it has and will repeat itself. Humans not versed in history will be surprised with painful irony. The short attention span and hubris of mankind now pervades the culture of this planet. This is a culture than runs on short-sighted capitalism measured by quarterly earnings. A materialistic, disposable culture that rebuilds stadiums after only few a decades of use. That burns through fossil fuels with reckless abandon. The nuclear arms race taunts us with the possibility of bringing in a new dark age with one doomsday event. In a less dramatic fashion, global warming, deforestation, fascism, crony capitalism, and greed, and the environmental impact of overpopulation may again reverse progress. But I digress. And, if history repeats itself, why not temper the frustration with humanity with the hope of each new Renaissance? The best show, season after season.

16

EPHESUS

At daybreak we sailed for Ephesus on the crystal-clear sea. On the ship were Simon Peter, James, and his mother Mary who had come to join myself, and about a dozen other Christians on our journey to Ephesus. We embarked on the journey in the last part of 56 A.D. before the winter months. Luckily, we did not encounter any treacherous winter storms at sea. It was so pleasant and clear that occasionally James and I would casually wave at other ships that passed by. The ship's route took us past the island of Cyprus and stopped on the Greek island of Rhodes. As the ship took on fresh water, we walked along the beach of the crescent bay and up the rugged hill to purchase goods, the ship bobbing below in the transparent water. After Rhodes, we sailed along the coast beyond Miletus, and finally entered the bay and the harbor of Ephesus.

James had decided that once his business was done in Ephesus, he was going to pursue his own interests in Jerusalem as a church deacon and husband. This meant that he would no longer be able to provide long-term care for his mother. Since Mary was elderly and beloved by the church, James easily arranged for her to retire in Ephesus under the care of the apostle John. Mary would relish the independence that she would be given in Ephesus, so she had accompanied us on the journey. The tension between James and Mary while we were on the ship was palpable. I promised Mary that I would visit her frequently while I was in Ephesus. I had no other real commitments.

After we arrived in the harbor we divided into smaller parties. Mary, James, and I walked together to our housing. Ephesus was built around a single linear street that cuts through the center of the city with a zig-zag street that runs perpendicular. The main road that started at the harbor, divided the city center, and ended at the other end of the city at the inland gates. The harbor road was lined with Greek columns and surrounded by baths, a gymnasium, and a massive U-shaped amphitheater carved into the side of Mount Pion that could seat nearly 25,000 people. We took a right turn at the amphitheater down a road lined by colonnades.

Mary shared her admiration of the marble road and estimated that it must have been quite expensive.

"What is this over here?" Mary asked, pointing to a large grassy open area to our right.

"Don't you know what an agora is? That must be the commercial agora," James explained with a hint of condescension in his voice. "See all the people conversing and interacting in trade?" James pointed out some of the people as he explained impatiently to his mother.

Further on we marveled at three arched passages and inscriptions on the Gate of Mazeus and Mithridates. Then we hooked a left onto Curetes Street, the main drag that most of the city was built around. Indeed, this was another spectacular metropolis.

Curetes Street was packed on both sides with public toilets, baths, temples, and opulent houses. Eventually we made our way to the housing district where John was putting us up. James and I would be living in the same building as Mary. James was going to stay with us only temporarily before traveling to Jerusalem. Our house was like so many other houses in Ephesus, which were built into the hillside, such as the famous houses on the slopes. John's building was much more modest, but the architecture was still pleasing, and it was in a prime location.

When we arrived, John's servant met us on the street and showed us into the house. The servant led us to where Mary, James, and I would eat and sleep. He informed us that John had left on a short trip and would be back in a week or so. We sat together at the table in the house to rest our tired legs.

"James, do you need to go to the toilets?" Mary asked.

"No, mom!" James replied. He got up and left. I presume he was heading for the public toilets.

Oh, the famous public toilets of Ephesus. The toilets were nearby on Curetes Street. In those times, these were popular places for men to socialize. Much like in Rome, the toilets were arranged in long rows where the men sat side by side, doing their business in close enough proximity to rub elbows. Not my scene. I have always preferred solitude.

"I have missed you, Lucius," Mary said. She gave me her classic smile.

"I have missed you too," I said. "We were all happy to hear that you will be joining us in Ephesus. It is a beautiful city with a thriving church community."

"Yes, so I've heard. But that doesn't matter much to me. I don't get out much. I'm not young anymore." Mary wiped her tired eyes. "I do not always understand your Christian mission, but I know you have good intentions. How is James doing? I worry about him, you know."

"I'm not sure. I think he's fine," I said. "He told me that he's going back to Jerusalem to become a deacon."

"Oh, dear. I hope you're wrong," she said. She put her hand on her wrinkled neck and her face tensed in discomfort. "He won't be safe in Jerusalem. The Sanhedrin do not approve of the Christians and their preaching. They are threatened by this movement and they have power. And they will act violently against him. Sarah's boy, Josiah, he was nearly stoned to *death* by the Sanhedrin in Jerusalem last year. I heard it myself from her . . . from the butcher."

"Are you sure that is a true story?" I asked.

"I heard it myself from her butcher. Before I left Nazareth," Mary said, holding on to her story.

"Don't worry, Mary," I said, changing the approach of the conversation "He will be safe in Jerusalem. It is a holy, peaceful place, for the most part." Oh, my poor reader, the irony is too heavy to bear. "Don't assume the worst from just one bad story. Some small village gossip. Anyway, I think James is really going there to track down his wife."

I had said the wrong thing. The one thing that made things worse.

"Rebekah, that hussy! How does James even know she is in Jerusalem? She is always getting around you know. Do you know for sure if she is really living in Jerusalem now?"

"I don't know. I am certain though that James has made up his mind. There is nothing we can do to change that. If we try to talk him out of it that will only push him away more. He has confided in me about these things lately. So, I know he is troubled about his marriage. Jerusalem will give him a purpose."

Mary sighed. "I suppose you are right, Lucius. You are a smart boy." Again, her classic smile. "But I will always be his mother, and I never stop worrying about him."

Mary and I chatted for a while longer about James until we were both tired. Then I went to my room for some desperately needed solitude. A lot of different thoughts raced through my mind. Still a young bachelor, I yearned for mischief and adventure. I wasn't sure what I was doing next with my life, but I would stay in Ephesus until it no longer amused me. As Euripides wrote, "Youth is the best time to be rich, and the best time to be poor." Since I no longer had a source of income, either from my father or from my previous labors, I was going to need to find an occupation in the city. I knew that eventually Martinus, or someone sent by my father, would catch up with me. I tried not to worry about that too much, but it did cast a thin cloud over me. At least I had important connections here. I wanted to follow Simon Peter and the Christians in earnest, but I was also interested in meeting new people in Ephesus and immersing myself in the local culture.

MY FIRST DAY WITH the Christians in Ephesus began with James and I walking together to the local church. The congregation had been meeting in a large hall just off Curetes Street. We sat down among an assembly that was sizable, diverse, mostly gentile, and of various levels of affluence. I gave credit to Paul for the diverse crowd since he had welcomed gentiles into Christianity. And now Simon Peter and James had come around to the same opinion. I gave myself a little credit for that, too.

Simon Peter was just completing his address to the congregation. "We are chosen people, all belonging to God. We were all once in darkness, but have by His glory been brought into the light! My devoted friends, I urge you all to fight against the sinful desires which war against your soul. After all, we are aliens among these pagans. We are tempted by greed, arrogance, and false gods." Simon Peter beat his fist on his chest, impassioned by his speech. "We must live good lives among those who worship false gods, even though we may be accused of wrongdoing. We will all find mercy in the Holy Spirit, and the glory of God on the day that he comes."

Simon Peter rubbed his beard and sat down in the front row. Then the local deacon stood. He was a younger man.

"And now for our community news and updates," the young deacon addressed the crowd. "The neighbors are complaining about the waste we are leaving behind the hall. One neighbor said, and I quote, 'Your garbage is stinking up our place to the depths of Tartarus. The rubbish pile is piled so high I can see it out my window. Please dispose of it more frequently so we don't have to make a formal complaint to the authorities.'"

There were a few grumbles from the crowd. The deacon continued, "Do we have a volunteer that can frequently take the waste and dispose of it away from the hall?" He paused. "Thank you, John."

He paused for a moment to collect his thoughts. "Moving on. A church member, who requested to remain anonymous, has goats for sale. So, I ask any of those who are interested in the goats to speak to me directly and I will put them in contact with the seller. And last, but not least, we have received a message that Tabitha, Simon Peter's wife, is coming to visit."

Simon Peter looked as if he'd just seen an evil spirit. Quickly, he feigned a look of cheerful anticipation. He might have corrected his reaction before the congregation noticed, but I had.

"Simon Peter is married?" I asked James quietly, surprised by this news.

"Oh, yes. Rocky, has been married for many years. However, it has been customary for Tabitha to stay at his estate with his progeny, by that I mean his children. She does occasionally follow him on his missions to provide moral support and matronly love, and so forth."

"Let us all please give a warm welcome to the distinguished and honorable Tabitha when she arrives in Ephesus," the deacon stated, concluding the announcements.

Simon Peter must have felt a new sense of fire in his belly at this news, because he stood and in an impassioned speech, he rallied us all to visit the local synagogue. So, we assembled out in the street, zealous and determined to carry the news of Christ. And we walked, shoulder to shoulder, heads held high, facing the blazing sun and blustery wind, with the glorious swagger of the Holy Spirit. Marching down Curates Street, we charged brazenly, prepared to defy thousands of years of Jewish tradition. We were fearless, fervent, and ready to spread the Christian fire of illumination to the synagogue.

Simon Peter flew through the doors of the synagogue and the rest of us followed closely behind. We all rushed in and filled out in ranks. An old rabbi was reading to a sparse group of fewer than twenty older Jewish men.

Simon Peter marched to the front and gently moved the old rabbi aside. Then he looked up to the heavens, clenched his eyes, and pounded his fist on his chest. His lips moved as he said a quick prayer to Jesus for spiritual support.

Then, holding out his hands, Simon Peter began his sermon to the group in the synagogue. "Behold! I bring you all good news! The Son of God, Jesus Christ, has come to bring salvation to the world. I am here to bring you his good news, so that you may all repent—"

"Shut up! Go away!" the Jews yelled.

"Are you one of Paul's men?" the old rabbi asked, annoyed but not alarmed.

"We have heard this all before from Paul! Go away, you Paul followers," another Jewish man in the crowd yelled.

"No, I'm Simon Peter. I'm not *with* Paul," Simon Peter replied with indignation. "I'm the *rock* upon which the *church*—" Simon Peter was cut off by the unruly crowd.

"Oh no, not another troublemaker! Go on, tell us about your new messiah of the week," the old rabbi said. He looked exhausted, as if he had done this often.

Simon Peter took a deep breath and soldiered on. "Praise be to the God, the Father of our Lord Jesus Christ! In his great mercy he has given us new birth into a living hope through the resurrection of Jesus Christ from the dead. Christ, the Son of God, is kept in heaven for all of you, who through faith may be shielded by God's power—"

"Blasphemy!"

"Who through faith *alone* may be shielded by God's power and love . . . until the coming of the *salvation* that will be revealed—"

"Blasphemy! He is a blasphemer, claiming the crucified Jesus is the Son of God."

"I bring good news!" Simon Peter switched tactics from love to fear. "Repent! Before the coming . . . of the end of *times.*"

"Jesus Christ is the Son of God! I have witnessed!" James cried out, soaked in emotion. He was trying to come to the rescue but was taking it way too personally. "He is my *brother.* The virgin mother, Mary, is my own dear *mother.*"

"Your mother—is a virgin? That doesn't make sense. So, are you saying you are also a son of god?"

"No, no," James said, "My father, Joseph, is a carpenter from Nazareth. And, so, Jesus, *his* father is—" James did not have time to explain before the small crowd of Jews erupted.

"Blasphemy!"

"We should stone him for blasphemy!"

"Now, that won't be necessary," Simon Peter said diplomatically. "Though you suffer in ignorance, I come here to bring you joy and faith, which has worth greater than gold—"

"Why don't we call some of our strong young men? Then they can take care of these blasphemers out in the street?" requested the tired old rabbi. The Jewish crowd agreed.

"Jesus Christ brings love!" Simon Peter said with great

passion. "Love your neighbor! Love your enemy as you love your friend!"

"Well you are really going to love Silas, our local Hebrew pankration champion. When he gets here, he's going to kick the loving shit out of you."

"Please, please, this is still a holy place of worship. Be respectful," the rabbi said, trying to maintain some civility, "Silas will summarily kick his Christian ass. Go out in the *street*, not in the synagogue."

Simon Peter still had fire in his belly, and he lit that fire under us, but he told us to exit the synagogue immediately. The love of Jesus shone too bright in our hearts and souls for an ass kicking from a big Jew named Silas. The battle was lost, but the war could still be won.

We fled the synagogue and ran down the street, afraid to look back. Simon Peter ran in front, his arms, legs, and beard akimbo. I followed him closely, watching his hairy legs kick in full strides. Looking back to find James, I noticed him falling behind, his rotund midriff gyrating with each stunted stride. I fell back to make sure he was alright. His labored breathing digressed to wheezing, followed by painful moans and grunts.

"I think we're safe, James, you can slow down, they were mostly old men," I said and looked back. "I don't even see anyone following us. I think we'll be alright to walk from here and meet them back at the church hall."

James pinched his side with his left hand, still huffing heavily. His face had changed colors.

"I recommend," James said, huffing and wobbling. "I recommend we call it a day."

"James, you do not look so well. I am going to walk you

home, then I will go back to the church hall. I want to see how everyone is doing."

Fortunately, we were not too far from our house. As we entered, Mary met us.

"What happened to him?" she asked. "He doesn't look too well. James, what have you been up to?" She seemed a little worried, but in a casual way, as if this was commonplace.

James sat down and took a drink of watered wine. He let out a big sigh before answering his mother.

"We had to run from," James took a few deep breaths, "some unruly Jewish men at the synagogue." He wiped his mouth and sighed heavily. "I don't think they are ready for the good news of our Savior."

I helped him out, getting him a wet rag to wipe his face.

"James, I have told you since day one that your little mission is nothing but trouble . . ." Mary lectured James with many more strong statements.

He did not acknowledge her with a single word in return. He was in rare form. Being short of breath, he was also short of words.

"Thank you so much," Mary said to me. She patted me on the back. I nodded and made my exit.

I left the house and quickly went back to the hall. When I arrived, it appeared as if they were already wrapping up.

"Lord, please forgive them since they do not know what they have done." Simon Peter was saying to the assembled Christians as I walked in quietly. "And so, to show our devoutness to Christ, and in solidarity against those who resist his love, we shall all fast for seven days, until a new week has come."

There was a protest from the congregation. I was mildly confused since I was catching up with what had occurred.

"Alright, we shall fast for five days," Simon Peter proclaimed. There were several groans from the congregation.

"OK, I declare we will fast for . . . three days," Simon Peter, the rock, ordered the members of the church. "As devout followers of Christ, we shall fast for three days and three nights. Just as Christ suffered on the cross for three days and nights before his resurrection, so shall we fast for three days."

Simon Peter walked out without another word. We bowed and prayed silently. After we had said amen, the young deacon who I had seen earlier that day thanked everyone and wished us a good night. The congregation began to leave, walking out in pairs. Today had been a long and unsuccessful campaign.

"What did I miss?" I asked, to no one in particular.

The deacon turned to me. "Simon Peter lectured about the blindness of the Jews not coming of Christ. Did you come to the synagogue with us today?"

"Oh, yes, I did," I said, feeling dejected. "That did not go so well."

"Indeed, it certainly did not," the deacon agreed. "No surprise."

"You have experienced this before?" I asked, conversationally.

"Oh, yes. That was not my first gladiator fight," he joked. His smile was very friendly and warm. "I'm Jason by the way, the deacon."

"I am Lucius. I arrived with James, Mary, Simon Peter, and the others from Antioch. We originally came from Judea."

"Oh, that's awesome! I'm from Ephesus originally, myself. Hey, listen, I'm about to go grab a drink. Would you like to join me?"

I could tell Jason was an extrovert and enjoyed talking to people.

"Yea sure. But aren't we supposed to be fasting?" I asked.

"Fasting means not eating food." Jason smiled again, but more devious this time. "Drinking wine is a fasting loophole."

"You sure?" I asked. "Never mind, you would know."

"Hey, are you Jewish? You kind of look Jewish to me," Jason asked me.

"No, not that I know of."

"Are you sure you're not? Like, at least, part Jewish?" Jason asked.

"Yes, I'm pretty sure I'm not. My ancestors are all from Italia."

We walked together down Curetes Street, this time inland towards the upper agora, known as the State Agora, where I had never been. Before we entered the agora, we hooked a right, passing a temple that was under construction, and some public buildings on the left, and kept walking until the street got very narrow and dark. Jason escorted me into a small but lively tavern where we sat down and were served Greek wine.

"So, tell me about yourself! What brings you to Ephesus?" Jason asked with genuine interest. "I hear that you are friends of Mary and James."

"Funny story actually. I'm from an extremely proud Roman family, well, my father is extremely proud, and I was not living up to my father's expectations. He wanted to teach me a lesson by sending me to Judea to perform manual labor. I was a carpenter's apprentice there. But my father never expected that I would get caught up with Christians and go on an evangelical mission as a result of my travels."

193

"So, you are a Roman and also a baptized Christian?"

"Actually, no I'm not a baptized Christian. But I am a dedicated follower, so to speak. James says I have a purpose, but I won't get into that." I desperately wanted to have a purpose. To be part of something. To be needed by the Christians. I wanted to learn more about the world and meet different people, just as I had set out to do. Yet, I was unable to commit exclusively to Christianity.

"How about you?" I asked him, just trying to match his friendliness.

"Oh, thanks for asking," Jason said. "Really, I just wanted to join some kind of cult, you know? I'm half Greek, and half Jewish. As a half-blood Jew, Christianity just made sense. It was the right fit for me. Also, it was a lot easier for people to accept the Greek and the gentile side of my lineage. Paul himself recruited me into this church. Paul was quite prolific in this area."

"So, you knew Paul?!" This grabbed my interest.

"Yea, Paul is the apostle that really put things into motion here. He spread the good news of Christ around this city," Jason said.

"So, he was the founder of the church here?" I asked.

"Well, there were some different Christians here before Paul. They had some fascinating ideas, but they didn't really take off here like Paul's ideas on the church did. There are many groups still around, with differing views. We can go meet them if you're interested."

"Yes, let's do that. I'm very interested. But, for now, tell me more about Paul. His name comes up all the time. It is like when Simon Peter's name comes up in a conversation, Paul has already been there and done that."

Jason paused to think of the right words. "Yes. Simon Peter is quite . . . passionate about his place in the church."

"Well," I agreed. "He was a disciple of Jesus and commanded by Christ to be the rock of this church. Wasn't Paul just like a wealthy criminal or something?"

"No, not exactly. Paul was a Jew and an enemy to the Christians. He was born in Tarsus of Cilicia as a Roman citizen. He was well-educated and deeply religious. As a young man he was a hard-nosed member of the Pharisees. During his time as a Pharisee, he spent much of his energy persecuting the Christians and inflicting punishment on them."

"What was he like when he was here in Ephesus?" I asked.

"He was lecturing on and on about the resurrection of Christ, and constantly writing other congregations to warn them against false worship. Paul was much more articulate than Simon Peter, but much less likable, especially to the Jews. He was erudite and well spoken, and he had a way about him that won over the gentiles. Although . . ." Jason paused again, this time to laugh. "This did not always go over so well. I have a good story for you."

Jason went on to tell the story. "So, Paul was going around the city to lecture halls and public places, preaching that there was just the one and only one true Christian God. There was this silversmith in the city named Demetrius that was raking in money selling silver coins with the image of the goddess Artemis stamped on them. He was selling them to locals and tourists by the boatload. They put these coins on the shrines in their homes as part of their worship to the goddess. Demetrius called a meeting of fellow craftsmen to remind them of the enormous profits made from these coins. He claimed that Paul was leading the people of Ephesus astray, convincing them to turn away from their local Greek gods. By claiming that Paul was out to discredit their local goddess Artemis and attempting to take away their livelihood, Demetrius incited a riot."

"Were they going to attack Paul!?" I asked.

"Oh, yea they were! Demetrius rallied his crowd and took to the streets to go after Paul and his companions." Jason provided an animated pantomime of mob and the riot. "The angry mob dragged them to the amphitheater. The Christians were in grave danger until a city clerk broke up the mob. The clerk informed them that they were breaking Roman law and that they should take their grievances to court."

"Then what? Did they find Paul later and go to court, or what?"

"No, Paul assembled his disciples, wished them luck, and left town. Nobody has seen him since then. I heard he went to Macedonia."

"That's a great story. So, what happened to Demetrius?" I asked.

"He's still around. I saw him a few weeks ago still selling his silver." Jason finished his wine and looked out the door of the tavern. "Hey, I've got an early morning tomorrow, but let's get together again some time. This was fun."

"I had a great time too. I want to stick around for a bit and finish my drink, so I will catch you later."

Much later, I crept out of the tavern and sauntered slowly through the city by moonlight, enjoying the eerie silence and shadowy figures. The soldiers walked in drunken disarray. One man shuffled by, arguing forcefully with himself. By the time I got back to our house it was very late, technically very early. Nearly dawn. I walked into room and collapsed into bed. Then I heard some rustling noises in the other side of the apartment. I lit a small lamp and went over to see what was going on.

"Ah!" James jumped, surprised by seeing me coming out of the dark.

"Ah!" I jumped too, startled by him jumping.

"What are you doing?!" James asked. He didn't make eye contact. He wiped a few crumbs from his beard.

"I thought we were fasting. James, were you eating?"

"No, uh, I was just tending to some housekeeping. You know, custodial duties."

I shook my head in disappointment. He must have been informed by the other church members of Simon Peter's declaration that we were fasting by now.

"Give me some bread then, I see it," I said. I was famished, and slightly hung over, and feeling mutually less devout.

James handed me the bread and then awkwardly embraced me.

"I'm going to miss you," James said, dramatically. "After I am gone, I hope that you think of me kindly."

"You are leaving so soon? When?" I asked. I was saddened. I had assumed he was going to stay much longer than this. I tried to hide my emotion.

"I am leaving tomorrow," he said. "But I owe you one favor. I'm going to help you obtain gainful employment."

"That would be greatly appreciated on my part."

I patted him on the back, took my little handful of bread, and went back to my bed.

JAMES NEVER MET A stranger. He quickly made connections with the local construction community. He put me in contact with some of the major employers. Having a selection of short-term gigs to fill my days, I mostly took general laborer jobs that did not pay much, but still gave me free time to explore the city and follow the Christian evangelists. The mission was highest priority during that time of my life.

James left the following morning for Jerusalem. His mother wept. I thanked him for everything. I didn't know if I would ever see him again.

I'VE MADE ENORMOUS PROGRESS *up here on this year of 1998, writing down this story, despite the constant interruptions from my heavenly companions. Yes, Simon Peter, James, and even Paul have caught wind of my little project. My loyal reader, I must protect you and this history from these biased influences, however well-meaning they may be. As I told you from the beginning, this is my own story, and it will remain that way.*

But, a couple of spoilers before I get on with the story. Up here, James has moved back in with his mother again. Paul is still writing letters and lecturing. I cannot tell you what Simon Peter is up to, as I think it could affect the integrity of this story, but I can dispel a few myths. Simon Peter does not sit at the pearly gates to the entrance of heaven. Do you think heaven is a gated community? There is no crime in the kingdom of heaven, so there are no gates. People take the scriptures way too literally!

After fending off these fretful heavenly distractions, I would be remiss not to share a most salient point of history from Ephesus. The Temple of Artemis. One of the Seven Wonders of the ancient world! This massive temple of enormous proportions stood on flat land just right outside of Ephesus. The city itself was a cult to the god Artemis. As the daughter of Zeus and twin sister of

Apollo, the eternal virgin goddess Artemis was one of the most sacred and widely respected. Imagine the figure of Artemis, the chief goddess of hunting, armed with silver bow and arrows, accompanied by a hunting dog and a stag, roaming the forests with nymphs, in godlike unison with wild animals and nature.

HOURS TURNED INTO DAYS, and days turned into weeks, until life in Ephesus had grown more routine. I moved rooms after James left, but still shared the same housing with Mary, and John. John had returned from his trip, and he was taking care of Mary now. I had settled into the spartan life of a young bachelor. I continued to take manual labor jobs around Ephesus without making any long-term commitments.

One day, as I was just finishing up some repair work, I noticed two Roman soldiers running down the street, still a distance away but coming in my direction.

"They mean business," I thought out loud. They wore plumed helmets that partially shadowed their faces. They were running hard, kicking up dust on the street. I decided to stick around and see what would go down, ready for some free entertainment. As they approached, I stepped away from the curb to give them room to pass, but then they closed in on me and grabbed me by the arms. My heart raced, and my throat closed with panic. I was too startled to react for a few moments.

"What are you doing to me?" I asked, indignantly. "You know my father is a distinguished Roman citizen . . . and so am I." My voice broke on the last words, ruining the effect of my defensive tactic. It never comes out like you planned.

"We know who you are," the taller soldier said. He had bad breath. "We were sent here by Martinus. He has orders from your distinguished father to apprehend you. You're coming with us."

"My father can't hold me hostage without cause. You do not have the right to do this."

"Let me show you my right." The soldier with the bad breath held up his right fist for me to see. He struck me on the side of my head.

"And then I'll show you my left."

He did the same thing with his left fist, a sense of pleasure in his beady eyes, striking the other side of my head. This man really loved his job. That second blow made stars explode across my vision. I did not lose consciousness, but my legs were wobbly. That made the other soldier, the quiet bashful type, hold me up. The soldiers then started dragging me away from the work site.

They took me on all the way past the State Agora, up into the hills. After passing several Roman buildings, we went into a small structure which I assumed was some sort of government or military office. I didn't know which, thanks to the blows to my head. After walking down a long hall, we entered a small room with bare brick walls. I immediately recognized Martinus sitting behind the table with a Roman centurion sitting across from him.

Martinus stood, showing his typical stoic expression. He walked towards me, looked at my face, and asked the soldiers if they did this to me. They answered in the affirmative. His expression went from stoic to stern as he went over and brusquely spoke to the centurion. The centurion pushed his chair back loudly, walked around the table, and waved the smelly-breathed soldier towards him. The soldier let go of me, approach him and as soon as he was close enough, the centurion slapped him across the face.

"Now leave! Both of you," the centurion commanded.

The soldiers obeyed, quickly. The centurion and Martinus sat down. The centurion then politely told me to sit down.

"I'm terribly sorry about that. Those brutes didn't need to rough you up. You can't blame them too much. We train them to be violent animals," the centurion explained to me.

"Can I have a moment with the boy, please?" Martinus asked.

"Sure, no problem. I'm going back to the barracks. You let me know if you need anything." The centurion stood and left the room.

"Lucius, it is good to finally find you." I almost thought I saw Martinus smile, but again, I had been hit in the head. "I apologize for those soldiers hitting you. Your father and I used our connections, deploying the military to track you down, but they were ordered not to do any harm to your person. How are you doing?"

"I'm doing fine. Well, I was doing fine until I those two brutes showed up. So, you are here to take me home? I finally thought I was free." I shook my head with frustration, realizing my lot in life and all the ramifications of the situation. "What took you so long to find me?"

"I knew that I was hot on your trail in Antioch. I might have been able to catch you there, but by the time we arrived you had already set sail for Ephesus. I had to resupply the Hippopotamus, and when we set sail for Ephesus, the ship was caught in a storm two days out. We were in imminent danger, so we decided to go to Cyprus. That time in Cyprus gave me time to think, and I came to a self-realization."

Martinus looked down and away, avoiding eye contact. He took a deep breath, rubbed his stubbled chin, then he stood up straight and proper to address me, crossing his arms behind his back.

"When I was young, I was an outstanding student and great Roman soldier. I went on to become a decorated commander. After retirement, I went into business for myself and became a successful merchant. Your father and I are very similar, and I've always respected him and his wishes. Overall, he is a good father, something I cannot say myself, since I do not have any children."

He paused and took another deep breath. This must have been really exhausting for him to speak from the heart. It probably would have been less stressful for him to track me down and beat me.

"What I'm trying to say is, I've done all the right things in life and followed orders, followed the right path, earned respect from my peers. But, my life has mostly been miserable. I see that you are trying to escape this way of living. I see the passion you bring to your life. Although you are often misguided in your choices, I find your way of living to be genuine and inspiring. In a way, you are brave and dignified by standing up for yourself, to your parents, and not conforming. I envy your freedom and curiosity. I find it refreshing."

I was baffled by his soliloquy. It made me feel better, but I was not sure what he meant by it at that time.

"Thank you," I said after a moment of stunned silence. "I just want to live my life unfettered by my parents, or any authority figures." I said this without any sense of pride. "And so, here we are. So much for freedom."

Martinus cleared his throat and crossed his arms over his chest. "Lucius, what I'm saying is that I've decided I'm going to let you go. I will tell your father that I was caught in the storm, which is partly true, and by the time I arrived in Ephesus you were gone."

I was about to say something, but Martinus held up his hand and stopped me. "Wait, I'm not done. You must avoid communicating with your parents until after you find a new location. You can stay here for a while. I doubt they will send someone here again soon, but do not get too comfortable. In case you are concerned about me, which I doubt but anyway, you need not be. Your father has merely used our past relationship to influence me, but I don't need his money, and do not fear him. He does not have any power over me. If he discovers the truth and gets angry, there is no real risk for me. This is for the best."

"Well, thank you again."

"You are welcome. Be safe and best of luck." Martinus patted me very firmly on both shoulders. He showed me out of the room and pointed with a strong arm straight down the hall towards the door. I wondered if that was the last time that I would ever see him.

17

GANG OF FOUR

My days passed by pleasantly in Ephesus through the early summer of 57 A.D., which brought in warmer weather along with some peace of mind. Martinus was not on my trail, I had some more time off from work between jobs, and I was enjoying my social life. Things were really looking up.

I made my way to the church hall for our usual midweek gathering. Jason and Simon Peter were in the front, addressing the congregation. I arrived late, and Simon Peter had probably been lecturing for some time. I was greeted by some familiar people in the back and soon I settled in to focus on what Rocky was preaching about.

"In summary, men must become submissive to their rulers and masters. And so, in the same manner, wives must be submissive to their husbands. If our wives are truly holy, they will put their hope in God, as did the women of the past. The great wives of the past were submissive, such as Sarah, who obeyed Abraham and called him master."

Simon Peter searched his thoughts and then resumed his sermon, "Wives must be—"

I heard the hall door open loudly as another follower entered. Thankfully, I was not the latest person to come.

"Must be what? I'm sorry, Simon Peter, can you speak up?" Asked an older man, cupping his ear.

"Wives must be . . ." Simon Peter paused, cleared his throat, and nodded to the back of the crowd.

Then he started over. "Wives, your beauty should not be presented from the outside through adornment, jewelry, and fine dress, but from your inner self."

The person sitting next to me nudged me on the side. "That woman who just came in is Tabitha, Simon Peter's wife." The man smiled at me and nodded over his shoulder at the back of the hall, appearing amused by sharing this big news.

"In God's sight," Simon Peter said, "there is no greater beauty than the gentle beauty on the inside. That inner beauty is a quiet and tranquil beauty."

Then Simon Peter cleared his throat again and scratched his beard. "Now shall we sing a hymn?"

The congregation sang together a joyous song of praise. I relaxed and tuned out the music, letting my mind wander up into the clouds like the notes of the majestic hymns.

AFTERWARD, JASON STOOD IN front of the congregation to share announcements and news. More goats, another reminder about the rubbish and a thank you to the volunteer.

Then James pulled out a scroll.

"James has sent us important news from Jerusalem. I will read his latest letter to you all.

> 'Our devout and divine apostle Paul has been imprisoned in Jerusalem. I have been told by my most trusted informant that he will be judged harshly by the Sanhedrin for what they consider to be his many wrongdoings, and that we should expect strict punishment and imprisonment.
>
> This troubling event began after Paul gave notice to the end of the purification days. Paul and his men went to the Temple where offerings would be made for each of them. He had also brought with him several gentiles including Trophimus of Ephesus. The unruly crowd began shouting that he was bringing foreigners into the Temple and attempting to turn the people away from their laws. They dragged Paul and his followers out into the street and began beating them. This caused a riot and the whole city was in chaos.
>
> Thankfully the Roman tribune was notified, and soldiers were called in to break up the riot. The soldiers tied Paul up in chains and took him to the barracks. We have heard from Christians that were present that the mob demanded Paul be executed. We must praise God, that by His mercy and protection alone, Paul was not murdered on that day.
>
> I have been informed that the Roman commander has released Paul. He has ordered the chief priest to

assemble the Sanhedrin where he will face trial. We all fear that Paul will not have a fair trial from the Sanhedrin. The Sanhedrin are enemies of Paul. Remember Paul's history as a former Pharisee turned believer in the resurrection of Christ. Please keep Paul in your prayers.

In lesser news, I have established myself as an esteemed deacon in the church here in Jerusalem. There is great strife and conflict between our church, the Roman authorities, the Pharisees, and the citizens of Jerusalem. I praise Paul and look up to him as our leader, but his arrival and capture in Jerusalem has only caused more unrest.'"

The congregation let out sounds of fright and dismay at this news.

"We should rally some men to break him out," one zealous member yelled. Others began to shout their opinions.

"Calm down," Simon Peter said. "One at a time!"

"We should plot an escape!"

"What if we poison the Sanhedrin?!"

"We shall not inflict any violence on them. We are not murderers," Simon Peter objected, then he addressed the crowd again, trying to maintain order and calm the waters, "I am a reasonable man and I value everyone's opinion. I am always willing to listen to suggestions from the congregation."

"Oh, so this is what you tell people?!" Simon Peter's wife Tabitha interrupted, "That you are great at listener?"

"Shut up!" Simon Peter shouted back at Tabitha. "Nobody cares what you think!"

A powerful silence fell over the hall.

"Now, does anyone have any other suggestions—that are not violent or sinful?" Simon Peter asked.

The congregation was frozen. The silence was broken only by the scorned staccato footsteps of Tabitha leaving the hall.

"Then we shall all be vigilant and pray for Paul." Simon Peter said swiftly. "And pray for me, too." He turned and followed Tabitha out of the hall.

Jason looked at the congregation, started to talk, but couldn't find the right words. A laugh burbled past his lips, but then Jason forced a serious look. He held his hands up in a silent prayer to the heavens.

Before leaving that night, I caught Jason in the back of the hall for a quick chat. He was always friendly and interested in others. I told him about my summer, my life.

"You mean you are not working anymore?" Jason asked me.

"I just take part-time jobs. I am between jobs." I answered lazily.

"You are always between jobs, Lucius! I love your style. Anyway, does that mean you're not busy tomorrow?" Jason was greeting church members as they filed out as we were speaking, without missing a beat in our conversation as he bid them a good evening

"Not at all busy." I replied.

"Then I'll take you to meet some of my other friends, you know, from those other congregations." Jason motioned with his hands facing down, as if to say, we cannot talk about it too much here. I agreed discretely, and it was decided he would swing by my house mid-morning.

JASON AND I WALKED together from my house towards the houses further up on the slopes. He was taking me to the gathering place where I would meet Christians with differing views who were around before Paul's had come to the city. We came to an upscale Greek house where we were greeted by a servant. The servant took us through the grand entry way and out to a lovely peristyle courtyard. The courtyard was lined on all sides with a tiled roof portico above rows of Ionic columns. There were four people relaxing in a seating area which was beautifully tiled and surrounded by a luscious garden of vines and flowers, stone fountains, and decorative statues. The sun shone over the roof to light the very far side of the courtyard. Jason and I approached the four distinguished people, who seemed to be engaged in deep conversation. When they noticed us approaching, they stood to greet us.

Jason introducing me. "Good morning everyone. I bring with me Lucius, a Roman citizen from the great city of Rome, a traveler of the world, a fellow follower of Christ, and a pursuer of knowledge."

Then the others followed Jason by giving their own introductions.

"I am Megakles." He was very tall, dark skinned, had a long dark beard. He wore a long cape and a hood which covered his head. "I am learned in the arts of cosmology and magic. I am also known as a follower of Zoroaster. I will not refute that, but it does not define me."

"Welcome Lucius, I am Sophia. I seek knowledge and wisdom, as we all do here," said a woman with long curly brown hair and wearing a Greek chiton. She shone with the inner beauty and serenity that Simon Peter had often preached about. "As a fellow Roman, do you not agree with Cicero? As he once said, 'If you have a garden and a library, you have everything you need.'"

Sophia smiled hospitably. I returned her smile.

"I am Heridion, originally from Sparta. I am a lover of life." Heridion said. He laughed, and asked rhetorically, "Tell me what is more important to love than life itself?" Heridion looked strong, broad shouldered, and able bodied. He looked like a warrior, as the Spartans were famously known as, so his word regarding love struck me as odd.

"I am Gnipho," said a meek elderly man. As he stood, I realized that he was had a large hump that deformed his spine. He had thin gray hair and a short beard. "I also follow Christ and his teachings. I seek a divine and secret knowledge."

This eclectic group fascinated me, but I was also taken by surprise. Jason had given me the impression that this was another Christian sect, but it seemed much more than that. Perhaps he thought that if I knew what I was getting into I would not have joined him. Or, even worse, perhaps Jason had worried that I would share this secret with Simon Peter and his congregation.

"Lucius, I assume you also seek a *divine* knowledge?" Gnipho asked.

"I seek knowledge," I answered. I adjusted my posture uncomfortably. "But I'm not sure how divine that knowledge will be until I find it."

Heridion laughed and rubbed his clean-shaven face. "Good man. My mutual sympathies on this dubious so-called divine knowledge."

"Where were we in our discussion before our new guests

joined us?" Gnipho asked seriously and dismissively, "Ah, yes. We were discussing the mortality of Christ."

"Oh, not again," Heridion complained. He stretched out his arm, grabbing one of his sandal-clad feet.

"Would you share your view with us again, Jason? Or shall we let Lucius add new thoughts to this conversation." Gnipho dismissed Heridion.

"Don't put him on the spot. I will speak, then he can speak his mind if he feels like doing so." Jason replied. Clearly, Jason was familiar with the flow of these group discussions.

"Lucius," Jason turned to me to explain. "We are a group of freethinking men and women who are passionate about knowledge. We gather for discussion and deliberation in order to seek knowledge and illumination."

I acknowledged Jason and the group, but gestured with positive body language that I was open to all ideas and for him to continue.

"Jesus Christ was born a mortal man from the Virgin Mary, suffered, was tempted by Satan, and died on the cross at the hands of the Romans, and rose from the dead in three days, walked the earth again as a man, and ascended into heaven where he now sits as the son of God," Jason summarized with conviction.

"I admire Jesus as a prophet, magician, and healer of many in the land of Galilee," Megakles stated, finding common ground. "However, I do not understand this narrative. It is much more likely that he was a magician who had prophesied of the coming of the kingdom of heaven. His fate was to be executed as a mere mortal before fulfilling this prophesy. This created the need for a new narrative of the resurrection."

Megakles could see that I was disturbed by this trivialized explanation.

"Allow me to walk through this briefly," Megakles explained. "We know Jesus was traveling around Galilee, healing many people, and preaching that the Kingdom of God was at hand. Jesus did not come as a king to rule God's people, but was executed by the Romans as a mortal man. Therefore, a new narrative was created, and a more figurative definition of the Kingdom of God was assumed."

"Jesus was not a man like you and I, in the physical sense," Gnipho said, holding out his small shaky arm with his palm facing up. "Jesus would cast no shadow, as I do." Gnipho's bony hand cast a shadow on the tiles. "We should not be mixing up the material world with the spiritual world. His crucifixion and resurrection were mere illusions. The fallacy is in following Jesus as a man, fixating on the material world, and making divinity of the mortal. Through Jesus we should seek spirituality through enlightened knowledge."

"I do agree with part of that last statement," Sophia leaned forward, gesturing with her hand. "As a philosopher, there is no higher pursuit than the pursuit of knowledge. Jesus offers much wisdom through his teachings and powerful words to live by through his parables."

"You are all lost in the thick weeds of the life of this one man! I have never been able to reconcile your one true god with all of these other immortals!" Heridion joined with a frustrated and dismissive tone. "God the father, the son of god, the holy spirit, the angels and archangels in heaven. Not to mention Satan, who is clearly acknowledged as a most powerful god. Satan, in your own words, often has more influence on man than god does."

"You speak of the Holy Trinity," Jason said. "God is God the Father, God the Son, and God the Holy Spirit. All three are one God almighty. Satan is merely a fallen angel."

I thought about this abstraction of the holy trinity, of the angels, and the fallen angel. I became more confused myself. I was impressionable at that time, so Heridion had caused me to no longer be convinced either way.

"Tangentially related to the concept of the holy trinity is the topic of faith. You all demonstrate such faith," Gnipho mused. "Jason, this is where you and I, both followers of Christ, do not agree. Your Christians put too much focus on belief and faith. Why is faith a good thing? Is faith in something without knowledge not counterproductive? How is this enlightening? Faith without knowledge is mere ignorance and wishful thinking."

"I also agree with that sentiment," Sophia said. "As the Romans say, 'dedicate your life to truth.' I value empirical evidence and truth over blind faith and ignorance. Although, I will add one subtle but significant nuance. In order to seek knowledge, like the beloved Plato, one must pursue and cherish ideas and ideals. Those ideas are not always existent in the material world, but form in our minds."

"I can't entirely agree with you, but there are shared parallels between my spiritual pursuit of knowledge and your idealism," Gnipho added. "The material world is not where we will find salvation. It is empirical and self-evident that all men are evil because the material world is evil." Gnipho was speaking to this topic which would later be referred to as dualism. "Would you not agree with me that salvation comes through obtaining special knowledge?" Gnipho asked Sophia, trying to use gentle charm.

"What other world is there besides the material world?" Heridion interjected, shaking his head.

"Please, Heridion, let her answer the question and then we will let you speak," Gnipho said.

Heridion crossed his arms and scowled.

"Well, I agree that knowledge is . . . the highest pursuit. I do not intend to equivocate . . . so I will try to answer your question." Sophia gathered her thoughts. "I do not share your pursuit that is so focused on salvation. This seems so singularly focused, as if the pursuit of this secret knowledge is a road to one specific destination. Through my study of philosophy and search for knowledge, I would rather travel many paths on my journey to discovery. The journey is much more worthwhile to me than the destination." Sophia shared a smile of delight. "I'm not convinced that there is a singular destination."

Gnipho seemed less than satisfied with this answer. Jason appeared to side with Gnipho. I was trying to keep up with the conversation, building up my nerve to contribute.

"May I share my thoughts now?" Heridion asked in a caustic tone.

Gnipho flicked one of his old hands at him and looked away.

"We speak of this spiritual world and salvation. What other world is there than the material world? You speak of empiricism and then wander off into your imaginary ideals and secret knowledge." Heridion stood and walked over to the garden, "See this flower. Smell this flower. This flower is beautiful because I can see it, I can smell it, and I can touch it. Do we not want to experience the pleasures of life to the fullest? Why forbid the pleasures of the flesh?" He held up his hand as if to preemptively counterattack the first argument. "Assuming that you do not deliberately inflict harm or suffering on others."

"You sound like a hedonist," Gnipho said, somewhat disgusted.

"Is that supposed to be a derogatory term? Would you rather have the Christian heroes that will suffer and die in vain?" Heridion laughed without malice.

"Ovid wrote, 'There is no such thing as pure pleasure; some anxiety always goes with it.'" Jason quoted.

"That's a great point Jason." I said. Encouraged by Jason, I attempted to contribute to the conversation. "I have met some hedonists in the Daphne suburb of Antioch. They seemed like really happy people." Heridion raised his eyebrows at me in solidarity, then scowled at Gnipho.

"As a follower of Socrates, I am familiar with his pupil, Aristiphus of Cyrene," Sophia shared harmoniously. "Aristiphus thought a central goal in life was the pursuit of pleasure and that through pleasure we will seek happiness. In other words, he followed a philosophy of ethical hedonism. I also believe that pleasure and virtue are not mutually exclusive. That being said, I cannot imagine that Aristiphus' numerous courtesans and lovers were always treated with the highest sense of virtue."

"Numerous courtesans and lovers? Now you are speaking my language, Sophia." Heridion looked at her suggestively.

Heridion did not get much of a reaction from Sophia. She merely gave him a look of distaste, and we each took a moment to silently reflect. When the conversation resumed, the servants served food and drink, and the pleasant exchange of ideas went on well into the night.

These wise people humbled me with their erudite and philosophical deliberations. I realized that I had been isolated up until this moment. I had not been exposed to the world beyond Rome, beyond the Roman gods, and my fledgling knowledge of Christianity. The more that I learned, the more I realized there was so much more to know. It became liberating and more fulfilling to know that being wise meant accepting that you know less, not more. To claim to know all would show prideful ignorance. I would have never come to that realization as a wealthy young patrician in Rome.

JASON AND I FREQUENTED the courtyard numerous times in the next weeks to engage in respectful discourse. One evening the group found itself back on the same topic of the physical and metaphysical.

"Megakles!" Heridion said, calling him out when the conversation had lulled for a minute. "You've been awful quiet today."

Megakles stood up in front of us, theatrically tossing his robe behind him. "Where does the material world end and the mystical world begin? A magician must travel on the continuum between the material and mystical world. The endless cosmos reveals the mystical truths to man." Megakles waved his hands towards the heavens. "As magicians use their mystical powers to physically heal the sick." He made the motions of a spell, pointing his fingers towards my abdomen.

"I will not truck in your sorcery," Gnipho said, turning away.

"The Christians are so dismissive," Megakles sniffed. "When Paul first came to Ephesus, did you know that they gathered up many of the magical books and writings and burned them?"

I felt that Megakles was directing this question towards me.

"You Christians are so hypocritical about magic and sorcery," Megakles continued. "Let me tell you about a great sorcerer named Simon Magus who draws his magic from the holy spirit."

The hair on my head stood up. Simon Magus, the sorcerer. Simon Peter's nemesis!

"Have you seen Simon Magus? Have you witnessed him performing magic?" I asked Megakles, almost choking up with excitement.

Sophia tightened her lips and glanced back and forth between us.

"Do you not know?" Megakles asked. "I was a pupil of Simon Magus. Through Simon Magus I learned of the universal principle, a new cosmology where fire is the first principle of all things . . ."

I grabbed Jason's arm. I needed to warn him about Simon Magus.

". . . of the incarnation of Ennoia," Megakles went on, quite animated, unaware of my tension.

Jason noticed my change in mood from relaxed to something dark and worried. He simply asked Megakles, "Do you still receive these mystical lessons from Simon Magus?"

"I knew him long ago in Alexandria. Simon Magus and I studied together there under the same philosopher. Then I met him several years later and he became my tutor. He had taught me many lessons, and I was his loyal apprentice and follower. It is funny that you ask," Megakles did not laugh in the literal sense, "I recently saw him here in Ephesus."

I did not want to be rude or indiscreet, but I was youthful and impetuous. I whispered to Jason, urging him to come with me to come private place so we could discuss this revelation.

"Young man," Megakles said to me. "You look as if you've seen an evil spirit. I do hope I did not offend you. I've always found Simon's cosmology overly complicated, but not nearly as offensive as many of our recent conversations."

"He's fine," Jason said and he patted me on the back. "His mother is ill, so he has not been himself."

"Yes, my mother has been ill." I imagined Mary being ill so I could put a touch of genuine sadness into the lie.

"I'm so sorry to hear that," Sophia said with heartfelt empathy.

"Let us go now, and care for our things, and we will come back next week." Jason said with masterful diplomacy.

We shared hurried but amicable goodbyes. Then we made a swift exit so we could talk openly in the street.

"What was going on in there?" Jason asked. He sounded friendly, but concerned.

"Do you not know of Simon Magus? He is the rival and archenemy of Simon Peter. I have seen his powerful magic with my own eyes, and he wants nothing more than the downfall of our beloved Simon Peter."

"Then we must go warn Simon Peter at once," Jason said, purposefully but without panic.

We walked together to look for Simon Peter but could not find him anywhere. After we searched some more, and after some calm and composed reassurances from Jason that he would set off first thing in the morning to resume the search, I went home to try to rest my worries.

18

SILVER AND GOLD

The next morning, I ran straight to Jason's house. He was not at home. I was told by his neighbor that he had gone to the church hall already, so I rushed through the streets in that direction. I was hot, sweaty, and breathing heavily as I walked into the hall. Simon Peter, Jason, John, and many other Christians had gathered there. Jason gave me a nod in his typical affable fashion. Tired from running, I sat down for a moment to catch my breath.

I had only been resting for a short time, when I heard loud noises coming from out in the street. I stood and rushed for the door along with Jason and several others to see what was causing the commotion. A crowd of Ephesians had surrounded the church hall.

"Great is Artemis of the Ephesians!" the crowd yelled in unison.

"That's Demetrius, the silversmith," Jason pointed to a man in the center of the crowd, carefully remaining inside the church.

"Great is Artemis of the Ephesians!" the crowd shouted again.

The man who identified as Demetrius stepped forward and shouted directly at us in his deep voice. "Cult of Christ!"

"We prefer the title Christians," Jason corrected him agreeably.

"Fine. Christians! You have a new leader named Simon who is called Peter, who was assigned to succeed Paul. Any man here to replace Paul, the temple robber and defamer of our goddess Artemis, must answer to us." Demetrius addressed us.

"I am Simon Peter." Simon Peter stepped out of the church hall to confront Demetrius. Simon Peter kept a safe distance. Demetrius was almost a head taller than him, and he had a large mob backing him up.

"We will run you out of this great city just as we chased off Paul," said Demetrius.

"I am the leader, the rock of this church, and have always been so. I am not merely Paul's replacement. I speak for myself and this church, and serve our Lord and savior Jesus Christ," Simon Peter said, with frustrated pride.

"None of that matters to us," Demetrius snidely remarked. "If you Christians have any courage or conviction, meet us at the theater before sunset this evening so we can resolve this once and for all."

Demetrius and his followers did not wait for a response. They marched off swiftly while shouting their protest slogans in unison. We went inside the hall to formulate a plan. It was decided that as many Christians as possible would assemble on the seats of the theater several hours before sunset. We would not bring any weapons. We were not to engage in violence or inflict harm on Demetrius or his mob. Instead, we would stand up for our faith in Christ at any cost.

THE ORANGE SUN BLAZED that afternoon and heat waves shimmered over the streets. Arriving at the theater, I climbed the steps to stand with the other Christians. As I walked up the middle aisle, I noticed hundreds of Christians had already assembled in the theater. The turnout looked sparse inside the massive theater. Simon Peter and Jason were sitting up in the much higher seats. Jason acknowledged me, and I could sense his apprehension even from that great distance.

Waiting for sunset that evening felt like an eternity. I would sit down to relax and think, then walk up the stairs, talk with others, pace around, and go sit down again. I eventually took a seat much higher in the theater for a better vantage point with a view out to the sea.

"What do you think is going to happen?" I asked another man sitting next to me, trying to calm the butterflies in my stomach.

He gave me a smile. "I was here for the last altercation. There was no fighting or anything. The city clerk came and broke everything up before anything happened. I tell you, it was all just shouting and posturing."

I stood again, and time passed, waiting. Waiting.

I noticed John, so I walked through the rows to greet him. He told me that Mary was safe at home.

"Look! They approach!" A man standing on the top row pointed in the opposite direction of the city center. I ran higher up to get a view, looking to the harbor and the sun setting on the sea in the horizon beyond. Demetrius and his mob of angry tradesmen were marching towards us.

"They are approaching from the harbor as well." Another man directly behind me shouted. I looked towards the harbor and could see another group approaching from there as well. There were two groups approaching the theater! The one from the harbor, the one that would reach the theater first, was being led by none other than Simon Magus!

Simon Magus and his company sped up into full stride and quickly approached the theater gates. They entered the theater and converged in the orchestra section beneath us. Simon Magus took center stage and addressed the crowd, his powerful voice projecting throughout the theater by its acoustics. "Simon Peter, we meet again. Demetrius and I share a common interest. We both want to see your demise!"

Simon Magus was wearing an elegant robe of the most fabulous cloth of gold, trimmed with violet and platinum, all of which reflected brilliantly in light of the setting sun. In addition to his jewels and other fashionable accouterments, the decorative shoulders on his robe pointed dramatically outward. The men who accompanied Simon Magus were similarly dressed, eccentrically, but not as richly. They all must have been his acolytes, and magicians as well.

Simon Peter was speechless, taken by surprise. Apparently, Jason had not had time to warn him about what we had learned the prior evening. Demetrius and his tradesmen arrived at the theater and blocked all the exits.

"Demetrius arranged this trap for us. Looks like you all fell for the bait," Simon Magus said.

Simon Magus held out both of his bejeweled hands, his fingernails curling almost as long as his thin fingers.

"Simon Magus, we all know of your black magic and false prophecies. You have claimed to speak for the Holy Spirit, but your allegiance is with Satan." Simon Peter addressed Simon Magus with strong conviction. "You may attempt to use your dark powers to tear my men away from our faith, but it will be futile, since they have the love of God in their hearts. In the name of the Lord and Savior Jesus Christ, go away in peace and seek redemption for your sins."

"You have been warned and do not take heed. Now prepare for your demise!" Simon Magus laughed off any theological debate. He returned with equal fiery conviction.

Then he strode from the center of the stage, stepped down into the middle of the orchestra section, and began his incantations. His acolytes started to march around Simon Magus, forming four circles moving in opposite directions around the magician, which created an unnerving illusion of depth. I could see the entire performance quite well from high up in the theater seats.

Also, I did not need to strain to hear the incantations coming from Simon Magus, as the acoustics in the theater were truly outstanding. I wondered if they were spells to summon demons or magical powers.

"AAA IEO IA NEEA NOUS."

Simon Magus began to slowly levitate until his knees were almost at the height of the shoulders of those that circled the closest to him.

"PLUMA XOYO BORO AER IEO," Simon Magus chanted with crossed arms. His body began to rotate in the air, stiff as a board.

Simon Peter's face changed dramatically from a serene countenance to one of panic and fear. Overwhelmed, Simon Peter moved quickly for the aisle and towards the theater exit.

I was still standing near John, and his heavy sadness was palpable. "And so it is written, 'Strike the shepherd and the sheep will be scattered,'" John said, plaintively.

The Christians fled down the theater steps and scattered in all directions. Terror gripped them as they sensed the dark magic of Satan.

"Where are you going?!" Jason yelled at them, facing the onslaught of magicians. He attempted to inspire bravery in the face of fear.

"Have faith, in the name of Jesus!" Simon Peter pleaded to the Christians. He had made it to an exit and had engaged the tradesmen attempting to block his way. The rest of us bolted, running down the aisles and towards the exits. In pure bedlam we fled, trying to move around Simon Magus and the magicians only to run directly into Demetrius and his tradesmen.

Surprisingly, I made it past the mob out into the street unharmed. Not far in front of me, I watched a young Christian being attacked by the crowd. He had been knocked to the ground and his head was being bashed in with a stone. I turned to run the other way. Another group of Christians were being savagely pummeled right in front of me.

I was grabbed from behind. Startled, I turned to defend myself, and saw that it was Megakles who had pulled me away from the fighting and into an alley.

"You and Jason need to flee the city! There is no safety here for you." Megakles said.

That was an understatement. He must have seen the look of betrayal on my face.

"I would not wish harm on any Christians," Megakles explained. "I was not informed of the ambush until today and I came to find and warn you."

I spotted Simon Peter across the street. Many Christians gathered around him, including Jason and John. None of the mob were around. I turned away from Megakles and ran for them.

"Simon Peter, what should we do?" Jason asked.

Simon Peter did not answer. He appeared overwhelmed by the situation.

John caught up to the group and said, "We should run for the harbor. We have a head start," John said. His old age made him look vulnerable, but at least he had a reasonable plan. "Let's head that way. It is not safe for some of you to stay in Ephesus, especially not Simon Peter."

We ran towards the harbor. John started having difficulty keeping up. He tripped on the cobble stones and fell hard face first onto the street. He hopelessly attempted to push himself up from the street. I went back to help him up.

"Do not wait for me, Lucius. I am an old man. Follow these instructions and you can leave safely. Go to the harbor towards the left, and find a large blue boat in the docks. It will have 'Soter' painted in red letters on the white sail. The captain's name is Johnathan, the same as mine. Tell him that I have sent you and that he must help you leave Ephesus immediately. I will arrange to pay him later. Johnathan will know my good name and my reputation."

"You must come with us before they catch up. Let's go, I can help you." I pleaded with him.

John shook his head and painfully sat up. "No, I must stay and take care of Mary. They will not beat a harmless old man like me. Now hurry up and catch the others."

I knew what I had to do.

"Say goodbye to Mary for me," I said tenderly, then rushed to catch up with the others.

I ran as fast as I could until I got to the harbor. Simon Peter and the others were already there, but they were all in a chaotic panic, uncertain about the next steps.

"John is staying behind," I informed them, "but he has let me know there is a ship's captain who will take us away from here. We just need to find to find the right boat and let the captain know that John sent us! Come on!" I said desperately.

"That's madness! Let's escape by foot down the coast. I know a good hideout," one of the others said.

"No, I agree with Lucius. We should flee by ship," Simon Peter said.

"Yes, listen to the boy!"

"The ship is captained by a man named Johnathan. The ship is called Soter, and it should have its name painted in red letters on its white sails. Come on and let's find it," I said.

And so, I convinced the fleeing Christians to head out onto the docks, looking carefully at all the ships tied up in the slips.

"That's it. The Soter!" Simon Peter exclaimed.

Once we found that particular boat, we were relieved. But that feeling did not last since there was no sign of any crew aboard, or near the boat. A sailor walked by us and Simon Peter asked him if he knew Johnathan, the captain of the Soter. The sailor rudely waved us off and went on his way.

A disheveled man walked towards us, carrying some heavy bags. He appeared to be heading directly to the Soter.

"May I help you?" he asked irritably.

"Yes, we are looking for Johnathan," Simon Peter said. "We have been informed that he is captain of this ship. We must set sail immediately on this vessel to avoid confrontation with some local troublemakers. We have instructions from John the Apostle that Jonathan will take us on as passengers."

"I am Johnathan, the captain of the Soter. I have some cargo that I'm transporting to Creta. We set sail today," Jonathan said.

"We must go immediately! There are evil men hot on our trail who wish us harm!" Simon Peter exclaimed.

"Slow down! Let me think. Yes, John, I know him and I know he is good for it. But I still need to make my shipment before I drop you off anywhere."

"I recognize you. You were a Christian and a follower of Paul?" another man asked Jonathan.

"I was a follower at one time, but I have not been to the church for a while," Jonathan replied. "It is a long story."

"Alright, men. Let's go. We will have time to visit once we are safely out at sea," Simon Peter said.

We quickly boarded and set sail for Creta. On the Soter were Jonathan and his crew, Simon Peter, Jason, five other Christian men, and I.

PART IV

WANDERLUST

19

AT SEA

And so there we were, out on the Aegean, winding south-wards. The glassy turquoise water was calm, and a gentle breeze blew from the north. The lines thumped lightly against the mast, accompanied by the ever-present, gentle sound of the boat cutting through the water. The bright sun glittered on the waves creating little sparkles all over the surface. I stared out at the sea in mesmerizing tranquility. The sea spray cooled my skin from the afternoon sun. Out at sea, I was lost in time, lost to the world, together with the other Christians on the small boat, but we were each alone with our thoughts.

As I gazed out at the sea and the shifting horizon, I was deep in my own recollections. Jason had been so warmly receptive of my friendship. In a way, Jason had replaced James as a mentor as I learned more about Christianity. In

contrast to James, Jason was more of a peer and friend. Jason
was also interested in many other philosophies outside our
Christian sect. I was fascinated by the concepts I had been
introduced to by that group in that lovely courtyard. Gnipho,
a different kind of Christian who had a metaphysical view of
Christ, was obsesses with a secret knowledge and believed
that the material world was evil. Sophia, the philosopher and
lover of knowledge, was so classically Greek in her manner
of thinking and living. Megakles, the sorcerer with a heart
of gold. And lastly, Heridion, who loved life and engaged
in worldly pleasure without guilt. I was impressed by our
scholarly discussions. How adroitly they had argued many
compelling topics such as philosophy, mysticism, and religion. I mostly admired how they shared many different
views and various truths on matters of god, life, existence,
morality, and reality.

Various truths? Wait a minute! How can there be various
truths? Is there not only one truth? Yes, there would be
different views and perspectives. It was self-evident that
there are limitless views and perspectives on any topic. For
any idea or physical thing, there would be multiple points
of view, but that did not change the core truth behind it.

Daydreaming out on the sea, my mind wandered deeper
into a sort of thought experiment on this analogy. I imagined
a building that was a perfect square. All four sides were of
equal length and height. If one were to approach it from
the sky directly above, it would be evident that this was a
square building. Yet, from other angles, it could appear
trapezoidal rather than square, or just appear to be one
wall. From many other perspectives the building may not
be in view at all and would not exist to the observer. What

remained true is that the building was square, no matter the perspective of the viewer.

I understood that perspective mattered significantly. To be objective is nearly impossible. I must be aware, I thought, that many observers may not see a building at all. Just like so many people did not know the good news of Christ. I told myself that I must be aware and empathetic of the perspective that pagans and others have on Jesus and the kingdom of heaven.

But to go full circle, back to the origin of the analogy, the perspective will not change the truth. No matter how much Jason, Gnipho, Simon Peter, or other wise men explored universal topics, it would not change the underlying truth. Either there is one true God, or there are many gods. I was coming to my larger concern over the matter of faith. If I did not have any evidence of something, I would rather not believe in it solely on blind faith. Perspective was not going to change truth. I wanted to seek truth. Faith could lead anywhere. It did not rely at all on truth. Faith could be held up through contradicting evidence or proven falsehood, so it is inherently flawed.

As I thought more about seeking truth, I became warier of men who confidently explained the universe without any evidence. My mind could not possibly grasp what the absolute truth may be. I had such limited perspective on the cosmos. But I became more confident that with more age and experience, I would be less sure that I would have all the answers. This also made me less confident in other men who claimed that they had all the answers.

How would this apply to Simon Peter, Paul, and the followers of Christ? Well, I knew that they were not able to change the absolute truth as mortal men. On the other hand, Simon Peter, James, Mary of Magdala, and the disciples had lived with Jesus Christ and witnessed his teaching and miracles. Many of them, such as Mary, had seen Jesus suffer on the cross, die, witnessed his resurrection, and then his ascension into heaven.

MY LOYAL 20TH CENTURY reader, I must interrupt the narrative of my past youthful musings on faith to share my present thoughts. These two thousand years have worn on me. I find it tiresome and pathetic watching humans try to identify one singular and absolute truth. I cringe every time I hear the Nicene Creed recited mindlessly by a congregation. As if God, the universe, and everything else was designed by committee, by a council of men in 4th century Asia Minor.

I'm endlessly frustrated by people being so earthcentric. "So, God created man in His own image." Is the author of this statement not doing the opposite by creating God in man's own image? Seven days to create the heavens and the earth? We accept that a day is defined by the rotation of the earth. But did the earth not yet exist?! We know that the universe contains countless other solar systems and planets, and that time is relative and not universal. How can we even measure such a massive creation event in earth days? Also, what about the continents and mountains that shifted and formed over millions of years?

While we ponder the vast cosmos, ever wonder how many other earth-like planets with intelligent life exist? Perhaps you've heard of the Drake equation? The equation estimates the number of civilizations in our galaxy that would be capable of communicating with humans. This may be the least earthcentric estimation by mankind that I have ever observed. I've heard the *solution up here, but I can't remember. Of course, I can just go look someone up here and get the exact answer.*

Wait, hold on.

I need to stop this.

Sorry. I owe you an apology.

I promised myself to set some boundaries. To tell this story without any heavenly spoilers from the afterlife. I have crossed the line again and I will not do so anymore.

My rant is over and done with. I am stepping down from this heavenly soapbox.

In all fairness, I cannot be completely unsympathetic to humans. I must set realistic expectations on mankind. It is reasonable to expect humans to search for answers and the purpose of life. If humans cannot seek existential answers, or the purpose of life, what else should I expect from them? Humans are blessed with remarkable imagination and intelligent thought. How about just embracing doubt and uncertainty? What about simply enjoying the beautiful, high stakes drama of mortal life?

"LUCIUS LOOK OUT! COMIN' right at you, lad." A sailor shouted at me and woke me from my daydreaming. A line was swinging towards me and the crew was moving to try to tie it down. The wind had picked up and some clouds were crossing the sky to hide the sun.

I walked over to where Jonathan was addressing the Christians who had gathered together at the stern.

"So, do we all agree with those conditions?" Jonathan asked, brusquely. "If so, I will move on with the itinerary."

We all acknowledged him. Although I missed what we were agreeing to. Something had been decided while I was daydreaming.

"Our next stop, which should be very brief, is on the northwest coast of Creta. From there we will set sail for the city of Lasea further down the coast. There we will drop off our cargo. I also have some other business to attend to in Lasea, so the ship will stay there until my work is done. Then we will leave Creta we will make our return to Ephesus."

I noticed the looks of uncertainty and concern at the mention of returning to Ephesus. Simon Peter was biting his tongue.

"That is the ship's itinerary—do you all understand it?" Jonathan asked us in a short-tempered tone, waiting for acknowledgment before sharply turning and walking away.

We all huddled around Simon Peter.

"I recommend we go back to Ephesus and face our enemies. After all, we have God on our side," one of our men suggested.

"Do we?" Simon Peter asked.

"Well, I think after some time has passed, and assuming Simon Magus has left Ephesus, we can engage in diplomacy with Demetrius and his followers. As long as their business is prosperous, they won't look for trouble. Simon Magus was the real instigator," another man said.

"I don't know," Simon Peter said. "I think once Johnathan has made his delivery in Lasea, we can persuade him to change course to another destination."

"I agree," said the Christian. "I think we should join James in Jerusalem. We can provide spiritual support to Paul during his trial."

"Jerusalem is far too dangerous for, you know," Simon Peter said, trying to find the right words. "What I mean to say is—we would have so much more to offer as evangelists in a new church community rather than an older establishment."

"We could stay in Creta and establish a new church," Jason suggested, "Or, there are other Christian communities where we could seek refuge. What about Rhodes, or Cyprus, or Corinth?"

"Corinth is a great suggestion." I chimed in, speaking up as a knee jerk reaction. As blood rushed to my head, I remembered that Daphne had moved to Corinth with her father. I wondered if she was still living there. Perhaps I would find out.

"Yes, Corinth sounds like a prudent destination for our new mission." Simon Peter agreed. "The Corinthians have a reputation for sins of the flesh and idolatry. Our evangelical efforts would benefit them greatly."

The entire group reacted with positive enthusiasm for a mission to Corinth.

"Yes, there would be plenty of work for all of us. As far as addressing all that immorality," one of the men agreed wistfully.

"I will speak to Johnathan privately regarding changing the course to Corinth," Simon Peter said, confirming our plans with the group, so we all disbanded.

IN LITTLE TIME WE arrived at Creta, a very big, wild, but tranquil island. It was covered with a fascinating variety of gorges, mountains, beaches, and forests. The diversity of vegetation was astounding. It was overgrown with palm trees, pine trees, olive, oak, cypress, citrus, fig, tall grass, wildflowers, and herbs. The locals believed that some of the herbs had special health and healing powers.

My days were idyllic, residing near the beach in a small lean-to, living all by myself away from the town of Lasea like a hermit. The crescent-shaped coast of Creta provided views of the sea and land from any vantage point. In the morning I would relax under a palm tree, watching the waves splash against the black rocks which jutted out of the beach. A steep craggy cliff surrounded the beach, splotched with bushes, trees, and tall grass. The dark stones eroded in spots revealing reddish clay where the sea splashed. Occasionally, goats would climb those cliffs with astonishing agility and fearlessness.

During one of those relaxing days, I was pondering the implications of the upcoming Corinth trip. Was Daphne still living in Corinth, or studying elsewhere? How long had it been since I saw her? By now she could be long gone, married to some brute, transformed into a wife and mother.

A Christian shipmate came to inform me that Simon Peter had updated our mission plan and had asked that we congregate in Lasea as soon as possible. The man told me to plan never to return to this side of the island. There were about ten Christians that met at the Lasea house that afternoon to break bread and discuss our itinerary. Philip was also in attendance at the meeting, to my surprise.

"Yes, I spoke with Jonathan about our mission. He has agreed to take us to Corinth before returning to Ephesus," Simon Peter announced.

"Perhaps I can accompany you and at least see you safely to Corinth. At some point I will need to return to Samaria, to attend to my church and my family duties," Philip said.

"Do you, uh, have any news for us from our brethren?" one of the men asked.

"Indeed, I do," Philip replied. "The Samaritan congregation is as strong as ever. We are a peaceful community. We do not have nearly as much conflict and struggle as the church of Jerusalem," Philip said confidently, but without boasting.

"Speaking of Jerusalem," Philip continued, "I have news regarding Paul. A group of forty Jews formed a conspiracy and plotted to kill Paul. The conspirators approached the high priests and elders, taking a solemn oath to fast until they had succeeded in murdering him."

"Is he in danger? What have they done with him?" Jason asked.

"Please, my brothers, I did not mean to alarm you," Philip said. "As a Roman citizen, Paul was rescued by a Roman captain. The Romans transferred him to Caesarea under the protection of hundreds of Roman soldiers. His case will be held in a higher court under the authority of the Roman governor."

This was not the first time I witnessed men being cast out by their own people. The closer one was to his own home and people, I thought, the less welcome they were. Not only Paul and the other disciples, but Jesus Christ himself. Conversely, I was increasingly struck with the occasional pang of desire to return home to Rome. I hoped I would be welcomed back someday.

"My brothers, I also have news about Ephesus from John. Jonathan received a letter from him this morning. Lucius, my eyes are sore and weary, would you please read the letter aloud?" Philip asked.

I took John's letter and read it to the group:

Jonathan, I hope and pray with all my heart that the Holy Spirit finds you again. As painful as it may be, see that God had a plan for your son. Pray for the soul of your dear child. Know that your son is at His side in the kingdom of heaven. Our sympathies are always with you. I pray that you live a life of love rather than a life plagued with anger and bitterness.

I will pay for the success of your journey, and that you may safely deliver Simon Peter and the Christians to their final destination. Whatever the cost may be of their passage, I will cover it. I am merely a humble old man without a family and choose to give my worldly wealth to support the work of the church. If you do reach any of my Christian brethren share the following passage with them as a favor to me.

We are working to bring Ephesus back to normal after that horrific attack at the theater. We have resumed regular attendance of services at the church and our congregation is thriving again. Demetrius and his men have not attempted another out right attack, but they still use tactics of fear. These men are greedier than they are violent. We have learned to coexist by not interfering with their business such as Paul did in the past. They do still intend to teach Simon Peter a lesson through slander or intimidation.

Simon Magus and his acolytes went all around town amazing people with their sorcery, and stirring up many new followers. They are certainly aligned with Satan and are truly evil. Their magical incantations make my spine crawl. Simon Magus left Ephesus not a fortnight after the theater brawl. He announced that he had a score to settle in Samaria. This sounded quite ominous. We are praying for all those good Samaritans.

During our escape I tripped and fell hard on the street. I was very sore for many nights but thanks be to the Lord that my aging bones were not broken. Many of our Christian brothers were badly beaten and at least one man will be crippled for life. Simon Peter, if you do return to Ephesus, we will ask that you heal his injuries in the name of our Lord Jesus Christ.

Mary is doing well and is in good spirits. Some days she is her old self, but on bad days she can be forgetful. The other morning, she forgot where we live now, believing she was still back home in Nazareth with Joseph. Mary says she has heard happy news from James about his family life and his thriving church in Jerusalem. It warms my heart to hear that he is back with his wife in that holy city.

Mary and I will pray for a safe flight for all of you. I will also pray for the sinners such as Demetrius, Simon Magus, and the souls of those that follow them. As Christians we must learn to forgive their sins. Please pray that our wounds will heal. Travel safely with the Lord and the Holy Spirit. Peace be with you all.

Philip then announced to the congregation, much to their disappointment, that he was not going to join us in our mission. He was needed at home in Samaria. "Simon Magus is probably coming after me," he said. "I have always stood up to him. I declared him a sinner and a heretic in front of the community. I must return to Samaria, posthaste."

"I should not go back to Ephesus. Demetrius will surely come after me. I will accompany you all to Corinth." Jason said. I was extremely pleased to hear that my new friend Jason was joining us.

"We set sail for Corinth at sunrise," Simon Peter announced. "Please prepare for the last leg of our journey."

"Let us pray," Jason said.

20

FIRST CORINTHIANS

Corinth was an ancient city located on the northwest side of the narrow isthmus connecting the mainland of Greece to the Peloponnese peninsula. The city could be approached by ship from two ways. The Gulf of Corinth provided direct access to the city, but required going around the Peloponnese peninsula. Instead of taking this route, Jonathan took us on the shorter route to Corinth by way of the Saronic Gulf on the opposite side of the isthmus. In those days it was common that ships would arrive on the opposite bay. These ships would be dragged to the gulf side of Corinth over a paved road. The Soter was too large of a vessel and Jonathan was leaving. Anyway, knowing Jonathan, he would never have agreed to that. The Soter dropped all the Christians off in harbor and we walked into the city across the land route.

The acropolis of Athens is the most well-known of any of the acropolis built by the Greeks. Yet the acropolis of Corinth, known as the Acrocorinth, is by far the most naturally impressive. The Acrocorinth sits high upon a rock cliff, dwarfing that famous hill in Athens. On our journey into Corinth we trekked close enough to view the Acrocorinth, but never attempted to make the daunting climb up to it.

I spent several months in Corinth following a steady routine of work and socializing, with the occasional involvement in the church. I had found employment as a tekton. The city had been growing quite steadily for the last few decades as a thriving trade center in the region due to its centralized location and construction work was in high demand, so I was able to capitalize on this opportunity.

Simon Peter poured himself into the church in Corinth. The local Christian community had struggled mightily with divisions within the church; there were followers of Simon Peter, followers of Paul, and followers of Apollo. The first thing Simon Peter did was to forbid the prevalent pagan practices. The followers of other gods were forced to abandon their idolatry, or they were no longer welcome in the church. Simon Peter and Jason were steadfast in their efforts to bring solidarity to the church. Some of these pagans left the church, but most of them were welcomed back after they destroyed their false idols and abandoned their pagan practices.

The church community had also been rife with sexual immorality. These sins of the flesh were addressed famously in Paul's letters to the Corinthians, several years before the Soter had arrived. Paul had preached to the Corinthians in shameful frustration, instructing that the body was not meant for sexual immorality, but for the Lord. Paul scolded them specifically, "A man has his father's wife. And you are proud!"

These fleshy conditions had become more rampant since Paul had last lectured the Corinthians. One of their most outspoken leaders, Gregorius, was a male prostitute. He was overtly and proudly pan-sexual. The followers of Gregorius were allegedly dabbling in ceremonies that incorporated sexual rituals, paganism, and idolatry. As the chaplain of these sexual rituals, Gregorius blended the worshiping of Christ with pagan deities. Simon Peter was vehemently opposed to these activities, calling them wicked and sinful.

As conflicts within the local church were addressed, I felt myself drift away from the church. Yet my social life did not suffer. I was still a young bachelor. I was a Roman citizen in a Roman world. Jason and I would spend nights together, carousing in our own deft fashion. Jason continued to show his dedication to the church, but also was able to compartmentalize and enjoy other aspects of life. Occasionally we would chase after the fairer of the Corinthians, Jason being the more skillful of the two of us. I was always more introverted and self-conscious than Jason, and doubly so around women.

Yet, I had noticed that I was becoming more comfortable with age in social situations. I had not suffered a spout of depression in my recent memory. My internal struggles had evolved from self-consciousness and insecurity to merely doubt and uncertainty. I was much more content to simply be who I was, Lucius. Still, I remained less certain about who I should be, and what I should do with my life.

Also, over time I had increasing pangs of desire to return to Rome. I wanted to start a new life, but at the same time some of the comforts of home were calling for me. My view of my parents had become less harshly critical. Although still strained, my empathy towards them had grown. I had not yet realized that we shared an unconditional love, and that I was taking this love for granted although it had been there all along. But I was now able to reconsider our differences. In a more mature and dispassionate perspective, I realized that the conflict of my parents was reconcilable. In short, I began to miss my family and my home country.

ONE MILD AND SUNNY afternoon I was leisurely wandering through the agora of Corinth. I had just strolled past the bustling central shops, looking for something to eat. I took a relaxing break to watch the crowd of pedestrians, leaning on the raised marble platform of the bema. The bema was used for hearing cases and addressing the public. This was the same place where Paul's case was judged not so many years ago.

Standing in front of a shop I noticed a lovely woman with dark straight hair. She was holding a little girl, swaying her, while she was speaking to a shopkeeper. The little girl rested her head on the woman's shoulder. She was the type of woman that attracted me, strikingly like Daphne. She was about the same height as Daphne, but had a fuller figure. A figure that came with motherhood.

Could this be Daphne?! My heart was struck. Who was the child? In a rush of excitement, I calculated the years that had passed, and the age of the child. I had not seen the woman's face, perhaps I was mistaken. She said she was going to move to Corinth. So, it was possible.

Should I go speak to her? I was quite a mess that day, my hair disheveled from a morning at work and my face not cleanly shaven in a week. My clothes were covered in sweat, dirt, and masonry dust from work.

Should I walk by to determine if it was truly Daphne? I must, I decided, but in a way so that she would not see me. I stepped stealthily past the shop at a safe distance, facing mostly away from her. Occasionally, I would discretely glance in that direction in an attempt to catch a clear glimpse of her face. The child looked up at her and the woman swung the child around, blocking my view. So, I continued walking on by, as if I was just passing through, just another lunchtime customer on the agora. After a moment I turned around to walk by again to try one more time. The woman had just paid the shopkeeper and he helped her with a small sack as she shifted the girl to her other hip. The little girl hid her face. The woman then smiled at the shopkeeper in thanks, showing her prominent teeth and slight overbite. I noticed her distinct profile.

It was Daphne!

OK, I thought, what is the plan? What do I say to her? Act casual. Wait, casual? Running into my long-lost summer love in a foreign city was not casual. Act surprised. Casually surprised, but friendly, and happy to see her. But don't act presumptive. Don't act like I'm overwhelmed with . . . with whatever I'm actually feeling. Essentially, don't show any excited panic. Stick with, "It is just so nice to see you after all these years," and, "how are you doing," and such.

I took a few deep, calming breaths and commenced my approach. "Lucius, it is you! Look at you! How are you doing?" I was startled that someone nearby addressed me unexpectedly. Daphne was still not facing me, so we had not made eye contact. Turning, I realized it was Daphne's sister, Cornelia, speaking to me. She approached me promptly, not carrying any pretense or emotional baggage.

"Cornelia, hello! It's nice to see you," I said politely as I could muster. I was surprised and literally blindsided by her. "It's been so long. I didn't know you were living in Corinth," I lied, then winced when I realized what I had said. She looked much the same, with her curly hair. She seemed shorter and fuller than I remember. She seemed more familiar and friendlier than I ever recall her being in the past.

"Daphne, look, it's Lucius. Remember, Lucius from Rome?"

Daphne turned, and then we were facing each other.

"Of course, I do," Daphne said, looking into my eyes and smiling. Her smile gave me a jolt. I was working hard to be casual.

Cornelia walked up to Daphne and the young girl in her arms immediately latched onto Cornelia. Cornelia took the child, and Daphne took a graceful step forward and she casually held an arm out to greet me. I wrapped my arms around and pulled her against me. As we embraced, my head went over her shoulder. I turned it towards her, felt her warmth and her familiar smell. I tasted her raven colored hair as it touched delicately against my lips. I experienced that guttural feeling that was not simply lust or visual appeal, but holistic and magnetic attraction. That old, familiar dichotomy of exhilarating warmth and crippling ache.

While I was not nearly as excited to see Cornelia, I was so grateful that she was there to mediate this strained interaction. Daphne and I had not really spoken yet. Occasionally, we made eye contact as we stood there.

"Lucius, this is my daughter, Julia." Cornelia introduced the child in her arms, relieving me of some burden. The little girl smiled at me. She had dark brown eyes and long eyelashes. I smiled back, and she bashfully hid her soft-cheeked face in Cornelia's shawl.

"You need to meet my husband. He is a Roman. I met him here in Corinth through my father's connections," Cornelia said. "Our family all live near father's villa. My husband is around here somewhere. Where did he wander off to?"

She scanned the crowd around the shops. I didn't speak.

"How is Rufus?" Cornelia asked as she continued to look for her husband, smiling comfortably in her motherly role. I recalled their dalliance on that starry night those years ago. It did not lead to anything. Typical Rufus, I recalled nostalgically.

"I wish I knew," I answered. I felt bad that I didn't have any good intelligence on Rufus. I did not feel bad for her, rather I felt bad for Rufus. And mostly, bad about myself. I had another pang of homesickness, reminded of my old friends. "My father sent me away years ago to work in Judea to teach me a lesson. I haven't been back to Rome in years."

"Oh, no!" Cornelia said, almost too sympathetically.

"I haven't seen my family, or any of my old friends in years. Last I heard from my parents they were doing fine."

Facing Cornelia, I sidled closer to Daphne. She bit her lower lip.

"Our father has a villa on a hillside not far from here. I live close by, and Daphne lives with father," Cornelia explained. "We have functions with friends and family quite often at our father's estate. We are entertaining this Friday, so you should really come join us."

Daphne tilted her head and smiled at her sister, mouthing some words that I could not make out. Perhaps Daphne did not want to seem too eager. Cornelia was a wife and mother, I thought, and was trying to project that same desire on her sister. What happily married woman would not want her younger sister to have the same happy fortune?

"So?" Cornelia asked, anticipating my answer.

"Oh, yes. I do not have plans, so I can be there Friday. At your father's villa," I answered. My newfound confidence lifted my spirits. I was the new Lucius, an experienced world traveler.

Cornelia kept chatting on and on about their family villa and directions on how to get there. I had a hard time following her details. I started to notice my surroundings, the people in the agora walking by, and the busy shops behind us.

Cornelia's husband walked up and introduced himself as Cato. He was very tall and dressed as a noble Roman citizen of the patrician class. He was not unfriendly, but we shared a mutual disinterest in each other. We greeted each other with baseline polite obligation.

"Goodbye Lucius, I will see you Friday," Daphne said. She appeared unaffected by this encounter, as if no time had passed since the last time that I saw her in Rome. If she was trying to play at being casual, she was doing so masterfully. She leaned forward and kissed me gently on the cheek. I touched her arm and held on to it for a fleeting moment before she walked away.

I strolled in the direction of the marble fountain on the agora, flying high with boundless energy. I observed the reflection of sunlight on the water. The clean sound of the splashing was so crisp and clear. I was admiring all the beauty that surrounded me. Life was a gift. I found completeness in everyone's face that day after meeting Daphne again. Each person I observed was a whole person inside, just like me. Jaunting by the Baths of Eurykles, I watched an old lady walking slowly. I was touched by the young man who stopped to help her along. My heart went out to that old lady and I wished them both well. I kept thinking of Daphne, of everything and nothing, and forgetting where I was going.

I turned the corner past the market and approached the Temple of Apollo. The priestesses inside would be attending to a ritual before the bronze statue of Apollo. I imagined Daphne, a graceful nymph of maidenly beauty, serving the gods. A loud voice shook me from my daydream. I turned and saw a small man standing on the steps of the temple speaking to a small crowd. His pronouncements had the tone of a confident orator, so I decided to listen.

"A strong wind will blow from the mouth of Eurus, as if he is blowing his final breath, pulling up trees and knocking down temples," the man proclaimed. "Thunderbolts, mightier than those hurled by Zeus, will fall from the skies and set fire to the cities! Terrible storms with hail stones larger than my fist will pummel our homes and kill all of our livestock!"

He was a soothsayer. Since I was in such a great mood, I gave him my attention. After listening closely, he sounded more like a raving madman than a confident orator. I was reminded again of the soothsayer in Messana and how he had accurately foretold some of my encounters.

"Great beasts twice the size of elephants, with the bodies of horses, and the heads and manes of lions, will come running from the forests, so starving mad that they will eat your children!" This guy was very dramatic. I'd heard enough. I was done with soothsayers for a while. And, also, magicians for that matter. I walked home alone with rejuvenated hope that did not fade as the sun went down and the stars appeared.

FRIDAY HAD ARRIVED LIKE an egg about to hatch, and I was getting prepared for a special evening at Daphne's family villa. My face was clean shaven, and I had cropped my hair. I adorned myself with a new toga made of fine Egyptian linen. I was going for the classic Augustus Caesar look, how he had been commonly sculpted in his statues.

I hiked my way up a winding dirt road that climbed a hill to the villa of Daphne's father. When I had first started walking, I thought I was lost, since I had not been paying close attention to Cornelia's directions, preoccupied by my encounter with Daphne. I eventually recalled the directions after finding the first landmark after some trial and error.

When I reached the top of the hill there was a magnificent view of the city of Corinth and the gulf, the miniature ships sailing across the horizon. I arrived at the villa, and I explained myself to the servant at the door. He showed me through the entryway and into the courtyard. There was already a large gathering of people and the ambiance was lively and convivial. People sitting and standing, laughing and talking, eating and drinking. Unlike our past social activities with the circle of young friends in Rome, this was crowd much more diverse in terms of ages, and familial.

There were brothers and sisters, cousins, parents, grand-parents, in-laws, friends and associates, neighbors, and no shortage of young children running around and playing.

I found Daphne sitting on a bench engrossed in con-versation with Cornelia, Cato, and another adult couple. Cornelia was laughing and blushing. Apparently, I was late to the party.

"Lucius, relax, sit down and join us. We were just talking politics," Cornelia said invitingly, tilting her head at the seat next to Daphne.

Daphne grabbed my hand and pulled me towards her. I sat down next to her, trying to act casual. She reached towards me and put her hands around mine.

"Your hands are cold," Daphne said quietly to me.

"Lucius is in construction, too," Cornelia said to Cato. "Lucius, did you know that my husband oversees Domus Maximus? Perhaps you have heard of it."

"Yes, I have." Of course, I had heard of Domus Maximus. It was only the most prolific construction outfit in the entire region. "I am a tekton. I was trained in Judea, among other places, so I am familiar with this industry." I explained, with a mix of pride and humility. Daphne squeezed my hand.

"A tekton? Why would you perform the labor yourself? That's what slaves are for. Sure, there's some up-front cost, but after that they are extremely economical," Cato said con-descendingly. "Anyway, most of my income is from trade. That is where all the denarius is made in Corinth. What projects are you currently working on? Maybe you've worked with some of my slaves?"

"Please, let's not talk about work anymore," Cornelia thankfully saved me, as this comparison between my work and the work of Cato's slaves was painfully unfavorable and condescending. "We were talking about politics. That is much more fun to talk about, and we can all participate in the conversation, not just the men."

"As if women can understand politics. Gossip? Yes, clearly so. But not politics," Cato said. He went on, expounding on this theory for several moments before I was able to return the favor to Cornelia by attempting to change the subject.

"My father is a politician in Rome. Recently he was awarded a position in the government of Britannia. He is a close associate to the governor there, Aulus Didius Gallus," I said, trying to embellish this position with names and titles. I shared every bit of the limited details that I knew.

"Britannia is a cold, dank dump. And, are you sure that you have your facts straight? Didius was sacked and replaced by Quintus Veranius Nepos last year, wasn't he? Hey, can we get some more wine over here?" Cato shouted at a servant.

"So, what were we talking about—before Lucius arrived?" Cornelia kindly attempted to change the subject yet again. She appeared a little embarrassed by her husband's pompous behavior.

"Oh yes, we were talking about Nero's singing," said the classy middle-aged lady who was sitting with the group.

"Yes, Nero's singing," said the classy lady's husband, an older gentleman himself.

"I have heard that he sings for hours on end at public theaters and that no one is permitted to leave, even under the direst of circumstances," the lady went on. "Women will give birth, men will leap from the walls of the theaters, or the elderly will feign death just to be carried out. Nero would bribe, slander, or assault his competition, in order to win a singing contest. Then when he did take stage to humbly accept his victory, he would speak deferentially to the judges."

A servant appeared, holding a silver tray. I took two goblets of wine from a servant for myself and Daphne, trying not to miss any of the conversation. When I passed the goblet to Daphne, she pulled me by my arm until I was sitting on her lap sideways. She was a strong woman who knew what she wanted.

"Has anyone heard Nero's 'divine voice' in person?" the older man asked the group.

"I saw him perform at a theater in Naples," the classy lady said. "He stood alone with his lyre in hand, sweating nervously, and performed a theme from a tragedy. He did not give a strong performance, but was still given a standing ovation. According to the local gossip, he had hired thousands of young commoners to fill the audience and praise him with extravagant applause."

I draped my arm over Daphne's shoulder and kissed the top of her head. She scratched the hair on the back of my head with her gentle hand. I felt dignified as well as emasculated.

"How was his singing? Does he have a good singing voice?" Daphne asked.

"Oh, it was awful. His lyre playing was sound, fundamentally speaking, but his singing was weak. His voice was shaky, and his tone was hoarse," the lady said with laughter.

"I heard he sounds like a nasally eunuch," the older man said.

"Oh, but some eunuchs do sing quite well," the lady responded.

Daphne whispered to me, and I quietly whispered back, beginning our own private conversations. I felt a strong connection between us and her friends and family.

"I'm sorry, I was late to the party. What brought all of this up?" I asked.

"A rumor is going around that Nero will attend the Isthmian Games this spring. If he comes, then surely, he will enter the events. Daphne intends to compete in the singing contest." Cornelia said.

"You are going to compete in the games?" I whispered, leaning close so that my lips brushed her ear.

"Yes, Lucy. You know I will," she answered softly.

"Daphne, are you going to sing for us?" Cornelia requested loudly, so everyone in the vicinity of our group could hear.

"Not right now. I'm not ready." Daphne was coy. "Aren't we enjoying this conversation together? I don't want to interrupt."

"Oh, come on, please. Just one song!" The raucous company all began to beg for a performance. After all, there was no better entertainment than friends and family. Daphne eventually acquiesced, agreeing to perform just one song. She got up and walked up the steps to the villa before turning to face her audience.

"This is called, 'Ode to a Long, Lost Love.'" Daphne stood up straight, posturing her hands in front of her, as her blue shawl fluttered in the breeze. A young girl with a lyre appeared and stood near to her. Daphne smiled and began singing as the girl strummed the lyre in sync. As she sang each poetic beat, she gracefully stepped one foot in front of the other to the rhythm of the song.

Oh, my long, lost love,
where have you gone?
To follow the spirit of
Alexander from Macedon.

Too far away Persia
with incense for trade?
On the road to Asia
which silk has paid.

Or in the footsteps of Flaccus
across the desert sand?
To a palm covered oasis
in a faraway land.

Has Aphrodite beckoned you
to a fair forest nymph?
Or has your heart grown cold
and our love gone dim?

Has Poseidon pulled you down
to the depths of the sea?
Or are you lost and alone,
calling out for me?

The crowd cheered for Daphne. Her performance was
truly enjoyed by all. There was not a dry eye in that courtyard.
The little girl with the lyre danced back and forth, capturing
every opportunity for praise.

Daphne came back to me and we sat together close and
contented. I was so proud of her and delighted to be with
her again. And so that night ended on a high note. I walked
home down the hillside alone, looking up at the stars. I mar-

veled at the Great Bear, as I had many times before. Again, I was feeling warm and hopeful, but this time I only saw the simple beauty of the stars twinkling above me.

ALTHOUGH JASON AND I had been in frequent contact since we arrived in Corinth, I had not been to the church for some time. And as I spent more time with Daphne, I had drifted further away from the community of Christians. Ostensibly, I was too busy with work, but I was mostly preoccupied with my rekindled relationship. I had warmed to Christianity and I was committed to helping them, and yet, I was still not baptized. I had learned the concepts of faith from the Christians, but I still had my doubts. And now my heart was consumed by Daphne. The concept of faith in one god and the pursuit of a single universal truth had been set aside for that mortal passion.

I could not wait to tell Jason about Daphne. I decided to go to the church at a time when I expected everyone to be congregating. I arrived just in time for the service. Jason was addressing the congregation.

"My brothers and sisters, Simon Peter is here today to bless you with his words. But before he speaks, I have a few items that I want to share. First of all, I am very proud to be accepted as the new deacon of the church here in Corinth. Thank you all for such a warm welcome. Regrettably, the division and sinful ways of this community have not been entirely resolved. Paul has warned you, Simon Peter has warned you, and now I am warning you again. Hopefully this is the last time. I've been informed that one of you has been stealing lambs from his neighbor, and sacrificing them to Apollo, and having them for dinner. This is sinful and wrong on so many levels, must I really have to explain this to you all?"

Jason paused to gain his composure as he rarely spoke negatively, and it visibly caused him discomfort. I saw many in the congregation turn their eyes away in obstinate shame.

"Although Gregorius was baptized in the church, he is no longer welcome to set foot on this holy ground," Jason continued. "Gregorius is a pagan idol worshiper. Anyone participating in his rituals or orgies will be banned from the church of Corinth."

Jason scanned the congregation, paused, and took a deep breath. "Simon Peter will now address the congregation."

Simon Peter stood and turned to face the crowd. He held his hands out and began reciting the Lord's Prayer. Then, clenching his eyes shut, pounding a fist against his chest, Simon Peter began passionately asking God for His forgiveness and for all their sins and transgressions. "I spoke of the one true God, warned against idolatry, and explained the roles of husbands and wives—"

"Has anyone even seen his wife Tabitha lately?" I heard someone whisper.

". . . of living holy, and the prophecy of the scriptures. Paul and I, disciples of Jesus Christ, have warned you all, mere infants in the ways of Christ, to be God-fearing. If you do not take heed, if you continue down the path of Satan, do not expect God's mercy. If God condemned Sodom and Gomorrah and burned those cities to ashes, will he not do the same to you? To all of you who are living in sin? God did not spare the ungodly people when He brought the flood. But He did spare Noah and the other righteous ones, just as God will spare the righteous on the day of judgment.

But God will not spare those who live in the sin of sexual immorality, who live in sin with their mothers-in-law, or who participate in pagan idolatry, who draw up frivolous lawsuits. Or, who steal lambs from their neighbors to sacrifice to pagan gods!"

Simon Peter's last words echoed, and then the congregation was silent. The only sound was Simon Peter catching his breath and the light rain dripping off the roof of the church.

"Praise be to the Lord, in the name of His Son, Jesus Christ." Jason gave the closing words of the service. "Thank you, Simon Peter, for those encouraging words. Everyone is welcome to stay for refreshments!"

Jason greeted me with his customary warmth, and I told him about my encounter with Daphne. Jason seemed very happy for me. I told him that he and I should spend some time together, but Jason made a lightly sarcastic remark that I was going to be way too busy with Daphne to have time for him. I replied that I would make time, but we didn't talk much after that.

DAPHNE AND I SAW each other nearly every day. We would walk around the city people watching, or I would come visit her at her father's villa. Occasionally we would spend time together with her family and friends. I got to know Cato and his arrogant friends better, but I did not always enjoy their company. Julia, Cornelia's daughter, was my favorite. She would run up to me on every visit, calling out, "Lucy" in her high-pitched voice.

Daphne and I sat alone and frequently talked all through the night, sometimes until sunrise. We would talk about our past, what she had been doing for those years when we were apart, her recent relationships, and family trials. I shared my journey and everything that had led me to the Christians and Corinth. We discussed the uncertainty of our future, and whether we really belonged together. We vowed not to take things too seriously. We were just going to appreciate this time we had together. This uncertainty over the future caused some strain in our relationship before, but it had never boiled over.

21

ISTHMIAN GAMES

Athletes and spectators alike flocked from all around the Mediterranean to Corinth for the Isthmian Games. Held every spring before and after the Olympic Games, these Panhellenic games paid honor to the god Poseidon. Athletes would compete in boxing, wrestling, pankration, and chariot racing. The rhetoric contests included singing, dancing, and poetry, and allowed women to compete in these events. To the victor went all the spoils, as there was no prize for second or third place. The winners would be adorned with a pine wreath (an improvement from the former wreaths of dried celery), and in addition to the eternal honor of championship the winners would also be able to attend the local university for free.

The Isthmian Games of 59 A.D. were in just two days. The events were to take place at the Isthmian Sanctuary on the other side of the isthmus near the city of Argos. Daphne and I had planned to attend the events together with her family and friends. The first day was dedicated to the pageantry of religious ceremonies and banquets. Traveling across that small bridge of land, we arrived in the Isthmian Sanctuary just in time to attend the opening day events in honor of Poseidon. Tents were set up all around the city in the fields and nearby pine groves for travelers and vendors, and lodgings had been quickly constructed to house the athletes from all over the world.

The streets swarmed with visitors creating an air of spectacle and grandeur. Mankind in that atmosphere generates a powerful mob energy that compels him to patriotism. To cheer madly for his own team. To love his friend and hate his foe. To go to war against an enemy. That competitive energy and anticipation was intense on opening day.

On the first night of the ceremony, Daphne and I crept out alone, a short respite from traveling with her family. The crowd had formed a parade on the walkway to the Temple of Poseidon. The line of people was still moving along as we joined them. We were at least a mile from the temple.

"We need to hurry if we want to see anything," I said. We started walking faster, pushing through the crowd, holding hands, but then letting go to squeeze through. A muscular boxer wearing only a loincloth was being paraded through the streets by his entourage. One of his men was waving a palm branch at him. Another held an impromptu sign that said, "The African Executioner."

"Oh, look at the theater!" Daphne said, pointing to our right. "That's where I will perform. Look at that beautiful marble." The outer stage wall was adorned with depictions of the games, chariot racers whipping their horses, all of which were illuminated by bonfires. The flames gave the illusion of movement to the figures.

"I know, that's beautiful!" I shared her enthusiasm. The adrenaline of competition was flowing vicariously through my veins. "Oh, look at the statues! Those are past champions of the games. Perhaps you will be immortalized too." We admired the statues of champions from prior games that lined the street as we approached the temple.

Two lines of soldiers had split the crowd that gathered in front of the temple. Priests and priestesses, adorned in sacred headbands, marched towards the temple. The priests led a procession of goats, cows, and swine. The animals were decorated with ribbons and medals, oblivious of their fate.

We moved through the crowd until we were close enough to watch the ceremonies being performed on the platform in front of the temple. Daphne and I were above average height, so we were able to see clearly. A cow was being prepared for sacrifice. A priest was sprinkling seeds on its head, and priestesses tossed seeds on the ground around the animal. After water was poured ceremoniously over the cow's head, a butcher quickly slaughtered the poor beast with one slice to the neck. The crowd responded with a deep and thunderous roar.

After the ceremonies were completed, the crowd began to disperse. A mother chased two giggling children. She was yelling and pushing through people, looking haggard and frustrated. Some priests appeared outside of the temple holding torches.

"Can you smell that? They are burning sacrifices at the altar for Poseidon," I asked Daphne, as the strong scent of burning flesh wafted in the air, covering up the stench of the warm crowd. Smoke began to roll out of the entrance of the temple and towards the night sky.

"Yes, I can smell, but I can't tell if anything else is happening. Can you?" She asked.

"It doesn't matter. The best part is over. Shall we join the others for dinner?" I pulled her away from the temple.

I didn't feel sinful or guilty about joining in this pagan ceremony. It just seemed so commonplace and it was how I was raised. In fact, I didn't really think about it at the time. All of my thoughts were with Daphne and the anticipation of the events to come.

THAT NIGHT A BANQUET was hosted by Daphne's family in a large open tent by the sea. Daphne and I sat at a long table with her family and friends. Trays were presented by the servants which were laden with poultry, rabbit, deer, goat, seafood, snails, nuts, cheese, and salad. Then desserts of fruits, nuts, honey, and other delicacies were served. I thought to myself, what would my Jewish friends think of me eating lobster and crab meat at a pagan banquet? The meal was pleasant, as was the atmosphere. There were musicians playing festive music on the drum and lyres, dancing through the tent and down the beach. The fresh scent of the food mixed with the stale fishy smell of the sea. The waves washed up near the tent, the sound of the tide like background noise as the foam crept up and slid away. It was nearly impossible to see out in the dark. The sea was nothing but blackness.

Guests were served copious pours of wine from a great cauldron. Some people drank as if these were their last day on earth, as if some of them would not survive the games. As I drank more and more, the volume of the talking around me became overwhelmingly loud, I lost track of what was being discussed. I fell into a daze, looking out at the laughing and shouting faces in the flickering light of the lamps. Cato and several of his boisterous friends were telling jokes, standing up and shoving each other around. The women would attempt to settle them down, but then become amused by their antics and start giggling. This only encouraged them to behave more outrageously.

AT SOME POINT I realized that I had drunk way too much. Somehow, I made it to my bed and I woke up the next morning with my head spinning. I had occasional recollections of the men boasting of the athletes that they knew and their prospects. Of Daphne, Cornelia, Cato and his friends helping me find my lodging. I remembered walking down the beach in the dark. Meeting a strange group of local teenagers and petting their dogs. During the walk, Daphne and I agreed that we were going to sleep this one off. We were not even going to try to attend the next day's events. And Daphne needed to rest, she was scheduled to compete on the following day. I said goodnight to Daphne, and then Cato and the others escorted her safely to bed.

TENTS OUTSIDE THE CITY were thrown up in droves by vendors and visitors across the expansive fields near the pine groves. On the following morning, per our arrangement, I went to go meet Jason, Simon Peter, and the other Christians at their tents. During the games the Christians were given the right to abstain from the pagan festivals, but they were still able to attend the competitions. So, Jason and the Christians avoided the opening ceremonies, and traveled out to join in on the second of the three days of competition. I planned to attend some day events with them, then meet up with Daphne's people for the afternoon competitions.

Jason and Simon Peter were accompanied by two middle-aged Christian men. Both greeted me kindly, accepting me as a fellow Christian. They did not ask about the opening pagan ceremonies as if they wanted to avoid the subject. The man named Dennis was portly, pale and freckled, with reddish hair. The other man called Cletus was dark, tall and thin, and hunched over. Cletus had a large Adam's apple, thinning hair, and a gaunt, malnourished face. It was safe to assume by their physiques that they were not athletes competing in the games.

"Praise be with you, Lucius," Simon Peter said, greeting me kindly. He looked askance at the mob of spectators walking past our group. "We find ourselves in a den of sinners and pagans. This is an important opportunity to share the good news of the coming of Christ."

"Praise Jesus! What do we plan on going to see today? Are there chariot races today?" Jason deftly balanced his evangelism with his social life in only a few sentences.

"No, the chariot races are always on the last day of competition," I replied. "Today there is boxing and pankration at the stadium. And this evening there is singing and dancing at the theater. My girlfriend Daphne is competing at the theater with music and dance. Daphne's sister's husband's friend grew up with a pankratiast. We should cheer him on and support the family."

Dennis and Cletus took some time sorting out my degrees of separation from the pankratiast. The pankration was a combat sport that was a mix of boxing, wrestling, kicking, and other fighting techniques. It was bare hands fighting that was as close to real combat as a sport could get. It was almost no holds barred. The only disallowed moves were biting, eye gouging, and direct attacks on the genitals.

"I dabbled in wrestling myself in my school days. Mind you, that was when I was a much younger man," Dennis said. To demonstrate, he squatted down, put both of his hands out defensively and began shuffling in the dirt around us. He looked more foolish than intimidating with his flabby arms and open-mouthed grin.

"Pankration is far too violent for me. I always feel a strong sympathy for the poor soul that is taking the beating," Simon Peter said. "But, for my loyal friend Lucius, I will do my best and endeavor to enjoy the match. And I will pray that nobody gets seriously injured." A pained look, a shadow of some inner turmoil, creased Simon Peter's features and he closed his eyes. He started pounding his fist on his chest.

"Please, Simon Peter, for my sake don't worry so much. These men are competing voluntarily and are trained for combat." Jason said, attempting to sooth whatever was troubling Simon Peter. But then Simon Peter covered his face, as if he was going to begin weeping, and said, "I'm sorry, my brothers, I'm terribly sorry. You see, this reminded me of an incident in my impetuous youth when I inflicted violence on a fellow man. When the Romans came to . . . came to, to arrest Jesus Christ I impulsively drew my sword and cut off a servant's ear."

"Jesus forgave you," Cletus consoled Simon Peter. "You had good intentions, and you have confessed your sins."

"The past is no matter. This is a festive event," Simon Peter wiped away a tear from his eye and took a deep breath. "And we have such a great opportunity to save the souls of many men during these few days."

WHEN WE ARRIVED AT the stadium, they were drawing lots to decide on the match-ups for the first round. Pankration was a single elimination competition. The luck of the lot determined the opponents for each round until there was a single final championship match. Daphne and her sister had not arrived, but I found Cato with his friend, the man who was friends with a pankratiast.

Cato saw me approaching and nodded. Cato's friend was rather large, like a fighter himself, but his soft face did not look nearly as accommodating to punches. Cato introduced his friend as Tadius.

"They call our fighter Prosopo because of his imposing visage," Cato said. Prosopo meant 'the face' in Greek. "He's drawn the third match today. The first round should be easy for him. We've placed a good wager on it." Cato pointed out the fighter Prosopo, who was down on the field. He was stripped down, surrounded by his trainers, getting warmed up. This was a formidable fighter, a beast. He was broad-chested and broad-shouldered, with a thick neck and ears that curled in on themselves like cauliflower. His whole face seemed flat and wide-shaped, as if it had accommodated to being punched.

"Better him than me," I said. I felt my hands shaking. I didn't have to fight, but just knowing someone who did caused me anxiety. The waiting was the worst part.

"I would probably do fine out there," Cato said confidently and dismissively, "but, I'm no Prosopo."

"Oh, by the way, these are my friends." I invited Simon Peter, Jason, Dennis, and Cletus to introduce themselves to Cato and Tadius before we found our seats.

"You and all of your friends are always welcome to visit the church in Corinth with Lucius," Jason said.

Cato whispered to his friend and they both laughed.

"I will say a prayer for Prosopo," Simon Peter said politely. He walked away from us, climbing the stadium aisle. The other Christians followed him.

"Hey, how old is that chubby, ginger-faced chump? He looks even older than my father," Tadius asked Cato. "Those guys give me the creeps. Where did you meet them?"

"They're in a cult with Lucius, I think. I don't know," Cato answered, again dismissively. "Don't worry. We don't have to stay with them the whole time." I wanted to correct him, but Cato started up the aisle before I could say anything.

After our group found seats, I with the Christians and Cato and his friend a few rows down from us, our attention was quickly focused on the first fight. The two fighters faced each other wearing only loincloths and leather-wrapped hands. They immediately began wildly throwing blows at each other. The crowd erupted in cheers and jeers. The stockier fighter was struck by a solid blow to the cheek. He fell, but quickly protected himself. As they grappled in the dirt, the pace of the fight slowed. The attacker had gained a position of control, locking his legs around the stockier fighter from behind his back. The stockier fighter underneath him continued to protect his head from the occasional striking. The judge, wearing a plain toga and a headband and carrying a painted rod, pivoted and shifted meticulously to get better angles on the fight. The man on top became frustrated at the stalemate and after pulling on his mouth, poked at the stockier fighter's eyes. The judge took his rod and struck the attacker repeatedly, warning him to stop the eye gouging. The grappling went on. The man underneath was in desperate need to free himself, knowing there was no time limit and he would eventually run out of strength to defend himself. He made a wild attempt to escape, but his movement was turned into a choke hold by his attacker. I held my breath sympathetically as the stockier man's neck was being squeezed, his face changing color. Before he passed out, he held up a hand and extended his one index finger, indicating that he had accepted defeat. The victor released the man, who immediately rolled over on the ground, coughing and heaving. He stood proudly and pounded his chest.

Cato and his friend Tadius shouted in pleasure from their seats. They shared some words between them and then exchanged some coins. Simon Peter was rubbing his eyes, perhaps saying another prayer. Cletus and Dennis had turned away, so they had not witnessed the end of the fight.

The next match was equally brutal, resulting in a knockout from a knee to the head. The defeated fighter fell face first to the ground, limp and lifeless. The crowd was ecstatic. Simon Peter had a look of complete terror on his face. There was a short intermission while they dragged off the unconscious body and cleaned up some of the blood.

Cato and Tadius walked up to our seats to boast of the next match. "This is our man, Prosopo! Break his neck! Knock him out!" Tadius shouted as he slapped Dennis on his large belly and laughed heartily. Dennis winced in pain, but said nothing.

"Oh, this should be easy!" Cato said.

They saw the opponent come out from behind his trainers, stripped down to a loincloth. He was very tall, lean, clean shaven, and did not have body hair. He looked relaxed, hair messy and matted, as if he had just woken up. He calmly shook his body to loosen up for the fight.

Prosopo flexed his muscles to the crowd. Then he bared his teeth at his opponent, growling like a rabid dog. He slapped himself several times, staring down the lean adversary and making more grunts and animal noises. Tadius channeled this energy with another slap across the Dennis's abdomen. Jason gave Tadius a look of disapproval.

The other fighter had a relaxed, disarming sort of serenity that was unfathomable under the circumstances. He looked at Prosopo with indifference.

"That man is doomed. I'll donate some of my winnings to his family for a proper funeral," Cato joked, getting a rise out of his friend.

When the fight started Prosopo wasted no time, charging like a bull at the lean fighter. He deftly moved aside at the last moment, tripping Prosopo so that his momentum slammed him into the dirt. Instead of taking the fight to the ground, the lean fighter stepped back, shuffling lightly, waiting for Prosopo to regain his feet. When Prosopo stood and was on the attack again, wheeling punches left and right, the lean fighter continued to nimbly dodge all the blows. So far, the lean fighter's strategy was almost entirely defense. His height and arm length were an advantage. Prosopo hadn't landed any blows and was starting to breath heavily. The lean fighter still appeared relaxed and calm.

This went on for four or five more furious rounds of attacks and Prosopo was breathing even more heavily. Now the lean fighter would snake in a quick counter attack. Prosopo put his hands to his side and bared his teeth. Then he increased the intensity of his assault. On his last swing he followed through wildly and the lean opponent made Prosopo pay, jabbing him quickly and powerfully in the eye, causing him to stumble away.

Prosopo kept his distance, trying to catch his breath. The opponent shuffled around again nimbly, looking no worse for the wear. Cato and his friend were silent and baffled. Simon Peter had covered his eyes. Cletus and Dennis appeared to be talking strategy with Jason, animating fight moves in the air. They were enthralled with the match.

Prosopo suddenly closed the distance with his opponent and locked up in a traditional face-to-face grappling lock. This went on evenly for a few moments until Prosopo pinned his opponent's long arms under his own thick, muscular arms. The lean fighter tried to release his arms unsuccessfully, his face showing increased concentration but not an inkling of panic. Then in one graceful move he shifted his body and threw Prosopo completely over himself. Prosopo slammed on the hard ground, landing on his back, and hitting with a loud thud. Prosopo shouted out in pain, the lean fighter pinning his arm painfully above his head. Hopelessly, Prosopo held his free hand up, pointing out one shaky index finger. The fight was lost.

For a moment, Cato was nonplussed. Incredulous. The lean victor stood smiling and then raised one fist in the air.

My Christian companions cheered along with the rest of the spectators. This match was a real crowd pleaser; a mob is always hungry for a surprising upset. But Tadius was incensed. He mumbled curses and paced back and forth in the stadium row.

I thought that Prosopo represented everything that seemed to look right on the surface. He was the obvious bet, the sure thing. He was the easy choice. But the tall lean fighter believed. He believed in himself. What else did he believe in? Faith? In a god? I did not know. But he had faith in himself. A belief in something had prevailed.

The Christians and I had our fill of combat sports for the day. We had also had enough of Cato and Tadius, and Tadius's friend Prosopo. I reminded Jason that we were to meet Daphne and her sister at the theater for the rhetoric contests. The Christians, except for Simon Peter, were looking forward to the theater events. Simon Peter, with all his virtues, was just not Panhellenic games material.

THE ATMOSPHERE AT THE stadium during the pankration events was thick with masculine intensity, the rows filled with men fired up for combat. The scenes played out by the athletes channeled that warrior instinct men have flowing in their blood. The competitive survival that is paramount for all living creatures. The ambiance at the theater was drastically different. The masculine heaviness of battle was replaced by a communal lightness of creativity and expression. Families with women, children and elderly walked by, chatting energetically with an amicable social buzz. The scowl of a pankratiast was replaced by the sparkling smile of a rehearsing dancer. Perhaps art was the only distinction between humans and animals. Yet the events at the stadium and the theater shared some common human experience that was both engaging and vulnerable.

A large crowd of Daphne's people, her family and friends, were visiting on the street outside of the stage left exit. I recognized the charming middle-aged couple from the villa party. I introduced my Christian brothers to her people, and then to Daphne.

"Are you nervous?" I asked Daphne. I seemed more nervous for her than she was, or maybe I was having a hard time connecting with her. She did not answer my question. Perhaps she was just too preoccupied, or just didn't hear me in all the bustle, or she was running her routine through her mind. I did not always appreciate all the energy she put into her performances. Selfishly, I was far more concerned about the energy she would put towards us. I wanted my friends to see that she was mine, obsessed with the idea of us together. This was also the first public performance that I had attended where she was performing. I ineptly tried to show her off and cling to her, but I could tell that it was causing us distress. Uncomfortable with the disconnected feeling between us, I turned my attention back to Jason and the Christians.

"It doesn't look like Nero is going to make it this year. It would have been a lot more crowded if he did. Anyway, at least now we don't already know who's going to win," I said to the Christians. Before anyone could answer, Cato and Tadius walked past us. Thankfully, they didn't acknowledge us. Dennis looked down at the ground uncomfortably while Jason wrinkled his brow.

We decided to go into the theater and found good seats in the front and center. We watched the first set of performances, which included tragedies and comedies, singing, dancing, and singing with dancing. As the night went on, Jason and I began consuming wine. We amused ourselves and our company with our antics, paying less attention to the performers as the night went on.

The musical ensemble prepared to play in the circular orchestra pit. I could see Daphne on stage right, ready to begin her performance. The civil applause and light chatter rose and fell as she posed to begin her act. "She's next! Everyone shut up and be quiet," I warned my companions, although I was probably the only one of us talking.

As the music began, Daphne danced across the stage, lifting her arms in the air and tilting her head back as she lifted her bare legs up in the air or behind her. She was wearing a rich colored silk gown, very thin and light, had make-up on her face, and anklets and bracelets that flashed as she moved. Gracefully, in the rhythm of the dance, she sat down and reclined on her side and lifted a bare knee. She rolled her head backward and forward. Then she lifted one arm back until she was lying almost entirely down on the stage, covering her face with her other arm. As the music swelled, she stood up and spun around and then pranced energetically around the stage, her fine silk gown gently flowing in the air.

"This is from the bacchanalia. She is performing a bacchanal dance, from the cult of Bacchus, the god of wine," Cletus pointed out academically.

"Are you quite sure?" Dennis asked. "She appears to be performing a Dionysian dance from the mystery cult of Dionysus."

"Not much of a mystery here," a man in front of us quipped. Daphne's dancing became more provocative and suggestive, her thin gown revealing her shape. The men in the crowd responded in approval.

"You can tell by her gestures that this is a Dionysian mystery. Observe as she is acting out the parts with her hands to the beat of the cymbals. Those hand gestures and sounds are symbolic, pardon the pun," Dennis explained. Daphne now used cymbals in her hands to play along with the music as she danced.

"But aren't the bacchanal dances of Rome based on the Dionysian mysteries?" Cletus asked.

"Yes, I see, good point," Dennis replied.

Jason elbowed me in the ribs and raised his wine in silent approval. I was proud of Daphne's grace and beauty, as well as her talent and fearlessness. Yet I was also embarrassed by her bawdy flaunting of her body in front of a massive audience.

"I am very impressed. Do you all like it?" I asked.

There were mixed reviews from my friends and those surrounding us. Simon Peter was the least impressed.

A stranger behind me mumbled, "Art that strives to please everyone can never truly please anyone."

"My Christian brothers, you are speaking of the outlawed pagan rituals of Bacchus that are commonly performed in a drunken stupor. This is not much different than Gregorious and his rituals we just banned from our church. Not to mention the suggestive nature of the dance." Simon Peter was working up his passion.

"Rocky, we understand, and we will not partake. We believe that understanding these pagan practices best equips us to engage with our hosts and bring them to the Lord," Jason said with calm diplomacy. "Also, this is Daphne, a dear friend of our brother Lucius. We all know he has followed a typical pagan lifestyle since childhood."

"Rocky, did you know that Daphne is from a long line of Phoenicians from Carthage? That dance could have been of a Phoenician persuasion, too." I tried to console Simon Peter, to no avail. And calling him Rocky only added to his irritation with us.

Simon Peter did not respond verbally. Instead, he shook his head at both Jason and me, then he covered his face to pray. Did my lack of devotion in that moment to Christianity hurt Simon Peter? It appeared to trouble him greatly. My loyalty was still with the church, but my heart was distracted. I didn't believe that Simon Peter condoned my heathen ways, and he was capable of forgiveness. He was taught to love his enemies. At least, I thought, I was much more faithful and loyal than any of his foes.

Applause set in as Daphne's act came to a finish, and another act had already started. We were no longer paying any attention to the stage. The Christians decided to go back to their tent, and Jason agreed to join me for the banquet being thrown by Daphne's family.

22

SECOND CORINTHIANS

Daphne's family banquet was arranged outside of the city near the tent grounds surrounded by massive bonfires. The higher-classes such as Daphne's family sponsored private banquet areas with tents, servants, and fancy couches so that the guests could recline in luxury. These parties were often ostentatious displays of social status, offering the best food, drinks, and entertainment. And, of course, social networking. Although this was a private family party, all from the public, except the unsavory plebeians, were welcome to join and mingle. At least a dozen similar bonfire banquets were placed in close walking distance so that they could be visited over the course of an evening.

When Jason and I arrived, it was already pitch dark outside beyond the large blazes. The main course of dinner had already been served. People were indulging in wine, fine deserts, and other libations. At least a hundred people were in attendance, including Cato and many of his friends. We were served wine from the cauldron and walked over to Daphne, who was standing in a circle of guests.

"You looked sublime on the stage tonight. My lady, you should have won the wreath," a tall distinguished man flattered Daphne. I estimated he was around thirty years old and he was dressed like Roman nobility.

"Oh, thank you, that is so sweet. The judges said that I was the third best performance in my category," Daphne responded.

"The judges must have been blind," he said. This provoked a smile on Daphne's face and her dark eyes lit up. She had changed into a heavier and more colorful gown. Although she had not won the official pine wreath, she had decorated her hair with a wreath of pink and white flowers for the party night.

"I'm Lucius Octavius Aurelius of Rome." I tried pushing into the conversation.

"Hello," the Roman man said in a monotone, not willing to return the favor and introduce himself. Daphne did not speak a word to me. Jason was disengaged, looking around at the rest of the party.

"Is he with you?" the Roman asked, dismissively.

"Yes, he's an old friend from Rome," Daphne answered. That's what I am? An old friend from Rome?

He gallantly reached for Daphne and took her hand.

Another man came up and introduced himself to Daphne, then began showering her with compliments on her stellar performance. Daphne was very popular at the party. I was overwhelmed, outmatched, and ill-equipped to compete with the aggressive onslaught of these alpha males. I retreated with Jason across the party. I drank more wine to settle my nerves, hoping it would relieve my anxiety, or at least bring on some calming apathy.

"Take it easy, Lucius, my friend." Jason grabbed my arm as I stumbled a bit. "What is wrong?"

"She's ignoring me. See all those men giving her attention? What can I do? How do I compete?"

"Lucius, relax. Daphne loves you, man," Jason reassured me. "She's a real diva and she put on a great performance tonight. Let her have her night in the spotlight to get showered with attention. Don't worry so much. You get jealous too easily. Women appreciate a man who is confident and comfortable with himself."

As I have already mentioned, Jason was more experienced and skillful with women. Even at that time, I suspected he was at least partly right. But in my impetuous youth, I could not control my heightened emotions. I was jealous and ill-equipped to compete for her attention. I was also still self-conscious and insecure to a fault. Jason noticed my pained expression and patted me on the back. We filled our cups again from the deep cauldron.

Jason and I left Daphne's banquet and went on to several other bonfire gatherings. I mostly watched Jason charm the people, try his luck out on the women casually, and even occasionally discuss Christianity. We returned to Daphne's party after several hours of wandering the bonfire scene. Acrobats and dancers juggled, flipped, and frolicked around the flames in their ludicrously colorful garments. They entertained the remaining smaller, but much more raucous crowd. Daphne was speaking to a couple male admirers when I approached.

"Hi Daphne, let's go away together. It's late," I said to her, tugging at her a hand.

"Lucius, I'm not leaving with you now. You're drunk. You should go and get some sleep. Cato will escort me back," Daphne said, irritated.

"Daphne, you want me to get rid of this guy for you?" one of her admirers asked, pointing a disdainful thumb at me.

"No, he's a friend. I can take care of him," Daphne answered and then turned to me, "Please go."

Stepping sideways to give the admirers a piece of my mind, I lost my footing and stumbled. I fell backwards into the dirt, spilling my drink all over myself. I remember vividly to this day the humiliation of the men standing over me laughing. Daphne looked down at me with shame, and then she walked away. Jason, who was also intoxicated, but in a more docile fashion, helped me up.

We walked each other home, helping each other along the way. We stumbled shoulder to shoulder, engaged in a disjointed conversation.

"No, the girl with the other girl, with the light brown hair. I think she liked me," Jason said.

"What did I say to him? To that jerk with Daphne," I slurred.

"The chariot race is the most popular, like but most popular for to who? I guess that means . . . the horses are doing all the work anyway," Jason rambled on.

"She treats me like just a friend, and I'm the bad guy?" I bemoaned.

"Yes, the men are skilled on chariots, but the horses matter the most, from the breeding, and, um. At least the horses . . . they are loved by their owners. How expensive do you think are uh . . . are those horses?"

"Is Daphne . . . is she still with one of those older men?"

BY SHEER LUCK JASON and I made it safely back to his tent that night. It was almost noon when we woke up in daze. I thanked and apologized to Jason at the same time. I thought I had overcome all those depressed feelings of youth during my travels, but all those dark thoughts came back to me in a spell of emotional and physical sickness that day. I took several drinks of water, trying to wash out the horrible taste in my mouth.

Jason mentioned that the rest of the Christians had already left to return to Corinth while I had been sleeping. I told Jason that I was not going back to find Daphne. That I didn't even want to see her today. The most anticipated event, the chariot races, was to take place on this third and final day of competition. I told Jason I was done with the games and just wanted to go back to Corinth. Jason clearly wanted to see the chariot races, but being such a loyal companion Jason agreed to return with me to Corinth.

DAPHNE AND I GOT back together the following week to attempt to reconcile our differences. We were sitting in her father's orchard when we started talking about our tenuous relationship. I told her how sorry I was. I admitted that I had acted like a fool, but I was still upset with her for giving so much attention to other men. If we were together, I thought we should be faithful and loyal to each other.

"Lucius, you are too possessive of me. I think you are obsessive. You are obsessively possessive." Daphne called me out with conviction.

"I'm not possessive. If, if I am, it's because of the way you act. You try to get attention from other men. You relish their attention, even when you know it hurts me." I reluctantly admit that I was obsessive and infatuated, no different than her other male admirers. It was hard not to be obsessed with the likes of Daphne. I was trying to protect myself, trying to turn it back on her.

"I love you, Lucius. But we are both too young for this," Daphne sighed. "We both still want to enjoy the remaining freedom of our youth. You do not even know where you are heading next. Do you really see us being together forever? Do you even know what I want? Do you know what I want to be? You plan things out in your head, but we never even talk about things."

"We could stay together. We could go back to Rome and I could start my business there. My father has many connections," I said earnestly.

"This is about us. What we have together, and what we don't have. I don't believe you are being honest with yourself right now, Lucy," Daphne said.

"Why are you . . . why are you making this so hard on us? Do you not feel what I feel?" I asked.

"I feel for you, Lucius. I love you dearly, but I am not sure that I am in love with you," she confessed with strain in her dark eyes.

I was devastated by her proclamation. I struggled to process everything she had said, and I had nothing to say in return. Overwhelmed, I wished this moment away. I wanted to escape from this situation that seemed to freeze time.

"I have to tell you something else," she said. "My father wants to arrange a marriage for me with a Roman citizen from Corinth. Initially, my father thought that you would make an eligible suitor because of your family. But then he recently changed his mind. Even though you are from a distinguished Roman family, my father no longer sees you as a proper husband for me."

"Wait! What? I come from a wealthy and noble Roman family. I have shown my loyalty to you and have properly courted you in front of your father." I turned redolent with indignation.

"He no longer believes you are serious about me, or about your future. He thinks that you are leading me on. So, if we accept that this was a passing fancy, he will not run you off. But, as soon as my engagement is announced, my father will confront you. Then we can no longer be seen together."

"This is . . ." Contempt overcame me and closed my throat.

"We still have a little time together," Daphne said. "I just wanted you to know that my father has plans for me. And, although I still want to be with you, Lucius, I need freedom to plan for my future. Unless you can prove to my father that you are worthy of my hand, this soon must come to an end."

We sat in the orchard silently for some time, thinking about our recent past and uncertain future. The cicadas screeched loudly in the trees. I looked down at all the figs on the ground, kicking them away. Many figs had ripened and fallen from the tree but had since become rotten over time. Daphne gave me a kiss on my head and then we parted ways.

We saw each other less frequently in Corinth and remained a couple after that. We still shared a strong personal connection, but our uncertain future because of Daphne's upcoming arranged marriage had created an undercurrent of instability. We experienced the challenges that are faced when two lovers were not fully committed, vacillating between affection, co-dependency, self-protection, and duplicity.

RETURNING HOME AFTER WORK one day, much to my surprise, I discovered a letter from Tiridata:

> Hello Lucius you shy Roman boy what you doing in Corinth you handsome devil I hear you are with your Christian evangelists like Simon Peter I know from him preaching in Antioch are you spreading the good news of Jesus do you no longer party like we do in Antioch you should come back to Daphne every night is a party here and we find a new villa party and stay up until sunrise and meet beautiful women because the Greeks in Daphne know me and know how to have fun and no I do not have a girlfriend but we see so many beauties and some are more easy than the ladies in Daphne but anyway Mary of Magdala was here and she is classy lady and beautiful for a mother but does not like us to really have fun she says I am not good for the church because I do not follow the word and I am bad influence but my father is patron of the church he is really Zoroastrian not just a Christian. You remember who is Zoroaster the prophet from my homeland empire? Yes I am still in Antioch and some of my brothers come to live here and join me in business but they are Zoroastrian and not Christians but sometimes we go to the cave church with Theo of Cyrene to discuss the teachings of Christ did you hear about Mary his holy mother not the other Mary

that is sad I am sorry but oh well she was very old lady we hope she is in heaven with Jesus you know she is like mother to many of Christians here and Theo is sad so it was hard on lot of people but anyway write back and tell me about Corinth and what your plans are you better come visit again and I show you a good party you Roman emperor.

Tiridata hadn't changed at all. I had to catch my breath after reading that letter. What was this sad news about Mary written in past tense? In heaven? Did he mean that Mary, the mother of Jesus, was dead? I already felt a wave of guilt passing over me. And a sympathetic pity for poor James. I needed to ask someone more reliable to confirm if that news was accurate.

I walked over to Jason's house and asked him directly. "Jason, did you hear any news about Mary, the mother of Jesus?"

"Yes, how do you know?" Jason asked. "She passed away last month, and now resides in heaven with Christ."

"What in the hell!?" I shouted. "You knew, and you weren't going to tell me? You know how close I was to her, and to James."

"I thought you were dealing with enough personal problems. We thought we'd wait to tell you." Jason looked surprised by my reaction.

"What problems? Do you mean my relationship with Daphne?" I was steaming mad and gritting my teeth.

"Lucius, calm down," Jason tried to console me, but I walked off before he could say another word. I felt so alone and so helpless. I did not want to share my sorrow with anyone else at that moment.

It was inevitable that my relationship with Daphne would come to a destructive final ending. That last afternoon came at Cato's estate, and it did not start out peculiar in any way. Daphne and I were spending time with Cornelia and Cato, as we did commonly. I cannot recall the chronology of events, what was said between Daphne and me, or how the agreement started. Perhaps I have mercifully been struck with amnesia so that I don't have to relive every detail of that incident.

What I do remember is that Daphne said she would be strong, that she would be fine without me, and that I had lost my dignity. A lot of shouting and ultimatums then began. My temper flared. I said some regrettable words in a fury without any self-control. Cornelia and Cato watched the entire argument and break up. Cato then forced me to leave, escorting me off the property. More than contempt, I saw pity in his eyes.

23

VINDOBONA

Once again, I embarked on a new journey, for central Europe this time to the new Roman settlement of Vindobona. This time I travelled by land rather than by sea. My reader may be left with any number of questions. Why was I traveling to Vindobona? If my story is ever studied as literature, I must leave certain aspects open for interpretation. Nevertheless, I will divulge some background. Cato witnessed my devastation and humiliation after my break up with Daphne and felt bad for me. After our breakup, I made a few desperate visits to his estate to ask about Daphne. Since Daphne would not speak to me, I told Cato I was leaving for good. As a favor, he used his influence to find me employment elsewhere. He showed me a map of his Domus Maximus projects across Greece and other provinces of the empire. I inquired about a distant region north of the Alps, in the Pannonia province. He described a land of barbarians on the edge of the empire that was only recently conquered. He was starting new projects in a settlement on the banks of the Danube River called Vindo-bona. He said it was only a military camp, not yet a city, but with enormous potential for growth. Impulsively, I made the decision to go there.

I made the trek with a caravan of mercenaries and other tradesmen traveling through the regions of Macedonia, Moesia, Pannonia, and finally following the Danube River to Vindobona. We stopped in Greek cities such as Athens and Thessalonica, then in new Roman settlements including Viminacium, Aquincum, and Carnuntum. We faced untamed wilderness, dangerous mountain passes, and hostile territory. It was a powerful journey that provided me solace during my sadness.

Although Roman roads made it possible to make this journey safely, most days were still tiresome and miserable. We hiked through the treacherous mountains, which were considered more dangerous than beautiful in those times. As we made it through one daunting pass, I pondered the rugged challenges of my past. Traveling through the alpine plains, I would find a stationary focal point in the distance and feel a sense of timelessness. Walking through narrow forest paths covered in trees, looking down at tree roots and ducking under tree branches, I would get lost in the moment. The forest canopy was a blinder from the outside world. When we arrived at the Danube, I felt the coolness of its water and a connection with nature. As I followed the rapid current walking along the bank, I reflected on how life will inevitably take its course.

We arrived in Vindobona in the late fall of 59 A.D. The original Roman military camp was just a primitive wooden fortress, quickly assembled from the local timber. Construction projects were transforming the temporary military camp into more permanent and formidable structures.

That was where we came in. As a foreman, I supervised a crew of men in Cato's outfit. The men did most of the skilled construction labor, and dozens of slaves did the back-breaking grunt work. Of course, Cato had arranged all of this for me, but to my credit, I took on significant personal responsibility, whereas other men just showed up to earn a living. I was able to use hard work to keep my mind occupied and escape my troubles.

Although I had become more solitary on my journey, I had made a few new friends. Particularly, with a local farmer and tradesman named Titus. Titus was born from the union of a local Celtic tribeswoman and a Roman soldier. I would frequently find him in the camp market trading his wares. My coworker, Salvius, and I, as confirmed bachelors, would spend evenings with Titus at the taverns or other social gatherings.

One night we arranged to visit Titus at his home for games and drinks. Titus took Salvius and me on his wooden chariot, wildly racing through the woods. We flew recklessly down the dirt roads and over small bridges, the cold snow blowing sideways and whitewashing the forest. Although the snow was beautiful and soft on my first impression, the blizzard strewn flakes burned my exposed skin with increasing pain as Titus drove onwards. The ride went on for almost an hour until we arrived at a stable in a clearing. From there, we jumped on horses and galloped through fields, becoming completely lost the few times the snow swallowed Titus who was leading the way. Salvius and I shouted for him to slow down. After several more miles on horseback we arrived in a meadow near a farm. We slowly approached several circular houses with thatched roofs covered in snow.

It was surprisingly warm and comfortable inside the main round Celtic house. Inside the house was one large open room with one thick pole in the middle. We sat at a low table and played games while drinking. Titus served us generously with delicious local beer.

I regarded Titus as he sat on the bench that circled the wall. He was lounging as he waited his turn, his legs spread out casually. He was very tall, had thick trunk legs, sloped shoulders, light blue eyes, dirty blonde hair, and a thick yellow beard.

"So, your father is a Roman soldier? And your mother is a native?" I asked, curiously.

"Yes, this is my mother's farm. My mother's family has lived in these forests for ages. She is from a long line of chieftains of this clan. Unlike your Roman culture, women are allowed more prominent leadership roles in our tribes. My mother is a distinguished leader in the clan. As Socrates observed, 'Once made equal to man, woman becomes his superior.'"

Was Titus a philosopher, or a barbarian, or both? Titus leaned back, his long beard resting on his chest. He could not have been sculpted as a better barbarian.

"And your father?" I asked, not completely satisfied.

"He was a Roman centurion. He was fighting for this territory when they met. He died in battle many years ago."

"Lucius is from Rome, you know. His father is a Roman nobleman, who is well known about the Forum," Salvius said.

"So, I've heard," Titus answered.

"Well, how did your parents meet?" I asked.

"I don't know the exact details," Titus said. "My mother was very beautiful, just like most of the local women. Tall and pale-skinned, with long hair that she wore in braids. She was a young maiden, beautiful, strong-willed, and from a noble line of chieftains. It must have been a wildly exotic attraction for my father, as our women are not only more beautiful than Roman women, but have strong personalities. She had male relatives who fought against the Romans. She has told me many stories of distant relatives who waged war against Julius Caesar in the Gallic wars."

"That must be strange having parents from enemy camps," I said.

"Yes, sleeping with the enemy!" Salvius chimed in, laughing clumsily to himself.

"I am extremely proud of both my parents," Titus said. "Our tribe has tried to maintain our way of life. Being raised by my mother, I identify more with the local ways of living. But, having many connections through my father, I am literate, and well educated in Roman and Greek history and culture. Although my father was often absent, he did pay for proper Roman tutors."

"It must be hard living with these barbarians when you have been exposed to Roman civilization," Salvius said, his wide head shaking awkwardly. He had enjoyed much of the good local beer.

"The atrocities that the Romans have inflicted on my people have been the most barbaric," Titus said without much emotion.

"By Romans like your father?" I asked almost reflexively.

"I think we are misunderstood. Don't confuse power with sophistication," Titus tried to explain. "Our culture of chieftains and druids are far more ancient and sophisticated than the Roman empire. However, we are not one empire like the Romans. Instead, we are many separate clans or tribes. Therefore, we are not empire builders. Our civilization, forced to unite for survival, has held back the Romans like none other. Would you say Egyptians are the most ancient and sophisticate civilization? Yet see how easily they fell to the Romans."

"But modern Egypt is no longer that same ancient civilization. They were as much annexed as conquered. Cleopatra was not from the same ilk as the ancient Egyptians. Cleopatra was from the ancient Greek line of Ptolemy," I countered Titus.

"That is a good point, although the Battle of Actium was a decisive Roman victory. Regardless, you see my point that the comparison of cultures is favorable to the Celts," Titus said.

I gestured, making a small concession with body language. Salvius had lost interest.

"Lucius, you should come hunting with us!" Titus changed the subject.

"Yes, Titus and I have hunted these forests many times," Salvius said, jumping back into the conversation by grasping onto a topic of which he could contribute. I'll give Titus the benefit of the doubt that he had switched topics in an attempt to be more inclusive of Salvius.

"That sounds like a great plan. What do you hunt?" I asked.

"Deer. Wild boar. Anything!" Titus laughed heartily and stood. "More beer?" He served copious pours of the dark brew before we could answer. It was truly delicious. As a Roman I was more of a wine drinker, but I was quickly acquiring a taste for Celtic beer.

We stayed late into the night, walking outside to encircle a huge bonfire long after the moon had set, joining many tribesmen already gathered there. Titus shared laugher, joking with his clan. I could not follow the local language, but I gathered that he spoke more freely with them.

IT WAS LATER THAT week when I was handed a letter delivered by courier mail to the military camp. It had been sent to Corinth first, and then forwarded from Corinth to Vindobona. It was a letter from James, who was still in Jerusalem.

> Lucius, my noble Roman friend, a veritable Caesar, a world traveler, and future Christian disciple, I hope this letter finds you well. I have recently received a warm letter of condolence from our steadfast deacon Jason and it reminded me of you. As you know, my beloved mother Mary has passed. She is now with our Heavenly Father and Jesus Christ in paradise. Although I know she is in a better place, I must admit I mourned for several weeks, weeping alone, not able to leave my room.

> I am otherwise thriving in Jerusalem, the Holy City, the center of our Godly world. I still serve deacon of the church here, leading the Christians, spreading the good news in regards to the life of Jesus Christ, his teachings and so forth, and the coming of the kingdom. The council of Jerusalem was held again

recently so I was blessed to see many familiar faces such as Mary of Magdala, Theo of Cyrene, and Philip the Evangelist.

Lucius, there is still hostility and unrest between the Christians and the Jews of Jerusalem. I fear that we do not always see each other eye to eye. I must admit, in my heart of hearts, that I am not always fond of those avaricious Jewish hypocrites. Every time I walk by the Temple, I see all the money changing hands outside. As the disciples witnessed, Jesus cleansed the Temple of the moneychangers, since it had degraded into a den of thieves. Lamentably, I still see bustling commerce just outside the Temple. The moneychangers take advantage by gouging all of those ignorant peasants on pilgrimage.

On that subject, I would be remiss if I did not share a pleasing pilgrimage story. I encountered Yohanan the carpenter from Nazareth, that cantankerous old geezer. He brought his entire family on a pilgrimage to the Temple with a sacrificial lamb. Much to my surprise, I really enjoyed our visit. That son of his is still a dolt, but his young daughter has grown up to be quite a beauty. It is no wonder why he was so protective.

Our beloved Paul has appealed to Caesar for justice. They will hear his appeal in Rome and so he is being transferred there for trial. He will probably be on route by the time you read this letter. Mary of Magdala has once again graced us with her presence and her patronage in regards to the church of Jerusalem as well as in Antioch. In addition to her patronage, Mary also served an indispensable role in my recovery from those dark times following mother's passing.

Since getting back together with my dear wife Rebekah, my family life has become everything that I had always hoped for. Lucius, it is imperative that I am a role model to my fellow Christians as it pertains to my family life and how I conduct myself with women and children. Rebekah and I would love to be blessed with children to cherish and provide for, but my sweet wife continues to be as barren as the Sinai desert.

Simon Magus, that wicked, sinful, idolatrous heathen, returned to Samaria where he is undoubtedly revered by the ignorant masses. Unfortunately, a few of the local Christians admire him. Many believe he is a son of God, or even the Holy Ghost. Philip had to run him off once again from beguiling them. Philip told me tales that would make your hair curl and skin crawl. Simon Magus performed dark sorcery before a considerable crowd of Christians, walking across hot coals, and levitating above the flames, chanting unspeakable incantations. His magical powers have increased to a new level of evil, as he now harnesses the powers of shape-shifting. In the city of Sebaste, he transformed himself into a black cat, a despicable creature with glowing demonic eyes. Simon Magus ran wildly through the streets in this form of a gnarly black feline, foaming at the mouth, attacking men fearlessly. One of his victims became possessed by demons, and days later was running the streets, shouting in tongues, foaming at the mouth, and attacking people. He eventually died in the gutter in spasms of pure evil. I pray to God the Father that we never have to witness such a foul metamorphosis.

I have heard news that you settled down in Corinth and have found happiness in a domestic life, exhausted your wanderlust, and no longer chase the dreams of your youth. Lucius, my dear boy, I imagine you are growing up to be a distinguished man. Please write back to me and pray for me as I will likewise be praying for you.

As I finished this note from James, another letter dropped to the dusty ground. It must have been rolled inside the scroll. I scanned it and saw that it was from Jason.

Lucius, I have forwarded this letter from James to you. He appears to be doing quite well. However, we are alarmed by the news of Simon Magus who continues to wreak havoc on our Christian communities. His sorcery has become famous across the Roman Empire. We have been informed that Simon Magus plans to travel to Rome to try to impress Nero with his magical powers. The inside news is that Nero is going through a fit of madness after his mother's death, and he is now more prone to the influence of magicians and soothsayers. We have also been told that Paul was sent to Rome and will be held there under house arrest.

Simon Peter is furious with this news and is beside himself with frustration. He realizes that the followers of Simon Magus view the pagan magician not just as a Christian, but as a true apostle. Simon Magus is competing with Paul and Simon Peter for leadership of the church. Simon Peter said to read the letters from James and the other deacons closely and see that Simon Magus's followers are numerous and growing, especially in Samaria. Simon Magus is not just seen as a magician there, but a true god with great powers.

We may need your assistance in Rome, as a resident citizen in high social standing, if the situation continues to escalate. I hope that this news meets you well and that you work out your problems. I've heard news about your separation with Daphne. You and Daphne were never meant to be, so it's a good thing that it has ended. Just give it some more time and you will feel better.

Holy shit! That was a heavy load of news. Jason was right. I knew Daphne and I were not meant to be. I knew it all along, but that didn't take away the pain. More importantly, I understood that the growing threat of Simon Magus was severe and sinister. I still considered the Christians as my brothers and sisters. I was conflicted between the fleeting liberation of my personal life and my sense of obligation to my fellow Christians. I had just gotten settled in Vindobona, so I wasn't ready to pull up roots and leave. I decided to write James and let him know how I was doing.

James, my good friend, I do miss you tremendously. It is with a heavy heart that I received the news of the passing of your mother. Mary was like a mother to all of us. You know how close I felt to her and how many good Christians will miss her. Truly she is in a better place.

I must be honest with you and inform you that I am no longer with Daphne. I now accept what I had known for some time that we were not meant to be together. I am still a young man and now enjoy my freedom. There is so much more to discover in this world before I ever settle down. I'm so happy to hear that you are together with your wife and serve as a leader in the church and the Christian community.

I am now in Vindobona, on the very edge of the Roman Empire. I am fascinated by this strange new land that surrounds me. Every day I walk through beautiful alpine forests, lush valleys, filled with clear running streams and moss-covered rocks. In the morning the sun shines on the white snow and this bright foreign world glistens all around me. This is a true adventure.

You would be proud of me as I am now supervising a crew building up this grand new city of Vindobona. Someday it will be one of grandest cities in the empire. I plan to stay here and finish my project. After that I am not sure where I will go or what I will do. Simon Peter and Jason have asked me to return to Rome to help in their cause against Simon Magus. I must confess I'm not entirely committed as a Christian, as I have never even been baptized, and I hold doubt in my heart, but I do want to help Simon Peter. I'm eternally grateful for your mentorship and would not be where I am without you.

I walked from my room to the barracks to drop the letter off with the Roman couriers. The camp smelled like men without women, of the complicit agreement of lack in hygiene and living in primitive conditions. Outside it was another cold and rainy day, so foggy it was hard to see the other people walking on the street. I trudged through the wet sloppy streets, splashing in mud puddles, my feet cold, wet, and wrinkled. As the wind howled, I shook uncontrollably, unable to keep warm, having never felt this cold in my life. A Roman soldier poured out a pot of human waste into the ditch. I jumped aside to avoid the splatter and gagged at the odor, overcome with disgust at the lack of drainage and sanitation in this awful, distant place.

24

CELTS

Vindobona was populated with around five thousand Roman soldiers and ten thousand civilians, which were an unusual mix of Romans, foreign tradesmen, and local Celts. The Roman soldiers spent most of their time in leisure rather than in battle. So, in the settlement there were a plethora of brothels, baths, and taverns. My coworkers, friends, and I would frequent the taverns where we would resort to drinking and gambling late into the night, and occasionally we would get into brawls. It reminded me of the good old days in Rome with Rufus and the gang. So much for personal progress. One evening Salvius, Titus, and I were playing dice at a tavern that we often frequented. We were accompanied by several soldiers and coworkers.

"Why don't you have your mamma come play with us, Titus?" a soldier asked.

"Is she the fiery red one? The one with the freckles?" A co-worker asked, and he elbowed me. With all these construction workers and soldiers, the onslaught of crude comments and profanity was almost insufferable. I suspected they turned up the volume just for me. They treated me like an elite, over-educated rich boy. As if I hadn't heard innuendo or dirty jokes before.

"Sorry, I don't want to offend the mamma's boy. I'm sure you love yer mamma and miss her at night," the soldier said.

"He loves his mother alright. Does he love his mother like Nero loves his mamma?" the coworker asked.

"Do you, boy? Love yer mamma like Nero loves his mamma?" the soldier asked.

"I love my mother. I don't even know what you are trying to imply with Nero." I gave my humorless answer. I didn't follow the Nero reference.

"The news from Rome is that Nero was having an . . . unnaturally loving relationship with his mother Agrippina," Titus explained to me in an even and cautious tone.

"I seriously doubt that," I answered. That sounded like a far-fetched rumor. One that would be propagated only by ignorant morons like these men in the tavern.

"Hey jackass, you haven't heard the latest news then?" the soldier asked.

"No, please share, my lady," the coworker coaxed.

"Nero has been trying to murder his mamma. He tried drowning her in a boating accident. He designed a self-destructing boat, but she swims too good. Well, and that was before she tried havin' him kilt off first," the soldier went on.

"How do you design a self-destructing boat?" I asked.

"Hades, I don't know! But it's only important that they know." the soldier said.

"Then what happened? Why are they trying to kill each other?" I asked, genuinely interested this time.

"Over a woman, a classy broad named Poppaea. Nero was all smitten in love with her," the soldier said.

"I still don't understand. Why did Nero try to kill his mother then? Jealousy?" I asked again.

"Nero needed her out of the way, so he could divorce Octavian and then marry Poppaea," Titus explained patiently.

"She's one powerful bitch, his mamma. Well, she killed Claudius, didn't she? And that other husband too," the soldier exclaimed.

"So, Agrippina survived? Are they still fighting?" I asked.

"Oh, Hades no! It's all finished. They were feuding and ah feuding for a long while, but finally, Nero sent assassins and they stabbed her to death," the soldier said.

"Actually, I believe that is accurate news," Titus agreed. "After her funeral Nero was openly congratulated by the senators and generals. They accepted that his mother had plotted to kill him, and that he had retaliated appropriately."

"I heard that she has been haunting him. Nero wakes up at night, scared his mother's ghost is coming to get him," Salvius shared spookily.

"Come on, roll the dice! Shall we play another, ladies?" the coworker asked.

"I am calling it a night," Titus said.

"I'll accompany you if you don't mind," I said to Titus. It was very late, and Titus offered more protection than walking home alone.

"Good night, ladies," the coworker called as we walked out of the tavern and into the night.

During the long walk, we further discussed our early upbringings, of which we were mutually curious. I had told him about Christianity, my evangelical story and travels, Mary, James, Jason, and Simon Peter. I asked him about his religious upbringing, as he mentioned he was raised by his Celtic mother.

"Lucius," Titus sighed, "you seem so preoccupied with the Christian personalities, these demigods. In our religion we have gods as old as time itself. We don't worship people. We worship nature and mother earth. Observe, it is self-evident, that there is nothing more powerful than nature. Does this Jesus dictate nature? Man is always humbled by nature and we all die, but the gods live on forever. Did Jesus not die by the hands of the Romans? You just said that, didn't you?" Titus asked.

"Yes, but he rose from the dead and ascended into heaven," I replied.

"Oh, did he," Titus responded with a sarcastic tone. "Unlike your newly invented Christianity, we have rituals that have survived since the beginning of man."

"I would love to see them. I am open for new experiences. I'll witness the power of your gods." I had a sarcastic tone now as well, but I was genuinely interested. I was much less defensive towards his doubts about Christianity than I would have been a year ago.

"Romans are not welcome," Titus snapped, turning towards me.

"Can you not sneak me in?" I asked. "If you do, I promise to return the favor. I can introduce you to Simon Peter, or the others who can perform healings or other miracles with the power of Christ."

"I'll think about it."

We walked on silently into the cold night.

THE FOLLOWING WEEK, I was awakened from a peaceful sleep in the middle of the night. Something shook me by the arms. I sat up startled, my heart beating heavily in my tired head. I saw Titus sitting next to me. He leaned close to my face, so that I could smell the sweet tang of good beer on his breath, and said in a slightly slurred whisper, "Get dressed. We go tonight to a ceremony like the days of times past . . . of past times."

"What are you talking about? How did you get in here?" I asked, still groggy with sleep. Titus had previously bothered me, on the occasion, after a late night of drinking, so I was not surprised at seeing him in that state.

"Come on, Lucius. You wanted to go to the ritual with us. Get ready fast. They are waiting outside for us."

That was how I found myself following the Celts into the forest, in the middle of the night. I was last in line directly behind Titus, and I had no idea where I was or where I was heading. I could smell the damp night air, the scent of the burning torches, and hear the crackling of branches and rustling of leaves. I could only see what was right in front of me in the flickering light of the torch held by Titus. Our hike led us deep into the primeval forest. I climbed over tree roots, mossy boulders, and felt my way over fallen logs.

We eventually made it to a clearing open to the star-filled sky. An ancient oak stood alone in the middle of the clearing. Its branches twisted from the ground and disappeared into the night sky. A procession of priests and priestesses clad in white hooded cloaks, adorned with clasps and belts of bronze, appeared from the edges of the clearing around us. They were primarily old men with long grey beards, but there were also woman with long braided hair coming down from their hoods as well. They circled around the oak, hands held up in the air, staring up into the starry night. They began swaying and chanting in unison in a foreign language.

The witnesses to this ritual, such as Titus and myself, remained standing at the edge of the clearing. After watching in silence for a while, I asked Titus, "Who are these clerics? And what are they saying?"

"They are druids. Druids are our dedicated teachers, healers, and magicians," he replied. "They are praying to the goddess of winter and darkness. The druids are also honoring the oak tree, the king of the forest, which holds the wisdom of the ages. The oak is being honored for his noble presence."

The druids swayed back and forth. Then they lit torches and passed them around their circle, speaking to each other ceremoniously as they passed on the new fire. They walked away from the oak, formed a line three across, and marched further into the clearing. The spectators then followed them while keeping a respectable distance. As I entered the clearing, I noticed large granite stones purposefully placed in the ground that indicated to me the permanence of this site. On the far side of the clearing the group circled around a giant cauldron. A platform stood next to the cauldron. One of the druids climbed up on the platform and spoke in a deep monotone, addressing the gods I supposed, his warm breath creating smoke in the cold night air.

From out of the woods and into the flickering torchlight came two warriors clad in armor, carrying oval shields, and wearing pointed helmets. Their mustachioed faces were painted white with dark figures starkly drawn on their cheeks and forehead. They wore golden torques around their necks just like Titus. They escorted a man between them who had his arms bound. The bound man was dressed in a cloak and wore a wreath on his head. He was ceremoniously led up to the platform. This did not bode well for him, I thought. His face looked calm and expressionless, but when he got on to the platform his chest began to heave as his breathing became heavy. My breathing sped up sympathetically with the prisoner until I became lightheaded.

"Druids have been banned from the Roman empire since the time of Julius Caesar. You must not repeat what you see and hear here tonight," Titus warned me firmly.

I was frozen with terror for what I thought was about to happen to the bound man. The druids began chanting, waving their torches upward, pacing around the cauldron. I could now see the wood piled underneath it and the platform. A bright full moon lit up the sky. The bound man knelt on the platform. One of the warriors handed a sword to a druid. The druid slit the bound man's throat. The man did not struggle. He choked and gurgled, bleeding profusely from the wound. Streams of blood poured into the cauldron beneath and he went pale. After he had bled out and collapsed, the warriors positioned him flat on his back, moving the cloak to expose the dead man's chest. Then they left the platform and nobly stood to watch from the ground. The druid sliced open the man's chest and abdomen, pulling out the man's organs and lifting them towards the stars and the moon, and raising his voice in prayer.

"Gods are like babies at the teat, hungry for nourishment," Titus explained. "We pour his warm blood into the cauldron of wisdom to appease the goddess of winter, before the cold darkness completely freezes the lands. Now the chief druid is performing an ancient practice of divination. During this examination, omens will be revealed to him." I was speechless, not able to form any questions, held captive by the sight before me.

The chief druid held up a string of entrails, the blood running down his hands and arms shining in the torchlight. The druids and worshipers all began to shout and sing. The hair on the back of my neck stood up.

"This is a good omen," Titus said and nodded, pleased with the outcome. I could not share his joy.

The druids threw their torches underneath the cauldron causing the dry wood to catch and a flash of fire to rise high up into the sky. I lost sight of the chief druid and the sacrificed man. I wondered if he was thrown into the cauldron.

"Lucius, next we walk to the great river to offer our swords to the gods. And then would you like to stay for the feast? There will be plenty of fresh meat to dine on. We brought jugs of beer as well." Titus was still elated from the news of good omens. "My mother was one of the druids in the ceremony. I want to introduce you to her."

I was suffering from the epitome of culture shock. I intended to have an open mind to this ancient religion and people. The Celts, brave and bold. Yet I could not do it. Perhaps, like the Greek and Roman gods, and the Carthaginians, the violence had turned me away.

"Lucius, my friend. You don't look so great."

I asked him to take me safely out of the forest and back home.

IN MODERN TIMES CELTS were commonly thought to have come from the British Isles, in particular Scotland and Ireland. We now believe that the Celts originate from central Europe. By the time of Christ, Celtic peoples had spread from Portugal and British Isles in the west and to the east as far as Russia. The territory of Gaul spanned modern France and central Europe and into Italia. The Galicians settled in what is now modern Spain and Portugal, and thrived in Asia Minor or modern Turkey. However, most of the Celtic culture in Europe was eradicated by the Roman Empire. Celtic traditions survived beyond the boundaries of the empire or on its wild frontier, in far flung places such as Scotland, Ireland, and Wales.

My 20th century reader, not much written history of the druids and their rituals survived from those ancient times. The Roman accounts of the Celts and the druids, such as those written by Julius Caesar and Tacitus, are exaggerated and defamatory. We do know that the druids were an honored class of men and women who served at least twenty years of training to become spiritual leaders. Many traditions of the Celts and practices of the druids were not entirely wiped out by the Romans, but were co-opted into Christendom. We have the jack-o-lanterns and spirits of Halloween borrowed from the Gaelic feast of Samhain. The mistletoe hung at Christmas was thought to be a magical plant by the Celts. Easter blended ancient pagan symbolism of springtime, such as bunnies and eggs, with new Christian beliefs.

In addition to my eyewitness account, significant archeological evidence supports that the Celts performed human sacrifices as part of their pagan rites of worship. If this sounds barbaric, I want to challenge my 20th century reader to consider the larger context. Animal sacrifice was a common sight in the temples of Rome. It was a common practice in Judaism as well, described *in the texts that became the Old Testament as a having a "pleasing aroma to God." Cain and Abel, the sons of Adam and Eve, brought animal sacrifices to the Lord. God himself asked Abraham to offer his own son Isaac as a human sacrifice. Jesus Christ, the Lamb of God, was to serve as the ultimate human sacrifice. Many Christians take communion every Sunday, and many believe they are literally eating the flesh and drinking the blood of Christ.*

25

NOSTALGIA

I spent some of the bleakest days of my life that cold winter in Vindobona. The snow came down and covered everything in a lifeless blanket of white. I would lie alone at night, trying to keep warm under heavy furs and blankets, wondering if Daphne's marriage had already taken place. I thought about my friends and family in Rome. I pined for the comfort of my Roman villa and the mild Mediterranean weather. I considered all my regrets and disappointments and what events had led me here. I worried about Jason, Simon Peter, Philip, James, and the other Christians facing the sorcerer Simon Magus. Not to mention, Nero. I had witnessed the power and charisma of Simon Magus, so I shared in their fearful concern.

AS I RECLINE IN these heavenly clouds now, recalling the next turn of events in my story, I realized what shook me out of my depression, what pulled me out of those dark days. At the time, I had become too introspective. Up to that point, I had always run away from my problems. But the best medicine for pain is alleviating the pain of others. Mortals ponder the meaning of life and why they must suffer and witness the suffering of the innocent. Man must survive affliction to achieve true comfort. The hedonist will focus solely on his own pleasure, but he will never realize true happiness. What saved me was trying my focus away from myself and on to other people's problems.

The word "nostalgia" is formed by combining the Greek words nostos and algos, meaning homecoming and pain, respectively. It's been two thousand years since I was among the living, so I have not felt pain or suffering for millennia. Yet, as I reflect on those challenging times, I am nostalgic for mortal suffering. That pain that I had witnessed daily on earth. I have only a distant memory of mortality. An old man can hold a baby in his arms but not bring back that experience of being a helpless infant. The experience of suffering, and the meaning of life for that matter, is not important for those in heaven. The mortal lifespan is infinitesimal, just a blip on the radar, compared to the afterlife. I have passed over two thousand years here, equivalent to twenty long lives, and I'm considered just a novice in heaven. Don't even get me started on those Neanderthals from cloud seven.

SO, I WAS READY to have a new purpose in life. I planned to go home to my family, my old friends, and rejoin my Christian friends all in one go. The Christians and I would join forces against the dark sorcery of Simon Magus. That black magic was not just a threat to my Christian brothers, but to Nero and to the entire Roman Empire. I wrote a letter to Jason to send word to the Christians that I was heading back to Rome, and how to find me there. Then I wrote a terse letter to my parents.

> Father and Mother, I am returning home to Rome. I have come around to at least some of your advice. Please arrange for uncle to find me a position in construction. I know this will never live up to your expectations but I have been supervising construction projects for some time now. I will make you proud. I need not ask about my friends and family since I will be joining you all soon. I miss you both and look forward to seeing you all. By the time you receive this message I will already be on my homeward journey.

I wanted to thank Titus for his friendship and all his favors and hospitality before I left for Rome. We met near a filthy trench on the edge of the camp. Titus smiled and congratulated me on my news.

"I will write you from Rome," I said. "Maybe you can come visit me and I can make good on my promise to introduce you to Simon Peter and the Christians."

Titus shook his head regrettably. "I would love to visit Rome and meet your magical friends, but I'm needed here with my mother and our clan."

"I understand, but I hope you change your mind. Anyway, send messages to me if you have a chance. Farewell, my good friend," I said.

"Likewise." Titus wished me farewell with a parting quote from Aristotle, "What is a friend, but a single soul dwelling in two bodies."

THE GRABEN, IN 59 A.D. *was just a muddy trench full of putrid waste outside the walls. Fast forward to modern times. The military camp of Vindobona transformed over the centuries into the modern city of Vienna, Austria. Vienna was home to the wealthy Habsburg monarchy for centuries, who left behind opulent palaces and gardens. Vienna of the 20th century is cosmopolitan with fashionable window shopping, Swarovski crystal, and the world-famous Vienna Opera. That muddy Roman trench is now the most famous street in Vienna. The street, called the Graben, is known for luxurious pedestrian shopping, its fountains, and festive lights.*

PART V

ALL ROADS LEAD TO ROME

26

HOMECOMING

All roads lead to Rome. In the first half of 60 A.D., I traveled on many of those roads over the Alps on my way home. I endured the remote Roman camps of Poetovio and Ravenna, followed the rugged coast of the Adriatic, and finally passed through scenic Umbria. I had returned proud and glorious to Rome, the Eternal City, the Capital of the World. Memories from my youth flooded back as I strolled through familiar narrow city streets, loud and crowded with rushing pedestrians. I had missed the familiar seven hills, the flowing fountains, the flat-top umbrella trees, and the old steady and reliable Tiber River. My 20th century reader is likely familiar with the expression, "You can't go home again," made famous by the Thomas Wolfe novel of the same title. A younger Lucius, almost two thousand years earlier, was not familiar with that sentiment. But returning to Rome, sweating with the nervous dramatic irony of the situation, I attempted to do just that.

I planned to first visit to my parents. I did give them notice through the letter, but I had not awaited any response. I visited their domicile in the city, only to find strangers residing there. My next impulse was to head to the Forum. That was the heart of the city—the legal, economic, religious, and political center. I strolled the Via Sacra, a main thoroughfare that ran the length of the Forum, which was used for processions of returning armies and coronations of emperors. In the valley by the Palatine Hill, I looked for someone to ask about my father or a family friend.

"Pardon me, my good man," I approached an older citizen whose face I found familiar, "I am looking for my father. Do you know Decimus Octavius Aurelius?" The old man walked away from me without a word, pompously flinging his toga aside. I noticed the purple stripe on his toga, called the tropa trabea, an insignia indicating his elite class.

I asked another elderly, gray haired man who received the question more politely. "You say, he is your father? That name sounds familiar," the elderly man said, and then he searched his thoughts in silence. We stood quietly for a while. He was not in any hurry.

"Do you know a man named Gallus Plinius Macro?" I asked. "Last I knew, he worked for some senators. I am close associates with his son, Rufus Arrius Macro."

"Oh, have you not heard? Gallus Plinius was murdered." The elderly man disclosed this information tragically, quieting to a whisper. I swayed on my feet. He tried helping me to sit down, although I ended up mostly helping him. He read the questions I was forming in my mind by my facial expressions.

"Young man, you sound educated. I'm sure you are well read in the history of politics and power. Plinius chose the wrong side of that fatal equation," the elderly man shook his head. "The dangerous business of propaganda. My boy, there have been men of much higher status that have been proscribed, pardon the euphemism. What I mean to say is, brutally murdered. We were powerless to do anything to prevent it."

"Can you help me find his son?" I asked, still in shock. I quickly found solace in the knowledge that the indelible Plinius, the abusive asshole, had flung his last insult. It was Rufus that I was worried sick about.

"I am so sorry. His dear son was killed in battle, too. Before Gallus Plinius was murdered," the elderly man said.

Deeply shocked and puzzled, so I asked for clarification. "Killed in battle? What battled would that have been?"

"I doubt I need to tell you that Tycho was a distinguished soldier who climbed the ranks with honor and distinction. He was last stationed in . . . Galatia? No, I heard that Tycho was killed in the Parthian wars in Armenia," he murmured.

"Do you mean his other son, Tycho, was killed?" This buoyed my spirits. "Rufus, Rufus Arrius Macro is the son that I am seeking."

"Oh, Rufus? You said Rufus, sorry, I lost the thread of my thought. That happens more with age, I'm afraid. I advise you—do not get old. No, my boy, I have not heard of a son named Rufus," the elderly man said. "But I know someone who can help you." At that time, I thought the old man was helpful and wanted a purpose. Perhaps he was just bored, lonely, and needed company. Either way he directed me to another old man, who directed me to another old man, and in this roundabout way, I found an old friend of Plinius and he shared with me the whereabouts of Rufus. This is how I ended up back in Subura, walking those narrow streets wafting with sewer smell, crawling with rough-looking ruffians and moaning feral cats. I was greeted at his door by Muntimer, that young scoundrel of my memory who had developed into an older scoundrel. His creased, worn out face told tales of his transgressions since we had last seen each other.

"Lucius, the boss, the world traveler! Hades, it has been years!" I heard Rufus shout from the dark dwelling. He approached the doorway to greet me. We embraced warmly. Muntimer crawled back into a dark corner.

"I'm so sorry, Rufus. I heard about your father, and Tycho."

"Oh, it has been a real bad year, Lucius. As soon as we make it through one funeral, there is yet another one on the way." Rufus took a deep breath and fought off the pain and sorrow on his face. "Anyway, whatever. Let's not talk about that. What you have been up to? Let's get out of this garbage heap. Muntimer, we're leaving. That food is mine, so don't eat the rest of it!"

Rufus and I took a walk through Subura towards the Viminalis Hill, our old haunt. We sat on the hill and drank wine just like old times, but it was not the same. Rome was still magnificent. In fact, only a few buildings had changed around the hill, yet I was less impressed. Everything seemed more common after seeing so much more of the world. The sun was setting over the horizon and it was getting dark. As the wine set into my blood, I did not feel the same youthful buzz of excitement. Rather, it only made me feel lethargic and irresponsible. It was harder to turn off my mind. I thought about the important work I should have been doing.

I told Rufus about my adventures and what brought me back to Rome. Rufus filled me in on all of his family tragedies. About how he was just trying to get by and stay out of trouble. Soteris had been killed too, by Roman cohorts, caught in the act of some crime. Muntimer, that scoundrel, was an old retired fighting dog, limping rather than brawling, drinking rather than working. Rufus wanted to help him, knowing that Muntimer's background was even worse than his own. Felix and Octavia were married and were now fat and happy.

"Lucius, Rome has been hard on us all. You should thank the gods and honor them for the good luck you were sent away this place."

"So, you didn't start a family? No wife and children?" I asked innocuously.

"No," Rufus said. "I didn't need anyone else to worry about besides myself. Felix and Octavia have a whole brood of kids. They're just busy and tired all the time. And so boring. Muntimer has a couple kids too, from different mothers, but they took them away from him, thank the gods."

Muntimer had children too?! I found that deeply disturbing. That is exactly what is wrong with the world, I thought. It was probably a blessing that his children were out of the picture, because it painted an ugly picture.

"I am just working every day and minding my own business," Rufus said. It turned out that Rufus was doing construction work as well. Plinius had surprisingly left Rufus a small amount of money in his will, and Rufus was able to use those funds to set himself up as a small-time contractor. I was proud of him. We talked shop, comparing the Roman architectural motifs to what I had observed across the empire.

"Rufus, I give you my word, if there is any way I can make it happen, we should go into business together. I will speak to my father who will connect me with my uncle. My uncle can set me up in his construction enterprises. We can work together and help each other out, like old times. You are like a brother to me. Like the brother I never had."

Rufus appreciated the sentiment, but I could tell how he had changed. He still showed remnants of a rough and wild edge, but that youthful energy and optimism had been beaten out of him over the years.

I FINALLY FOUND MY parents at their villa outside the city walls following directions from Rufus. They had grown noticeably older, feebler and more fragile, and thus less intimidating and authoritarian. My father was still taller than me, but he seemed smaller to me. The conversation was heartfelt but strained. I wanted to make them proud, but a rebellious resistance still lingered in me. My mother was most happy to see me. She looked up at me and smiled, but I saw unhappiness beneath her expression. She was worried about my choices, especially any choice that would cause friction with Roman society. Mother wanted me to be a normal Roman citizen and stop following these dangerous fanatics. I recalled the words in the letters I had received from home over the years as I spoke to her.

"You don't have to leave again so soon, Lucius," Mother said, glancing up at me, with a lifetime of disappointment on her face.

"I am going to live in Rome. I'll be in the city, and nearby to you Mom. I have a lot of business to do here," I assured her. I was staying close by in Rome, but I did not bring up my Christian mission. I still didn't think that my parents could distinguish it from Judaism.

Father and I went outside that night and spoke about my future. It was a surprisingly civil and adult conversation with my father. We formed an agreement that was not ideal, but satisfactory. Through family connections, specifically my uncle, we arranged a manager position for me in construction. I would be supervising the construction of insulae, or tall apartment buildings, in the city.

Through these means, I secured a modest apartment near the Quirinalis Hill. I had also formed my own personal vision that was twofold. After I had gained the necessary experience and capital, I would start out on my own business venture and bring Rufus in as my partner. And I would also join up with the Christians in Rome and take down Simon Magus.

SIMON MAGUS WAS MAKING himself known all around Rome and attracting enormous crowds. I headed for the Forum where he was rumored to be making an appearance on the Rostra, the large platform where orators addressed the people. From the Rostra, Julius Caesar spoke. And, after Caesar was murdered, Brutus and Cassius gave their respective speeches from the Rostra. When Marc Antony had Cicero proscribed, he ordered his hands and head to be displayed on the Rostra.

When I arrived by the Curia, there was already a large crowd standing in front of the Rostra. Simon Magus was in clear sight standing on top of the marble platform, behind where the prows of conquered enemy warships had been mounted for display. He was addressing his audience with his arms held up in the air.

"Yes, you might attend to the *temples* and *worship*." He pointed theatrically at the temples that surrounded us. At the Temple of Castor and Pollux, at the Temple of Saturn, then over our heads, at the round-shaped Temple of Vesta. The vain Temple of Divine Caesar stood behind the crowd. "So that the rain will fall heavily on your crops. And, so that your bellies will be filled with nourishment. So that your *coffers* are filled with gold. But those seeking *divine* knowledge . . ."

Simon Magus was a great orator and knew how to feed off the energy of the crowd. He would speak slowly, deliberately, using simple language. He would engage the listener with dramatic pauses, emphatic intonation, and the occasional eruption of passion. Standing by the lonely tree at the back of the crowd, I was able to take in the entire scene. The diverse and growing crowd consisted of wealthy citizens, poor slaves, politicians and businessmen, unexpecting pedestrians, and devotees of Simon Magus. I decided to approach the Rostra, pushing my way through the people.

"*Divine* knowledge can be found within *all* of us. First you must *release* yourselves from the bondages of your pantheon of gods." Simon Magus exaggerated his facial expressions, swirled his hands in the air, his fingernails mesmerized the crowd.

Some people held their hands up to Simon Magus in awe, trembling and teary eyed with passion. One man pronounced, "He is a wise man. A living legend! What profound words." Profound? What nonsense. He's not really saying anything, I thought.

Another man, moved to tears, proclaimed, "He is more than a wise man. He is a living god!"

I pushed closer to the front of the crowd. There was a large group of women crying and screaming near the foot of the Rostra. They must have been overtaken by his charismatic aura, because they were shouting wild exclamations, such as, "He is the most beautiful man in the world," and, "He loves us all! I want to meet him!" And, most unfortunately, "We must join him and bear his children! I think I am in love with him!"

Several of the women were disturbingly young and all were beautiful. They madly pushed towards Simon Magus, but guards prevented them from moving further up the Rostra steps. His magnetic energy was clearly irresistible to these women.

"God is in you. God is in me. God is in *all* of us!" Simon Magus declared. "My children. I will help you find salvation."

Simon Magus was in full splendor from my vantage point. His royal blue robe with its distinct pointed shoulder design was bedazzled with sparkling gold thread. His hair was much longer than it had been the last time I had seen him. His face was still gaunt, but he had a distinguished radiance now.

"God provides the *true divine* wisdom and knowledge. I am a mere guide, a vessel to deliver you on your spiritual journey." Simon Magus held out his hands, feigning humility, the gesture of a true servant leader.

A woman nearby cried out, "Please Simon Magus, help us! Show us your power!"

"Witness the powers of the mystical and magical *holy spirit*! I will hone those magical powers. The powers of Sun, Air, Water, Earth, and Heaven!"

Holy Spirit! That struck a chord with me. It was all just talk and nonsense up until that point, but then he brought in the Holy Spirit!

"Witness the power of *Air*!"

He began a magical incantation.

"PLUMA AAEEE BORO AER IEO!"

A hot wind began to blow through the Forum. As he continued chanting, Simon Magus began to levitate. He crossed his arms over his chest, and his body rose until his body was at the height of the rail that surrounded the Rostra. Then he remained motionless while he continued his evil chant.

"ENN EEE IEO IA NEEA NOUS"

"Witness his powers! Simon Magus, please help us! Show us this divine knowledge!" Some of the crowd shouted in awe, some cheered, a respectable few grumbled, and others were speechless. A woman nearby passed out into the arms of a friend. The women in front were still shouting and screaming for him. I was shocked by the display, profoundly concerned by the reaction of the people, and disgusted by the entire spectacle, so I left the Forum in haste.

SITTING ALONE IN MY apartment that night, I began to write a few correspondences. First, I wrote to Jason in Corinth, to share all that I had witnessed, and express my desire to join the Christians in Rome.

> Jason, I have finally returned to Rome after all these years. I have visited my friends and my family. Although I missed them, I am pleased to share that I made the right decision to leave this city when I was

younger and see the world. My parents have grown older and docile. The conversations with them are less strained. My friends are tired, complacent, or dead. In a way, it is depressing. I do have some good news. I have established my construction business here. I even rent my own home.

In more concerning news, I went to the Forum to watch Simon Magus yesterday. Simon Magus is not just trying to impress Nero, but the entire population of Rome. He attracted a very large crowd and is already gaining fanatical followers. I was not moved by his words as they didn't have substance, but I must admit, he is charismatic. Indeed, he incites a mystical aura.

I will dedicate myself to the cause of Simon Peter and the Christian church of Rome. Can you inform me where the church meets here? Has Paul arrived in Rome and where is he held as prisoner? Please let me know how I can be of assistance and I will join the cause here.

Jason, you would love this place. Rome is majestic.

I was also compelled to write Titus to share my exploits and to invite him to Rome.

Titus, my friend, my erudite half-barbarian, how is the wilderness of the north? I have arrived safely in Rome! Have you planted your crops already? Is your mother well? Here's hoping that Salvius has cured his body rash.

You should come to Rome to work with me in construction. Together, we can build great things in this city! Although I find your rituals disturbing, I truly do respect your culture. I was recently reminded that the Celts conquered Rome centuries before my time. In these times, however, the center of the civilized world is Rome. I have many connections in Rome and will share my hospitality with you if you come. As I mentioned, Simon Peter and the Christians are plotting to take down an evil sorcerer named Simon Magus. I promise I will introduce you to these Christians.

It is still painful to think about Daphne. The best relief has been the combination of hard work and passing time. I received a short letter from Cato. He told me that her father had already arranged her marriage. How is your love life? Do you have a girlfriend or any love interests? As the Romans say, 'amor vincit omnia' —love conquers all.

The ox carts rattled loudly down the city streets that night. The street noises banged through my open second story windows as memories echoed in my head.

27

PONTIFEX MAXIMUS

Just outside the city walls, between the Capitoline Hill and the Tiber, sprawled a swampy grassland named the Campus Martius, or the Field of Mars. The Campus Martius would eventually become one of the most densely built sections of Rome, home to temples, theaters, stadiums, and the famous Pantheon. But in 60 A.D. it was just a swampy field below the floodplain with a few old temples, occasionally used for army drills and public assemblies. A section of this land had recently been renovated with public pools, baths, and aqueducts. Temples had been built on this sacred ground many centuries ago, but not with the lasting architectural strength of the later structures of imperial Rome.

In a matter of days, I had received a short and terse reply letter from Jason. He and Simon Peter had arrived to establish the new church of Rome. Jason shared the church location as well as the meeting date and time. He instructed me to come meet them but cautioned me not to speak of the location with anyone. Outside the city walls, in a vacant old temple in the Campus Martius, the new church of Rome held their first clandestine meeting.

There was a very good turnout of both women and men, what looked to be Jews as well as Romans of the varying classes from servants to patricians and foreigners as well. Jason was standing up in front. We shared a familiar nod.

Then Jason addressed the church, "My dear Christian brothers and sisters! Today we are blessed to have with us Simon Peter, the disciple of our Lord and Savior Jesus Christ. Simon Peter, as you all know—"

"Simon Peter?!" a man in the crowd shouted, "We are here to see the great one, Simon Magus. Not this Simon Peter!"

Simon Peter's face turned red and his brow wrinkled. He charged to the front of the congregation, shouting furiously, "Who here is expecting to see Simon Magus!? Stand up and show yourselves!"

Many people in the crowd stood.

"If you wish to see Simon Magus, I ask that you excuse yourself straightaway! If you wish to be Christians, to accept Jesus Christ as the Lord, and reject false prophets such as Simon Magus, you may stay. The Lord will forgive your sins."

Many of those standing sustained their allegiance to Simon Magus, boasting of his great powers. Simon Peter sternly ordered his men, "Show these pagans out, and beat them summarily if they do not flee!"

A commotion ensued as the followers of Simon Magus were dragged out of the temple and chased off.

"Now, where were we?" Simon Peter shook off the disruption, but I had sensed that this had affected his mood.

"Prophesies are not just the creation of man. They are not only imaginative inventions, fabricated in the minds of mortals. Yes, there are many among us who benefit from the gift of prophesy. This gift of prophecy is brought to men through divine inspiration. But I must warn you, my brothers and sisters, of the false prophets who come to you appearing as sheep, but underneath are ravenous wolves. These false prophets invent their own creations to do their own evil bidding. Simon Magus has come to Rome with his false teachings and prophecies, claiming to invoke the Holy Spirit, and is leading men astray. If Simon Magus has the gift of prophesy through divine intervention—then it is only from the spirit of the antichrist."

The crowd had calmed down such that Simon Peter had their undivided attention.

"Not one week ago, I was traveling through the countryside on the Appian Way. As I was praying to the Lord," Simon Peter continued, "I became surrounded by a mist and I fell into a trance. Then I saw a vision! In this vision I witnessed Simon Magus and myself standing before Nero in his palace chambers. The emperor proclaimed that we were the greatest prophets in the land. Nero asked for us to demonstrate our magical powers, to rid his house of any curses, and speak to his mother in the afterlife. Nero asked us, who is the leader of your church, and we both said, 'It is I.'"

The entire crowd was silent in suspense. But that was it. Simon Peter shared nothing more of what he had seen in his vision. Many were visibly disappointed by the abrupt ending, before Simon Peter shook his head and went on.

"My brothers and sisters, this prophecy, granted to me through divine inspiration, informs us that Simon Magus is a threat to the Christian church. He will vie for the favor of Nero. We must all avoid the temptation of Simon Magus and his seductive powers. We must pray that he does not influence our holy church. Let us pray to Our Savior, the Lord Jesus Christ."

Simon Peter clenched his eyes shut, looked downward, and began to passionately pray, his lips mouthing without sound, holding his hands open towards the heavens.

Jason moved forward to address the congregation. "Simon Peter has been chosen by God to lead the church. Jesus Christ, the Son of God, informed Simon Peter that he was rock on which the church would be built."

I approached Jason after the meeting as he was speaking with some other Christians. They were talking about Paul. He was under house arrest in Rome, but was receiving the greatest care while he was a captive. He was free to worship, pray, and share the good news of Christ. Demas, one of Paul's followers, introduced himself to me. Demas informed us that Lucas, another follower of Paul, was taking care of Paul today. Demas also shared that other existing Roman Christians would join up and unite with Simon Peter soon.

"I look forward to meeting Lucas, Paul, and all of the other Roman church members," I told Demas.

Jason and I went to speak privately with Simon Peter. Simon Peter was pleased to see me again, but he got right down to business. "Jason, I need someone to infiltrate the cult of Simon Magus," Simon Peter said. "I need someone on the inside who can ferret out the details of his plans in Rome."

"I would be honored and proud to do that," Jason said, bowing slightly.

"No, that won't do." Simon Peter rubbed his beard. "Take this kindly, Jason, but you look too Jewish. And too Greek. Trust me, it takes one to know one."

"But what if—" Jason began to plead his case.

"Simon Magus is a Samaritan. He might catch on and investigate your past. You are half Jewish, half Greek. Just like Timothy, his mother a Jewess and his father a Greek. It is written all over your features, and eventually it would be found out that you are a deacon of the church. Please, don't take this wrong."

"No, I understand." Jason despondently gave in. Then he looked thoughtfully in my direction. "What about Lucius? He is a Roman citizen, highly resourceful. He would pass as a local here, another patrician youth, and be beyond suspicion."

"That is a tremendous idea! Lucius, you shall begin infiltration of the cult of Simon Magus promptly." Simon Peter patted me on the shoulder, then walked off to the front of the temple. Wait, what was I just enlisted to do? Was I going to be in danger? My mind vacillated between fear of the unknown and pride at being selected to help with this Christian mission.

I watched as church members gathered around Simon Peter, waiting patiently to greet him at the front of the temple. They may have been asking him for spiritual advice, or prayers for forgiveness, or requesting that he heal sick friends or family. This was the new Church of Rome, in that temple ruin, in the swampland north of the city walls. As I left the church, I looked out across the Tiber. Centuries later that was where St Peter's Basilica and the Vatican would be constructed.

MY CONSTRUCTION BUSINESS FLOURISHED in Rome. I was building insulae up to seven stories tall. Most of the residents of Rome in those times lived in these tenant buildings. Only the wealthy could afford their own domus. I was finally able to recruit Rufus to supervise one of my several building crews. He was leading the construction in the Subura slums, where insulae were built with taverns on the first floor. Taverns just like where Muntimer and Soteris fought many years ago.

In my insula, my own apartment, I received a letter from Titus in Vindobona. Anxiously, I unrolled a scroll to read the message, hoping he was on his way to Rome to join me and the Christians.

> Lucius, my dear Roman friend, I hope this letter finds you well. Vindobona is still cold and damp, but the snow has melted. The crops are doing quite well. My mother is now chief priestess of the druids, elevated to a highly respected role in our clan. Salvius, that fantastic beast, was in rare form during our Spring festival. He drank—a conservative estimate—twenty goblets of beer and devoured five whole chickens. He fights a daily battle with his body rash but has still not won the war.
>
> I do like women, and I meet them time and again. I was seeing a Roman woman, off and on. I do enjoy their company, but I do not get too close. Mother is the only woman who needs love in my life. In your love life, Daphne is still in your mind but not in your spirit. Lucius, you need to move past Daph-

ne—be sound of mind, body, and spirit. As the wise Plato cautioned, "Love is a serious mental disease."

It pains me to tell you that I will not be able to join you in Rome. I appreciate the cordial offer, but I must decline. My home is here with my mother and my clan. Rome may be magnificent, but I was not made for such a place. May you soar with the eagles and run with the wolves!

28

INFILTRATION

I was waiting for the right opportunity to infiltrate the circle of Simon Magus and his followers, who were now called Simonians. The right opportunity appeared after one public appearance. Simon Magus had just finished his grand speech and was leading a parade through the streets, his followers traveling behind him. I stepped from the crowd and into the Simonians, blending in by walking amongst them. I was dressed as a typical Roman patrician, and not one of the Simonians seemed to notice me as I walked with them out of the city. They traveled to a large country estate where many of them appeared to live.

Of all the beautiful Roman villas, Simon Magus's estate, Villa Gitta, was one of the most grand and opulent. It comprised of a kitchen and large dining hall, gardens and atriums, and couched sitting rooms. On the second floor there were numerous living rooms encircled with a balcony vista. The villa was surrounded by lush gardens, orchards with plum trees and berry bushes, olive groves, and a large stable filled with many fine horses.

I casually followed the crowd into the villa and took a seat in an atrium. The sun glinted off the tiny tiles of the mosaic floor which depicted racing horses. I was struck by the sight of a stout lady figure sprawled on a couch across the room from me. She wore a colorful dress made from a shiny silk, and all kinds of jewelry dangled from her ears, arms, and legs. Her short, thick body folded like a rhinoceros underneath the fine material. Most of her face was covered by a glittering cloth, revealing only her eyes. Those eyes were dark brown and bloodshot, and they were outlined with thick black makeup like an Egyptian princess. The woman lifted the cloth and uncovered her mouth to gorge on a bundle of grapes. This action also revealed her tanned and tattooed face and pierced nose. I could not take my eyes off her.

She caught me gawking, shifted her weight, and focused her piercing gaze on me.

"Can I help you, honey?" she called. Her voice was guttural, raspy. "Struck by my timeless beauty? Or are you searching for feminine companionship?"

"Uh, I—" I was blushing, fumbling for words.

"Camel got your tongue?" she croaked.

"Do you not know Helena?" another woman asked me with condescending surprise.

"Simon's loyal companion," a Simonian man stated.

"His muse," added the woman.

"A diva. A royal princess," the man recited.

"I'm the reincarnation of Helen of Troy," Helena claimed.

She sprawled on her couch, attempting elegance. "And I am the living embodiment of Athena, the goddess of wisdom and war. And Ruth of—"

"And Queen Nefertiti of Egypt," a younger woman said, "among others."

"You look surprised," the man next to me whispered. His name was Flavius. "When Simon Magus found her many years ago, she was a stunning beauty. Under all of that, uh, well . . . was the finest body to be seen."

"Where did he find her? Are the two of them a, uh," I whispered back to Flavius, gesturing with my hands, "an item?"

"Oh, no. Well, yes, in a way," Flavius answered, not so quietly. "Simon Magus has many concubines, boy lovers, mistresses, you know. He met her ages ago on the streets of Tyre. He was convinced that she was a princess reincarnate and wielded mystical powers." So, she was Phoenician, like Daphne, but she shared no resemblance to Daphne in any way whatsoever.

"No secrets, boys! No secrets," Helen screeched. "Do you want me to perform for you? Perhaps, you desire the mystical dance of the serpent."

"Yes, but . . . maybe after dinner?" Someone mitigated, thankfully.

"Well, let me tell you a story then." Helena stood up from the couch and wobbled to the center of the atrium. "During the time of Claudius, when I was a young woman, I resorted to working the streets of Tyre. I was the most beguiling temptress in all of the land."

"Start from the beginning, darling," a man requested playfully.

Helena cleared her throat and continued. "My father was born in a tribe of nomadic people. They followed the seasons, wandering the deserts with their camels, sleeping wherever they staked their tents. He was the poet of his tribe, carrying on the stories of his people which were handed down from times long before the Pharaohs of Egypt. His poems were epic tales of the battles against evil, of how his people were created from the sand and wind of the first great sandstorm from the east."

Helena reenacted the sandstorm creation story, tossed by the mythical storm, jewelry shaking and sparkling in the sunlight.

"My mother was a fortune teller, but she wasn't no good, otherwise she would have seen that my father was no good. My father's tribe was on its way to the sea when she met him in Tyre. Mom was instantly attracted to this foreign wanderer from the desert. She tried to tame him and hold him down, but he was a wild horse that could not be broken."

She was bucking and grunting like a wild horse trying not to be broken, her body jiggling, kicking her legs and flaring her nose.

"My father wandered during the nights, philandering and fighting. Mom bore him five children. I was the first born. All us children worked the streets since we were just this tall, begging for money or food, picking pockets. When we got older my brothers and sisters did musical acts or simple tricks. My mother told fortunes and then collected all our earnings at the end of the day. I raised them kids since I was the oldest.

"When I had matured, I survived on my feminine wiles. My father traded me to the sailors for coin. Then one day, my father wandered back into the desert. He never came back, and never was heard from again." Helena looked out into the distance, squatting and shielding her eyes against the glaring sun with her hand.

"When I was a child, mother would tell me the stories of a powerful man from Galilee, a Jew, who came to teach to the people and heal the sick. This man was named Jesus. The messiah, as they called him. I didn't think nothing of it at the time. Many years later, a powerful man from Samaria came to teach and heal the sick with his magical powers. That man was struck by my beauty. He saw in me the reincarnation of powerful women. He said I was an inspiration, his muse. That man took me in and saved me from a life on the streets. That man was Simon Magus."

As if on cue, Simon Magus entered the atrium, followed by two young men running to keep up with his long strides. As soon as he entered the Simonians rose began bowing to honor of his presence. "No, stop it! Please! You don't need to grovel. Carry on," Simon Magus said.

As the evening passed, I learned all about the estate and the people who worked there through continued conversation with Flavius, the man who had whispered to me about Helena. I ingratiated myself to Flavius and embellished my position in society. Flavius kindly showed me around and introduced me to the other Simonians, young and old, all from various walks of life. I saw more of the domus and the surrounding estate. I was invited to the activities that took place on the estate, such as Simon's teaching at the Theater of Christ, feats at the Fountain of Miracles, and ceremonies at the Baptismal Pond. After a few more visits I would be accepted as a familiar face, and I could let myself in to the Villa Gitta at any time.

The people at Villa Gitta freely told me what Simon Magus had done to improve their lives. He provided them with salvation, healed sick family members. And, to the chagrin of all Christians, he had blessed them all with the powers of the holy spirit.

A FEW WEEKS LATER, after one long day's visit, I was taken to a luxurious balcony room where I could stay the night and rest my tired head. As I walked by another open doorway, I noticed Simon Magus sitting inside.

"You there! Come back here," Simon Magus shouted after I had passed by. I turned and cautiously entered the room. Simon Magus was sitting, dressed in a fine robe. As I approached him, I saw his face up close for the first time. His strong features, dark slanted eyebrows, and aging creases were more noticeable, as well as the makeup he used to cover his aging skin. He was being groomed by two handsome young men. One man was standing behind him, brushing his flowing hair. The other was kneeling, polishing his long, spiraled fingernails. The two men were well dressed and had soft features.

"I've noticed you here before, but you haven't been introduced to me. I'm a very busy man. What is your name and what do you do? I must know. Tell me now." He spoke rapidly, but was not facing me, as he was still being groomed.

"I am Lucius Octavius Aurelius. I am a patrician from the city of Rome. I am a skilled tekton and I currently oversee the construction of insulae here in Rome." Just sticking to the facts.

"Oh, fabulous! I love it." Simon Magus smiled, looking away. Then he threw down his hand mirror in frustration. He turned directly towards me.

"Curius! Spurius! Leave at once. We're trying to have a conversation." Simon Magus commanded them in high pitched voice.

The young man on fingernail detail tried to kiss Simon's hand. "Oh, you don't have to," Simon said, and with a diabolic smile followed up with, "but it doesn't hurt." They both grabbed their grooming tools and quickly fled the room.

"So how can I help you? You must want something. Everybody that comes here wants something." Simon Magus crossed his legs casually and looked at me again.

"I am seeking salvation through obtaining the divine secret knowledge." I lied for the first time, repeating something that I heard him say.

"Bullshit, kid. Everyone that comes here wants something. Do you have a sick aunt or something? A demon possessed child?"

"No, I don't. I guess, I don't always get along with my parents," I confessed, with a sprinkle of truth.

"Naturally." Simon Magus laughed. "So, do you seek fortune or power, or fortune *and* power?"

"With all due respect, I only seek health for myself and the fortune of others. Personally, I would only like to hear your teaching. That would benefit me greatly." That was a truthful statement and a lie wrapped in one.

"Come back next week and join the group for my next lesson at the Theater of Christ." Simon Magus reached out and took my hand in his. I tried not to react to his touch. He looked at me closely, leaning towards me. "You are a strange young man. You do not show much fear or deference. You do not grovel like the others. Do you not believe that I am the great one?"

"No, I'm really, really impressed! I think you are a prophet and powerful magician. I am inspired by your teachings." I lied again. Maybe I was getting good at this. After all, he was so charismatic.

Simon Magus waived off these compliments dismissively. He paused, as if waiting for more flattery, then said, "You are Roman. Do you work for Nero? Has he sent you here? I have been informed that Nero wants me to help him. He seeks to obtain power from all gods and magicians—for himself of course. Just tell me what he wants and how I can help. You don't think I'd refuse granting favors for the emperor, do you?"

"I do not work for Nero. That I can swear to you," I said. "But, I do confess that I am a follower of Jesus Christ, the true Messiah and Son of God."

"I am a Christian too, kid," Simon Magus grinned. "I was baptized a long time ago in Samaria by Philip the Evangelist. I am the one true apostle of the Christian church. Don't forget to whom you are speaking. I am the great one, who wields the power of the holy spirit, among many, many other things." As he spoke his voice became increasingly grandiose. He wiggled his dark slanted eyebrows at me. I was at a loss for words. Hold it together, I thought.

Simon Magus leaned further forward and said, "There is a man called Simon Peter who has recently arrived in Rome. His an uneducated, smelly, inarticulate man without charisma, and yet despite these traits he's attracted a significant following. Do you know him?"

"No, I've never met Simon Peter, but I have heard his name," I shook my head, then smiled at him. "I came to you first."

"Please, if you will do me one favor, kid. Follow Simon Peter around and see what he is getting up to. Can you do this for me, Lucius?"

"Of course, I will," I said. And then I followed that statement as evenly as I could with, "Oh great one."

Simon Magus held out his hand so that I would kiss it. I did what I had to, for God's sake. He grabbed some of his effects and began walking out of the room. I followed him to the balcony. We both looked out at the view of the estate and the valley beyond.

Simon Magus took a deep breath, as if taking in all before him, then said, "Let me share with you one lesson in greatness. If you want a loyal following, you must give people what they want. You must tell them what they want to hear. Now, I must see to my people." And with that Simon Magus spun on his sandaled heel and quickly strode off. Curius and Spurius ran from the other side of the balcony, struggling to keep up.

"WHAT IS NERO WREAKING havoc upon these days?" Jason asked Simon Peter and me, just trying to make small talk. I had met Simon Peter and Jason that evening. We were at a tavern on Vicus Patricius, which was in a slightly better neighborhood of Rome than in Subura.

"I hear that he aims to marry again," Simon Peter shared. "But Poppaea, his next unlucky bride, is still married. She is of the most distinguished lineage, from a great general of Augustus Caesar. This will all end in tragedy, I'm afraid."

"Oh, did you hear about his aunt?" Jason asked. "The poor old bag was constipated, stuffed up solid for weeks. So, Nero ordered his doctors to give his aunt a fatal dose of laxatives. The dose was so strong that the old lady slowly shat herself to death. Nero didn't even wait until she was done evacuating herself to move in on her property," Jason laughed as he told the story. I was too disturbed to laugh.

"Speaking of poor aunts," I said, changing the subject quickly, "Simon Magus asked if I had a sick aunt or a demon possessed friend. He is quite the character. Get this, Simon Peter. He asked me to spy on you."

"Did you agree to it?" Simon Peter asked.

"Of course! And I agreed to return this week for his next sermon. I'm sure he'll expect a report on you. And just like that, I'm a Simonian. I'm part of the inner circle." I got a laugh out of them.

We were served watered wine and some bread and large bowls of stew. I offered to buy, since I was increasingly prosperous thanks to the boom in construction.

"First, we impress the masses. Then, we impress Nero. Simon Peter, you must know that this is a popularity contest. Simon Magus knows how to amaze the crowds and inspire the people," Jason said. I realized he came here to strategize.

"I agree with Jason," I said. "Simon Magus confided in me. He told me that the way to control the masses is to tell them what they want to hear."

"Not to mention, appearance is important. You need to work on your look," Jason said, causing Simon Peter to scowl.

"I agree on that as well. Simon Magus is always finely dressed, adorned with fine robes and flashy jewelry. He has two assistants that constantly groom him," I reported.

"I am not going to change my appearance. I was a poor fisherman when Jesus met me, and Jesus himself dressed no better than any one of us," Simon Peter said. Then, iron-

347

ically, he exclaimed, "Do you think the father of the church should wear flashy clothes!?"

"No, of course not. Personally, I find it tacky," Jason said. "But what about pleasing the masses? Let's think about that for a moment. I may have some ideas that may work. How about you, Lucius?"

"My brothers," Simon Peter cut us off abruptly, "I am here to share the good news of Jesus Christ and prepare mankind for the kingdom of heaven. I will tell them what needs to be said, not what they desire to hear."

Jason, never easily discouraged, tried a different angle. "Ok, how about we work on our strategy for impressing Nero? If we can impress Nero, then many people will follow us if only to appease him."

Jason and I both signaled for more wine.

"As I have already said, I am here to prepare man for the kingdom of heaven. I will not cater to the Empire of Rome," Simon Peter sighed.

"Rocky, you need to budge a little bit on this issue. I must insist. If Simon Magus caters to Nero and he turns the people against you, we will be outcasts. No, worse than that, the church will be destroyed," Jason said.

"Jason, remember the words of Jesus. 'Give to Caesar what is Caesar's; and to God what is God's.' I will not make it my mission to impress Nero. If I must face him, I will speak faithfully for the Lord our God, and then the will of God must prevail." Simon Peter said.

"Is it not God's will to end false prophecies? And there is no authority above God." Jason said, building up steam. "Remember the prophesy you had of appearing before Nero? Both you and Simon Magus—"

Simon Peter put a hand on each of our shoulders, and with melancholy, said to both of us, "We must obey God rather than man."

"Simon Peter, with all due respect, I think this is a bad decision. I hope that you are not making a fatal mistake," Jason said in a troubled tone.

Simon Peter clenched his eyes shut, said a short prayer, then got up and walked out of the tavern.

Once Simon Peter left, Jason said, "If Nero merely laughs about murdering his own family, what might he do to us?"

I waived for even more wine. We drank in silence for a minute as the wine soaked into our heavy hearts.

"Come on Jason, let's go to the Subura. I know just the place to take you tonight," I suggested to break the mood.

Jason and I walked through dark streets of Subura towards Vicus Longus. I took him to my old haunt, the Caput Porcus. We found seats in the corner, opposite the gambling tables. "Jason, this is where it all started for me. My friends and I got in a fight here and my father sent me away to Judea," I retold Jason my story, shouting it over the loud patrons.

"Rome is such an amazing city. You are so lucky to grow up here. The village I grew up in was so quant and dull," Jason shouted back at me. In that dark dive, we shook off the horrible thoughts from earlier. After Caput Porcus, I showed Jason some of my other old hang outs around the city.

SIMON PETER HAD FINISHED his teaching at the old temple in the Campus Martius, and a small crowd had gathered to watch a young boy who was possessed by a demon. He had been kicking and punching people uncontrollably. His mother just confessed that he'd knocked the wind out of Lucas earlier. Simon Peter invoked the name of Jesus, and the demon was cast out. Business as usual. Lucas and I walked over to Simon Peter to catch up.

"Jesus taught us that we must love our neighbors as we love ourselves," Lucas said properly. "Although Simon Magus is an evil man and a false prophet, we must find it in our hearts to love him."

"Yes, we must love our neighbors, and this includes Simon Magus and his followers," Simon Peter said. "Since we love them with all our hearts, we must show them the toughest kind of love. If we did not love them, we would be indifferent, and do nothing. Instead, with neighborly love, we will bring them down to a place of humility before the mercy of God."

"We have no other choice," Jason added.

"I will seek Paul's advice. Who among us would like to come with me?" Lucas asked.

"I need not seek council. I am the rock . . ." and so Simon Peter began another passionate sermon.

"I will go visit Paul with you," I said to Lucas, who smiled back kindly.

29

CONFRONTATION

In the late autumn of 61 A.D. Lucas and I went to visit Paul for the first time. The domus where Paul was being held under arrest was located in the central part of the city. It was not spacious, but it was tidy and comfortable. We were greeted at the door by a Roman soldier, a member of the elite Praetorian Guard. He was permanently stationed to guard Paul. The guard recognized Lucas and they embraced in Roman style.

"Paul and I were just about to say our prayers. Please come in and join us for dinner," the guard said, inviting us in warmly, behaving more like a host rather than a guard. We walked into a lamp lit room with a low ceiling. I saw Paul, a small man who was modestly dressed, sitting at a short table. When he turned to acknowledge us, I heard the shackles on his ankles rattle against the wooden floor planks. His bald pate shone in the lamplight. His dark eyebrows connected below his smooth forehead. Paul's gray beard was overgrown but not unkempt, and his clothes were threadbare but not dirty.

The guard knelt in front of him. Paul placed his hand on the guard's head and began to pray. After the prayer, Lucas spread the food that we had brought with us on the small table. Then Lucas examined Paul's neck, then his forehead, then asked him to open his mouth. Lucas listened to him breath and then asked Paul to cough. Paul accepted this routine patiently.

"Your condition has greatly improved. You are no longer phlegmatic, so I can report that your four humors are now in balance," Lucas said cheerfully.

Paul looked up at me and said, "Lucas has been my loyal follower and personal physician for many years. And he brings me a delicious meal on occasion." Paul smiled. "I wouldn't survive without you, Lucas. Please, please sit down, all of you. We shall have dinner together. There is more than enough for everyone."

We sat and began eating a sumptuous meal together. The guard sat at the table as well. We passed the food between us.

"Although I am under house arrest, they allow me to freely teach the word of God. Guests are more than welcome to visit me here. In fact, citizens are often the most hospitable. My visitors are necessary caretakers since I cannot provide for myself," Paul said as he pulled on his chains. "What with all these delicious meals they bring me, I am tempted to eat to pass the time and become obese."

"Did any of the local Jews come visit you?" Lucas asked.

"Yes, many of the Jews assembled here to listen to me, but most of them did not believe my words. Their minds were indecisive, their eyes were not open, or their hearts were hardened. They could not even come to any agreements amongst themselves about what they believed. Meanwhile, many gentiles came to listen and received the good news of Christ with open hearts and minds." Paul looked across the table at his guard, who bowed to him.

"We just came from the church where Simon Peter is preaching to the people of Rome. Those who come to hear him are from all walks of life, Jews and gentiles alike," I shared proudly. Lucas cleared his throat. We resumed eating in silence.

"You know of Simon Magus, the false prophet?" Lucas asked Paul.

"Yes, you know that I do," Paul answered sharply.

"What is to be done about him? Simon Peter and the Christians of Rome plan to go after him. They plan to take him down and break up his following," Lucas said.

"God's will be done," Paul said. "And pass the bread, please."

After dinner, Paul began writing a letter at the table ignoring us as if we were no longer there. He was deep in thought as he wrote, rubbing the skin of his bald forehead profusely. I tried to reconcile what I had heard of Paul and his teachings with the man I had just met. There was nothing at all grandiose about this man under house arrest. The articulate thoughts he expressed in his teachings were not demonstrated in person. I considered Simon Peter, who was less educated and intelligent, but a more charismatic leader and passionate public speaker when encountered in person. Simon Magus, however, was second to none when met in the flesh. I kept that last opinion to myself.

AFTER MEETING WITH PAUL, I walked back to the church alone, hoping to find Simon Peter or Jason. As I was leaving the city gates, which were frequently crowded with beggars, a man approached me begging. I reached out to hand him a denarius.

"No thank you, my good man," the beggar said. "I was only looking for a bit of food. I have no need for money."

"Well then, I will pray to God for your salvation."

"To whom?"

"God the Father of—"

"No, no. Which god?" the beggar asked.

"God the Creator of the heavens and the earth. The one and only true God."

"No, thank you," the beggar said politely.

"Then which god do you worship?"

"None."

"You do not worship any gods?" I was getting frustrated.

"No."

"Why not? Look at you. You are in greater need of divine intervention than most." I waved my hand at his filthy and ragged clothing.

"I worship no gods. There are no gods." The beggar itched himself like a stray dog.

"So, you don't believe in any gods?" I had confronted every kind of belief in god and type worship. But, to have none?

"No. All of the gods, you see, they are all just man's creation. For instance, have you heard of Jupiter?" the beggar asked.

"Of course, I know of Jupiter. He is the king of the gods," I replied.

"Well, then, do you know Zeus?" the beggar asked.

"Yes, I do of course I do. Zeus is the Greek god. They are one in the same." I answered.

"So, obviously, Zeus was an invention of the Greeks, then the Romans coopted the Greek gods and renamed him Jupiter. See? Man's creation. The Greek's created then the Roman's imitated," the beggar put it simply.

"That proves nothing. I'm not interested in the Roman gods or any other gods."

"Me neither," he said.

"You're not?" I asked, confused.

"I'm not interested in any gods. I've said that already," the beggar stated calmly.

"How can you not be interested in any gods?" I asked.

"You are not interested in the Roman gods and I am not interested in the Roman gods. We share a common disinterest. The only difference between us is that I am not interested in your god either."

"But my God is the one true god. God the father, the God of Abraham—" I started to try to explain, but the beggar cut me off.

"So, your God was the creation of Abraham? Who was a man?" he asked, tilting his filthy head in disbelief like a confused dog.

"Don't interrupt me. I wasn't finished," I snapped, becoming more frustrated. "The God of Abraham, Isaac, and Jacob. The one true God, Yahweh."

"Oh, I know that god. That god is the invention of the Jews. Who are men," the beggar stated and began walking away.

"Then if there is no god, why do people worship so many gods? Why do we have the power to invent gods?" I called after him, beckoned him back.

"Why not?" he shrugged.

"If there are no gods, why is there good and evil?" I pressed.

"One is only relative to the other. If you believe in only one god, why is there both good and evil? Wouldn't there be a good god and an evil god?" The beggar asked, confusing me more. "We're up to at least two gods already."

"Well, there is one true God, and there is Satan. Never mind that," I said dismissively, then asked, "If there are no gods then why does the sun rise every day? Why is new life created when each baby is born?"

"Why not?"

I had finally had it with the conversation, and the beggar's lack of a straight answer to any of my questions. "I'm in a hurry! I'm on my way somewhere, and you are making me late. I need to go," I told him, walking away.

"I am not holding you back. Wasn't it you that just chased me down?" The beggar asked politely. "Besides, I merely asked for a bit of food. Be on your way."

I turned back. "Why is man so conscious of his existence, so acutely aware of his mortality, and so different from all the other living creatures?"

"Why not?" he countered my question.

I began thinking about the best question to stump him. The beggar began scratching himself, stirring up the worst stench.

"Infernal fleas! Here, make yourself useful and hold my blanket for a moment."

"No!" I stepped back, covering my nose and mouth, my eyes already watering from the man's stench.

"Listen, I'm famished. So, if you don't have anything for me to eat, I must beg from someone else. This is the best time for prime handouts, so I cannot waste time talking pointless drivel."

"But, without God, what is the purpose of life? Why would we be here? How could we be here?" I asked.

"As mere mortals, we cannot answer those questions. So, we invent gods so that we have answers. Hence those gods are our own creations. They appease us with oversimplified answers to the difficult things in life we encounter. They offer explanation to the things we don't understand. They bring us comfort."

"You are a dirty, strange little man. Look at you, living on the streets, begging at the city gates for table scraps. What do you know?" I dismissed him.

"Great point. I am a homeless beggar. So, if you don't mind, I will continue begging for food. That is the only salvation I seek."

I rushed to the church to find Simon Peter, or anyone who could interpret my encounter with Paul. Paul was clearly devoted to the church and he poured himself into his letters. I was confounded by why he seemed so detached from the events in Rome, as if his letters to distant lands were more important. Maybe that was his only outlet from his house arrest. Perhaps he had decided to leave the local Roman matters to Simon Peter who was vigorously up to the task, and free to move about the city.

After I had walked for a few minutes a sense of compassion overcame me. I stopped and purchased some bread, then I turned back toward the city gates. When I arrived at the city gates, the atheist beggar was not there, so I gave the bread to other beggars. I went home with a full mind but an empty heart.

I RETURNED TO VILLA Gitta and went down into the valley on the estate to the Theater of Christ to catch the next teaching lesson from Simon Magus. After following a path through a wooded area, I found a small theater that fit cozily into the surrounding trees. The front rows were filled with the Roman upper-class Simonians, whereas the common people were in the back rows or standing. I recognized Flavius from my first evening at the Villa Gitta sitting in one of the middle rows. I scooted in and sat next to him and we greeted one another. As the small crowd socialized, Simon Magus took the stage. He was dressed in a fine, bejeweled robe of purple cloth with pointed shoulders. He wore a small head covering, but his long flowing hair was still on display.

"Welcome everyone!" Simon Magus began. "In my last teaching I discussed the elements of Sun, Air, Water, Earth, and Heaven. Were there any questions?"

There were a few coughs from the crowd, but no questions.

"Now, we shall revisit concepts of the great mother, and the first and second man. The great mother being Sophia, and the masculine form of god, being god the father and god the son, who was Jesus Christ. Of course, I am Simon, the figure masculine head, the apostle of the church of Christ, the great one!"

Simon Magus took a breath, then started in on the lesson, "Today, I will focus on Ennoia, a female spirit. Ennoia was my first thought, a creation that totally embodied the feminine spirit. She was created in the most exquisite and angelic form. I, Simon Magus, a god figure, created her in perfect femininity and heavenly beauty. Ennoia was such a ravishing beauty that the other heavenly beings, jealous of her perfect beauty, schemed against my female spirit. Together they conspired, employing all their wiles to plot her downfall. Oh, my perfect Ennoia was betrayed constantly! You folks know how jealous women can be," Simon Magus paused for the obligatory laughter.

"This perfect female form, Ennoia, was pulled down to and imprisoned in earthen form. She was a lost sheep among the mortals. Ennoia, imprisoned in human form for thousands of years, was reincarnated from one powerful woman to the next. She was Helen of Troy, wife of King Menelaus, whose abduction by Paris sparked the Trojan War. She was the daughter of Zeus. She was reincarnated as the powerful Queen Nefertiti of Egypt, the muse of King Akhenaten, a living god. In Persia, she became Esther, a beautiful Jewess who beguiled King Ahasuerus."

"More like Hagar," a man nearby joked, referring to Abraham's second wife and mother of Ishmael.

"Many years ago, on my way to Samaria, I made an amazing discovery. I had a fortuitous encounter with a beautiful temptress in Tyre named Helena. I found trapped in this sweet young girl, was Ennoia, my original feminine concept. To everyone else, Helena was just a poor working girl on the streets. Oh, but within her I recognized my original thought, the feminine spirit. Now, see her today in all her feminine glory!"

As Simon Magus carried on with his sermon, Helena waddled on to the stage carried by her squat legs. She dressed in the finest silk gown and was decorated and bejeweled as usual.

"I think she's about due for another reincarnation," Flavius joked, which gave us both a good laugh.

"Listen, my children, to all that you shall witness if you continue to follow my teachings." Simon Magus lifted his hands up in the air theatrically. Helena wiggled around the stage without much effort.

"In your lifetime, in the great city of Rome, I will release the Ennoia from Helena! And a force so bright, so magnificent and feminine in beauty, will shine across the entire world!"

The crowd was certainly interested in the events Simon Magus was foretelling. Yet, as Simon Magus had imparted to me, the more tactile or visual learners were in want of a display. Give the people what they want.

"Just as the brightness will shine from the release of the Ennoia, the spirit of light will spread across the land! Witness the spirit of light and the power of fire!"

Simon Magus then began his magical incantation.

"IGNIS AAEEE ZORO LUX EE!"

A hot breeze passed through the theater. Simon Magus started spinning round and round, his robe and hair twirling in a blur. He stopped with his back to the crowd, flinging his robe out dramatically, shaking his hips to-and-fro.

"EEEAA SOLIS XI VOX IGNUS!"

Simon Magus turned and squatted with his left arm pointing outward. Then, like a soldier throwing a javelin, he tossed a ball of flame over the crowd and into a pile of brush at the back of the theater. I turned and saw the brush pile erupt, the flames reaching high into the air. I felt the explosion in my chest. The Simonians were amazed by his sorcery!

Those in the back of the crowd, the lower classes and the ones closest to the explosion, were in awe. Again, some of the women confessed true love. In the front, the erudite crowd began asking questions about the Ennoia, Sophia, and god the father. Simon Magus stormed off the stage to avoid the onslaught of feedback from the crowd. Not discouraged, many of the people followed him. I went along. As we followed him down the wooded pathway he stopped abruptly and turned to face us.

"My children, I must attend to my work. May you be blessed with the holy spirit and be gone!" he cried. For an instant, I thought he made eye contact with me. I was startled and anxiously looked away.

Then Simon Magus turned around to resume walking down the path. But after three steps he stopped, turned back and looked at me again. "Lucius, my boy, come with me to the Fountain of Miracles. I have something to ask of you. This is a private matter so the rest of you must leave now."

The people began to disperse as Simon Magus strode down the path and I followed. Without looking at me I heard him say under his breath, "The people need their gods. They want to believe in miracles."

We arrived at the Fountain of Miracles. I sat by the small pool next to Simon Magus.

"Lucius, Nero has ordered me to go to his palace to appear before him. He has stated that I shall demonstrate my magical powers to him. Then, if I have proved myself worthy and capable, I shall be asked to rid his house of any curses. Most importantly, if I prove myself, he wants me to speak with his mother in the afterlife."

"Are you going to agree to his orders?" I asked.

"Say no to Nero? Kid, are you crazy? Nero, the emperor, megalomaniac, sexual deviant, artist, and musician. God, I love that man!"

Curius and Spurius approached us deferentially.

"Can't you see that I'm busy having a conversation! Both of you, be gone!!" Simon Magus yelled.

They were not just "Yes men," they were "God-yes men." They both turned and fled.

Simon Magus continued. "Besides, I need friends in high places. Oh, Lucius, but that is not what I wanted to talk to you about. Please tell me, have you caught up with Simon Peter and his ragtag group of followers?"

"Yes, I have met with Simon Peter and his church like you instructed," I answered, trying to share as few details as possible.

"Come on kid, tell me everything. Does Simon Peter talk about me? What does he say?" Simon Magus waved his long fingernails at me, eager for gossip.

"He does not believe you are the great one, or even a true apostle," I answered hesitantly.

"Well, I know that. I mean, what does he say about me personally?" Simon Magus was chuckling.

"Oh, nothing specifically. But I can tell that he does not like you," I said.

"That's terrific. I've gotten under his skin." Simon Magus wiggled his eyebrows. "What about Philip? He was a gorgeous man. Did he come with Simon Peter? And Mary of Magdala? Such a fine, fashionable dresser. How about that strange man, uh, the brother of Jesus?"

"You mean James?"

"Yes, that's him. What a bizarre character he was, but a sweet man too. I heard his wife left him."

"Simon Peter told me that they are back together in Jerusalem."

"Hah, likely story, kid." Simon Magus laughed. "Anyway, let's get back to Simon Peter. What's he after?"

"He's only interested in the church of Rome and spreading the good news of the resurrection of Jesus and the coming of the kingdom. He's not interested in impressing Nero, but he is entirely against you."

I could eternally debate whether Simon Magus was the great one, a powerful sorcerer, or just a powerful man. Regardless, take my word that he was a persuasive individual who had an overwhelming effect on people. To this day, I cannot remember what else I told him about Simon Peter's church in Rome. I tried to be vague, but I'm afraid what scant details I shared may have been too much.

I HAD NOT HEARD from James for a long time. One evening I received a letter written by James in Jerusalem. It warmed my heart to read this optimistic letter from him:

> Lucius, my protégé, a master tekton, and builder of the Roman Empire, I have faith in the veracity of the news that you are doing quite well in Rome. My fellow Christian brothers revealed to me that you have established your enterprise, constructing the finest high-rise apartments that tower up into the sky. You are my most accomplished mentee, vis-à-vis personal relationships and professional achievements, so I could not be prouder of you. As you achieve more success than me, the student may someday become the master, and so hence we all may end up working for you.
>
> Rebekah, my dear wife, whom I dote on endlessly, and I have found true domestic happiness. We have

adopted an orphaned daughter whom we call Naomi. She is a sweet girl, the apple of my eye. Pray tell me, you have spoken with your lost love Daphne recently? I urge you not to be too bullheaded regarding the fairer of our kind.

As deacon of the church of Jerusalem I have received formal word that Simon Peter has established the church in Rome. I'm eternally grateful that Simon Magus is no longer haunting our neck of the woods and we pray to the Lord that Rocky is ready to head him off. That being said, I do not see the fruitfulness of a Christian church in imperial and pagan Rome. Jerusalem, the Holy City in this Holy Land, should be the focal point of the church of Christ. Please do not take this viewpoint as entirely self-serving.

In respect to the church of Jerusalem and my deaconship, I am positive that I have truly found my calling from God. I serve my church above all else. Lucius, as you know, my greatest talent in life is my ability to build relationships, even with the most fatuous and uncongenial people. I continue to visit the Temple undeterred, to speak of the resurrection of Christ. But I must confide that the people who visit the Temple are the most hypocritical and hostile crowd.

You must make a pilgrimage to Jerusalem before you are old and decrepit like me. I pray for your good health and fortune and expeditious correspondence.

ONE EVENING, I WAS performing a walkthrough with Rufus of an insula that he and his crew had just completed. He had done such a fine job and I had complimented him on his work. We planned on going out that night to celebrate, but first I had to stop by the church in the Campus Martius to check in on Jason.

"If you don't mind coming with me, I can introduce you to Jason. He may want to come with us tonight," I explained to Rufus.

"Ok, boss. As long as we get something to eat soon," Rufus said indifferently.

When we arrived in the church, I introduced Rufus to Jason. I spoke to Jason about our plans that night and he agreed to meet us in Subura. I mentioned my letter from James and his face became pale.

"I'm sorry, but you don't know? James is dead," Jason said.

"What? How?" I asked. Panic, sorrow, disbelief clashed within my chest.

"You probably know about the ongoing conflict between the church and the Temple. James was speaking to the Jews at the Temple about the resurrection of Jesus. They accused him of blasphemy and forcibly threw him off of the Temple platform. He fell several stories down into the street below. When they noticed that the fall did not kill him instantly, they assailed on him in the street and beat him to death. May the Lord have mercy on his poor soul."

Rufus looked towards me with pained sympathy.

Lucas walked up to us, and solemnly said, "It has been confirmed. Simon Magus appeared before Nero, and the emperor has sought his council."

I was still too upset. I walked out onto the swampy field with Rufus. "I'm sorry, boss. I knew James was a great friend. I know how it feels," Rufus consoled me.

A band of Praetorian guards clad in Imperial armor, holding oval shields, marched in line up the street towards us. I spotted Simon Magus within the formation of the guards. I turned and rushed back into the church and shouted the alarm to Simon Peter and the others. Simon Peter, Jason and many others rushed out to the front of the church just as the guards arrived.

"Simon Peter, we meet again!" Simon Magus said. "I will offer you just one warning. Stay away from Nero and the people of Rome! Just mind your own business, you poor pathetic fisherman from Galilee. Stick to your own kind!"

"Simon Magus, you are a sinner and a fraud," Simon Peter replied. "You are no apostle of Christ. As long as you claim to speak in the name of Jesus Christ, or claim to invoke the Holy Spirit, I will make it my purpose to protect all the good brethren of Rome, both Jews and gentiles, from your evil sorcery and false prophecies."

"You are an obstinate old fool. Guards, teach them a lesson or two." Simon Magus threw his arms in the air, then turned and disappeared behind the guards.

"I really hate the cohorts," Rufus said to me under his breath. Then he shouted to a guard in the front rank. "Hey man! Why don't you pick on someone your own size?! Like your captain's fat mom."

That guard turned his head stiffly towards Rufus and then marched towards us. Rufus stepped forward fearlessly. The guard drew his sword, lifted it high, and with one fell swoop, sliced downward at Rufus's head, smashing his skull.

Bright blood gushed profusely from the gaping wound and the gray matter of his brain was exposed. Rufus's face and eyes instantly became lifeless, his body went limp, and he fell to the ground with a heavy thud.

My shock turned quickly into rage. I charged towards the guard shouting every threat and insult I knew. Fortunately, I was forcibly dragged away by some Christians to the other side of the church. I pushed away from them, my fight instinct switched to flight. I ran as hard as I could. I ran, and I ran, until I could taste the blood coming up from my lungs. Tired and dizzy, I slowed to a wobble. Too shocked to cry, I felt nothing but a painful and heavy void of numbness, then I walked slowly back to the city gates.

"You ok, man?" It was that begging atheist.

"Fuck everything," I said. I collapsed against the wall.

"You need a swig?" He handed me a jug of wine. I drank, pouring down my throat, down my chest, until it was empty.

"Goodness! Steady on, man." The begging atheist pulled back the jug, shaking it out, confirming it was empty. "What ails you, man? You owe me now! That was the finest vintage of Etruscan wine in the uh . . . Well, ok, I am exaggerating, but the jug was almost full!"

I handed him all the denarii I had on my person. His palms were only too ready to catch the coins.

"Oh, that'll do," he said. "I'll be back before an emperor can murder a family member."

He returned with an abundance of wine. I was feeling hit hard by all the wine that I had already gorged. When he began offering some of the wine he'd purchased to the other beggars, they flocked to us like pigeons. I don't care, I thought, as long as I have plenty for myself.

"I'm sorry I was wrong," I said, starting to explain.

"No, my newfound friend, you are spot on! This wine is terrific and you're a generous man. I'm sure your god, or gods, must love you, man!"

"No, I was wrong! There is no god. There's no god," I said.

"Well, I can't argue with that. You've gone through, uh," he coughed, moved his lips searching for the word, "a transformation."

"My best friend was just killed right before my eyes! By the Praetorian guards!" I wailed.

After mention of the guards, some of the beggars dispersed just like pigeons, or at least, they kept their distance.

"I'm so sorry," the beggar said. "I've seen too many of my good friends killed or died for no reason. Even beggars like me—I must ask though, are you wanted? I mean to say, is the cohort following you?" he asked.

"No, I don't think so. My friend, who's had the most difficult life, taunted one so he was the first man to die. I don't know if anyone else was killed. What loving god would allow that to happen? That is not fair. It's wrong. Forget it. Forget about everything."

The beggar nodded. "I understand, trust me. I, uh, it's not been fair for me either. I was a musician, a great artist, and I was blamed for stealing from my master. I could not find work after that."

I stood against the wall, and then steadied myself. I struggled to return his good favor.

I shook my head in confusion. "I don't understand. How do you know so much about the gods? Where were you educated? Were you tutored?"

"As a student of the world. I learned everything I know on the streets. I don't suffer from any formal education. I'm not engrained or indoctrinated in any social or religious constructs. That is why I have none of the trappings of your gods."

"There's no gods. There is no god." I grabbed a jug and started drinking again.

"Hold on, man. I will be back," he said and walked away. Apparently, he went to transact with his fellow beggars.

I stumbled, slipped and fell, then got up again and ran into the street. I deliberately collapsed in the middle of the road and then closed my eyes. I could hear a horse drawn cart approaching through the gates. Fortunately, I must have spooked the horses enough because I heard shouting and cursing from the cart driver as the horse reared and the cart stopped.

"Be careful. Do you want to kill yourself?" the beggar asked.

The beggar shook me and pulled me up out of the street. The driver shouted many more choice words. The beggar, I think I remember, said something to the driver about my father being patrician and looking for me, bless his heart, and kept him at bay. Then the beggar dragged me back to the wall where we sat by the gate with the rest of the beggars again. He gave me more of the medicine that would save me from my fatal illness. I embraced him as a friend. I felt the tension in his body as I embraced him, but he did not push me away. Pain and sorrow give no favor towards rich or poor.

Stumbling all over, I eventually leaned against the wall. I provided enough laughs that I stayed popular with the beggars that night. If I brought any bit of levity to the situation, it was to mercifully escape the deep darkness of losing two dear friends in one day.

30

RETALIATION

"Wake up, Lucius!" I was shaken from my slumber. Dark memories flashed through my mind. The rough, worn, weeping face of a grieving mother. Two women wailing as they walked in a procession. A man wearing the funerary mask of a haunting old man. The acrid smell of Rufus's body burning on the funeral pyre. Waking up on the gritty street, cold and wet. Wandering alone, desperate, and wounded. The brandished sword of a Praetorian guard, glistening with blood and gore.

Jason shook me again. "Wake up! We need to get you cleaned up and dressed. I'll take you to a bath house and then we are heading to the Forum."

"Go away," I said sharply, and then asked, "What do you want from me?"

"Nero has summoned Simon Peter. The Praetorian guards took him away this morning. He went without a fight, because he knew it was God's will. Simon Peter's vision is being fulfilled. This is the day that Simon Magus and Simon Peter will face Nero!"

As my pulse throbbed in my head, I slowly rolled out of bed and onto the streets. The bathhouse did wonders. By the time we arrived at the Forum, it was already late afternoon. We met Demas, Lucas, and a small gathering of Christians in the grove near the Temple of Vesta. We held vigil for hours, quiet and anxious.

As the sun was beginning to set, a Praetorian guard approached us. "Which of you is Lucas? I have a message for him."

"I am," Lucas answered bravely.

"You must go to the house of Paul at once. Paul's guard has news of the events that took place today. I must now take my leave and not be seen speaking with you. Travel safely."

The guard marched off.

WE ARRIVED AT PAUL'S house and were greeted by Paul's familiar guard. The small room was lit by a lonely, flickering candle in the middle of the table. Paul was sitting at the table with an unfamiliar guard. We gathered around him.

"Simon Peter will not be released today," Paul's guard said. "This guard will share what he witnessed in Nero's audience chambers today."

This captured my attention immediately. Paul and the others focused soberly at the guard.

The guard began his account. "When Simon Magus and Simon Peter were called into the chamber, Nero was lounging comfortably in his chair. The two men stood humbly before Nero, one more humble than the other. Nero's advisors stood by his side. On his left was Seneca the Younger, the stoic philosopher and his former tutor. On his right was Sextus Afranius Burrus, the Praetorian Prefect. The chamber was secured by the Praetorian guard, and more guards were protecting the emperor's person, or standing behind his advisors, or like myself, standing behind the two Simons.

"Nero began by talking about himself bombastically, sharing many exploits that I won't recount in detail. He then performed a bit, singing and playing his lyre. Peter stood expressionless, but Simon Magus flattered the emperor's performance with great charm.

"Then Seneca and Burrus began their posturing by introducing themselves and explaining their credentials, but Nero cut them off abruptly. He said, 'I seek new outside advisement. I've already had too many advisors that only desire to increase their own wealth and influence. Now I am looking for new blood. New advisors with novel capabilities, new forces that will enhance my power and influence. I want to learn how to harness this holy spirit power. I desire to possess these magical forces.'

"This accusation of Nero's struck Seneca and Burrus. Although Seneca is a stoic, he is hypocritically wealthy and self-serving. At that point Burrus, my fearless leader and a pragmatic military man, warned Nero, 'My emperor, these men are merely small-time sorcerers. They conjure cheap magic tricks. They are outsiders. Simon Peter is a poor fisherman from Galilee, and Simon Magus is a Samaritan who has performed in the streets and theaters.'

"Simon Magus then said, 'It is true that I am a Samaritan. As far as Simon Peter is concerned, you are also correct. He is a fisherman, poor, uneducated, and Jewish. My emperor, with all due respect, I consider myself a child of the Roman Empire. I was born in Samaria and then educated in Alexandria. Then I traveled the breadth of the empire to bring my knowledge to inspire many followers. Yes, proudly, I was born in Samaria. Was Seneca not born in Hispania? Was Burrus not born in a southern province of Gaul? Were they not born and raised among the barbarians also?'"

Jason asked, "How did Nero react to this?"

"Nero laughed heartily, amused by this counter point to his advisors," the guard replied. "Seneca and Burrus were visibly uncomfortable, but quelled their reaction in the face of the emperor's laughter. Simon Peter stood silently and did not deny his humble background. Simon Magus went on confidently, 'I wield my power by harnessing the holy spirit. More importantly I alone hold this divine and secret knowledge.'

"Then Nero cut him off, 'You lost me there. Secret knowledge? Not interested. Although the holy spirit sounds sexy. I seek to possess this spirit. Tell me, does this holy spirit also allow one to speak to people in the afterlife?'

"Simon Magus hesitated, 'Well, my emperor, that is not exactly how the holy spirit works—' Nero did not like that answer and commanded Simon Magus to look into it, which Simon Magus then whole heartedly agreed to do."

Paul asked, "Did Simon Peter not explain the true nature of the Holy Spirit?"

The guard shook his head, "No, he did not. However, after Nero was finished questioning Simon Magus, he then turned his focus on Simon Peter, who had kept silent until that moment but was clearly struggling to disguise his contempt. Nero commanded Simon Peter to share what was on his mind. Simon Peter answered, 'Simon Magus is an imposter. I have witnessed his false prophecies since his early days in Samaria. And unlike Simon Magus, any powers that I possess come only from the Holy Spirit and through God. And only by the name of our Lord and Savior Jesus Christ, the Son of God, do I invoke those powers.'

"Before Simon Magus could retaliate, Seneca interjected. 'I have learned of Jesus of Nazareth and his teachings. Many of the parables of Jesus contain great lessons and many of the values that Christians practice have merit. In fact, the Christian ethos rings with stoicism. Let us recall the history of Jesus. At first, he formed a loyal following as a wise rabbi. However, eventually he was overcome with his own greatness and claimed that he was equal to a god, that he was the living son of god. For this crime he was outcast by his fellow Jews and sentenced to crucifixion. These false powers of the holy spirit and dark magic do not impress me. Religion is true to the commoner, but false to the wise. I stand with Burrus. My emperor, with all due respect and deference, these outside advisors are not only a risk to the credibility of your rule, but will lead your greatness astray.'"

"Did Nero finally acknowledge his advisors?" Jason asked.

"No, he still did not. Nero merely glanced at Seneca and Burrus dismissively," the guard said. "Then he stood, walked in front of the two Simons, and paced between them imperially. In good humor, he told them, 'I would like to keep you both as guests here for two days. Then in a fortnight, we will meet at the Palatine Hill. There you will both demonstrate your magical powers not only to me, but to the entire city as well. And you will do so in the name of Nero! Not in the name of any of your other gods, spirits, or Christs.'"

"The Simons could not refuse, so they promptly acquiesced. At this point Seneca and Burrus, went on to expound their views on the Simon situation. Diplomatic and politic, they acted out this theater of advisement in front of the Simons. The tension in the room grew as Nero became more agitated. Nero then ordered some of the guards to show the Simons to their quarters and see that they were made comfortable. Nero, still annoyed with his current advisors, asked Seneca and Burrus to stay behind, and excused all but his personal guards. That is my account."

"Please, go on," Paul urged him.

"Since I was excused at that point, my story ends. However, I did hear that the Simons will be released in two days." The guard had finished his report.

The room remained silent as the candle flame danced in front of us. Paul was deep in thought. Demas was praying silently. Jason appeared as worried as I had ever seen him.

Lucas, calm and composed, asked, "Paul, what shall we do for Simon Peter?"

Paul answered somberly, "We must provide Simon Peter with moral support when he is released. And trust in God. I must remind you all, there is a church in Rome, in Corinth, Ephesus, Galatia, and many other places. I must remain steadfast and work to equally marshal efforts across our church communities. Let us pray for Simon Peter, for his safety, and for his faithful commitment to the word of God." Paul looked back down at the letter he had been writing before we had come to visit him.

TWO WEEKS PASSED UNBEARABLY, wearing down our patience. We took Paul's advice, and we all rallied behind

Simon Peter when he was released. Rumors abounded of encounters between Simon Magus and Nero that took place during those two weeks. According to the most popular gossip, Simon Magus spent several nights dining with Nero, establishing a closer relationship. Nero and Simon Magus, delighted by their mutual company, allegedly discussed showmanship, magical demonstrations, appeasing the masses, indoctrinating followers, mentorship, creating your own god-like myth, and even high fashion.

Much to our dismay, Simon Peter planned to resist Nero's order to appear with Simon Magus atop the Palatine Hill. Instead Simon Peter planned to appear with his Christians among the crowd of common citizens in the Forum. On the afternoon of the appointed day, we walked in solidarity with Simon Peter as Praetorian guards escorted him to the Forum where a tremendous crowd of thousands had already gathered.

In the distance, I could see Nero standing on a balcony of his palace. The unruly masses hushed as he raised his arms. Although Nero's gesture had caused the crowd to cease and listen, I could not yet make out what he was saying. The guards pushed the crowds apart and escorted our groups closer until we were standing within a distance that I could hear.

I had understood before that Nero was an artist first and an emperor second. I knew that Nero was young, educated, intelligent, and ruthless, killing off friends and family, yet no more merciless than his own mother had been. But before that day, I had never seen him closely with my own eyes. I looked on as Nero strode proudly across the balcony. He was still showing some youthful athleticism, he was not bad looking or out of shape, but he did not carry himself with a natural grace due to his slightly bent posture. His hair was short and wavy, a dirty blonde color. His head had the distinct shape of a Caesar, trapezoidal and wider on top, with conspicuous ears. His face was soft and youthful, with healthy eyes, but he had a weak, slightly double chin which was lightly covered with a beard.

". . . and so, my people, that is how I discovered these Simons from far off lands. I gather us all together today to witness these Simons as they demonstrate their supernatural powers. In this manner, we can observe them as one people and authenticate these magical feats of strength. I intend for them to be my new advisors so that I may harness their powers. If I, the emperor, possess their powers, then the empire will possess their powers."

Argumentative, I thought, but is anyone here going to argue with that?

"Allow me to present them. Simon Magus, come forward!" Nero commanded.

Simon Magus came out into view, stepping to stand next to Nero on the balcony. Simon Magus wore his signature flashy robe with protruding shoulders. He looked distinguished in the sunlight, his groomed hair flowing in the breeze.

"Simon Magus, a spiritual leader, magician, and candidate for the new imperial advisor!" Nero grabbed Simon Magus' arm and held it up to present the sorcerer to the crowd. The crowd erupted with cheers. Nero and Simon Magus shared a smile, ominous and complicit, reinforcing the rumors I had heard.

"Simon Peter, come forward at once!" Nero shouted. The crowd fell silent. The guards pressed Simon Peter to announce himself.

Simon Peter stepped forward and said, "I am Simon Peter and I stand with my fellow Christians. I am a poor sinner, a fisherman from Judea, who is not worthy to stand above the people of Rome. I possess no special powers of my own. I have only my faith, devotion to God, and love for my fellow man. All miracles that I have performed are through the will and power of God. Only in the name of Jesus Christ, the Son of God, may I perform any miracles."

The crowd again erupted. Not in cheers this time, but with taunts and insults. Jason tried to calm the Christians, who grew worried about reaction of the now unruly people surrounding them.

Nero raised a hand to silence the crowd, then said, "So be it. You make this easier on me. Simon Peter, I will deal with you later. Simon Magus, the empire is yours to impress. Demonstrate for us your feats of magic."

With that, Simon Magus changed his expression, wiggling his eyebrows and smirking. Then he crossed his arms as he began to invoke his incantations, and his body levitated until his feet were just below Nero's head.

Then Simon Magus started shouting his spells, the strange words coming more vehemently. Suddenly his body shot straight up into the air! I saw him lean forward and spread his arms out, soaring, flying at the speed of an eagle. He flew across the sky, robe flapping and beard parted by the wind. Then he dove and swooped just above the heads of the crowd before flying over the Capitoline Hill and out of sight.

The people went wild with amazement.

The Christians were speechless. Some of them looked truly afraid. I know I was. I feared many of them were losing faith.

Jason said, "We cannot show our fear, even if you are as terrified as I am!"

Suddenly, Simon Magus soared over our group of Christians, his robes flying behind him like demonic wings. As he flew close above us, I could hear him shout, "By the power of the holy spirit!" He probably did that just to agitate Simon Peter.

"This false prophet . . . this dark sorcery . . ." Simon Peter said under his breath. He was shaking with anger and I could tell he was losing patience.

"This dark power could only come from Satan himself," Lucas stated ominously.

"Simon Magus is the antichrist," Demas said. He knelt in prayer and looked towards the heavens.

Simon Peter began yelling at Simon Magus. As he shouted, the crowd moved away, until Simon Peter stood alone.

"By the power of the Holy Spirit," Simon Peter shouted as Simon Magus flew by another time. "In the name of the Lord Jesus Christ, spare us all from this spectacle, and bring him down to the dust from which he was created."

And then the dark clouds parted, and a bright ray of sunlight shone down on the Forum.

"See, over there! A white dove!" Jason exclaimed.

"The Holy Spirit blesses us with his presence in the form of a dove," Lucas said, pointing.

And then there were three, four—too many doves to count—flying from the other side of the Palatine Hill.

"Look! Look at the doves!" The people shouted, as the flock of doves came together to form a V.

In the distance Simon Magus shouted, "Simon Peter, I intended to duel you, sorcerer against sorcerer, but you have abstained. Now I see that you will die without putting up a fight. So be it."

The flock of doves turned in the air and sped up towards Simon Magus.

Nothing had prepared Simon Magus for that. He leaned back, his arms and legs spread wide in a braking motion, as the flock of doves began to pelt him. Simon Magus covered his face and screamed in pain.

The crowd watched in silent, enthralled horror.

"Good form, Simon Peter," Nero shouted. I turned and saw him clapping. Nero said, "Birds? What a novel approach. I'm impressed!"

The silence that had held the crowd broke. The people started to whisper, then to chatter, which then quickly turned to chaotic shouting and cheering.

I overheard people shout, "A magician's duel! Give us a magician's duel!"

Simon Magus was covered in squawking doves. He was shouting, swatting, and swinging. His long sharp nails clawed at the birds, pulling out feathers, but there were too many. Their wings flapped and unified into the most eerie cracking noise.

Simon Magus rallied his senses and began another incantation. Flames shot out of his arms and legs. The doves caught on fire, and squawked in horrific high pitch. They began to fall from the sky, leaving trails of flames and smoke. I could smell the burning of feathers from where I stood.

Simon Magus, now free from the doves, shot through the sky until he hovered closer to us. He threw more flames directly at Simon Peter. He was able to shield himself from the flames, but his hair and beard were singed. Simon Peter crouched and held up his hands, praying aloud, "Dear God, send an angel to protect me. I do not have the power to protect myself."

I heard a loud cracking sound. The people in the crowd gasped.

"Look, an angel!" Jason said, pointing to our right.

The angel stood dignified on the peak of the senate house. His long wings, the wingspan of two men, slowly flapped. They looked like the wings of an eagle, but with white feathers. The angel wore a white robe, had long brown hair, and a strong, but gentle face. I was astounded and terrified by the angel, as if his presence was too much for my mortal eyes.

"It must be an angel or archangel! Is it the angel Gabriel or Michael?" Lucas asked.

Simon Magus looked towards the angel. The angel cracked his wings and flew directly at Simon Magus. Then Simon Magus was on the run, hastily changing directions to avoid the angel.

"Why has the angel not struck down Simon Magus?" I asked Jason.

"I don't know. But I am sure he is an angel. Perhaps a guardian angel? A messenger from God, a defender, not an aggressive warrior," Jason said.

The clouds rolled across the sky and there was the rumbling of thunder.

A large black crow flew in from the direction of the Capitoline Hill. At least, I thought it was a crow, until it flew closer and I saw that it had a human face. Once in perspective, I realized that this creature was even larger than the angel.

"Is that Satan?" A Christian behind me asked.

"The antichrist!" Lucas said. Then he prayed loudly for salvation.

"I do fear that is a dark angel," Jason said.

"A dark angel?" I asked.

The dark angel wore a black robe. He had the wings of a crow, but the wingspan the width of three men. The dark angel chased the angel of God down, wrestling with him, until the two flew over the Palatine Hill and out of site. I never saw either angel again, and I feared the worse for the angel of God. Momentarily, Simon Magus was safe from harm.

"Simon Magus, I was worried about you for a moment, but great comeback! I am most impressed!" Nero said as he clapped slowly. "What was that a harpy?"

Simon Magus now had his bearings. He again flew towards Simon Peter, soaring gently through the cloudy sky.

Simon Peter cried out with all his might and passion, "In the name of the Son of God! The Lord Jesus Christ, our Savior!!"

Suddenly Simon Magus fell like a brick from the sky, dropping into the crowd and landing with a loud boom. I struggled to reach him through the madness of the panicked push of the people around me. He had likely been killed from the fall, but when I reached him, I could see that the people had turned on him and had been beating his body mercilessly as well.

I don't know why, but when I looked down at his bloody corpse, I felt sorry for him. But I knew that he deserved his fate, so that feeling of sorrow and pity was fleeting. I was then filled with a sense of pride for Simon Peter and the Christians. It felt great to be part of that congregation. And that we, the Christians, were victorious over evil that day.

Many of the Simonians in the crowd shouted, "The great one is dead! The great one is dead!" Opportunistic and fickle, many of the Simonians quickly changed allegiance, and were now shouting, "Simon Peter is the true great one! Simon Peter wields the power of the holy spirit."

My dear 20th century reader, it was in this manner in 62 A.D., that Simon Peter and the church in Rome overcame Simon Magus the sorcerer. That was what I witnessed of the famous magician's duel.

31

CONFLAGRATION

The "Pax Romana", if you will, for the Christians of Rome was the time between the death of Simon Magus in 62 A.D. to the first half of 64 A.D. During that time, Paul was released and allowed to rejoin the church. Nero never fulfilled his hopes of appointing a magically endowed advisor. Although Nero was frustrated with Simon Peter for not joining him in chambers, the superstitious side of Nero feared Simon Peter. Nero left Simon Peter to his own devices, with the provision that Simon Peter remained humble and inconspicuous. The Christian church thrived during those years. My life was prosperous and ordinarily routine.

I reached some closure regarding my personal relationships during those years as well. Through brief letters, Daphne informed me that she was married and had two young children. I realized, in hindsight, that my love for her was not complete. Instead it was a love that was unsophisticated, adolescent, and fleeting. Although I had busied myself with work and the church, I started courting other women, but nothing significant developed. My father attempted to arrange a marriage for me, but I stood my ground, wanting to make my own choice in the matter. Otherwise, I had an increasingly warm and civil relationship with my parents. As they grew older, and I maintained my own independent life, the issues of the past were less significant to me. When I visited my parents, which was infrequent and measured, we never tried to reconcile our differences. Instead, we enjoyed each other's company, living in the present, grateful for the lives we had. I realized that I had always tried to run away from my parents, to be different and better than them. During my journeys away from home, I discovered Jesus Christ, the son of God, and God the father, and our creator. Why then was I running from my own creators? And how can I alone be better than the parents that created me?

NERO'S ERSTWHILE ADVISORS, SENECA and Burrus, did not prosper. Although Seneca and Burrus had been Nero's advisors since the beginning of his reign, both appointed by Nero's mother Agrippina, their future turned out to be bleak. While many believed that their relationships soured when Nero had Agrippina murdered, the real turning point was the Simons. That would be one of their last times to appear as advisors before Nero. Nero increased his obsession with magicians and the supernatural and continued to seek outside advisement. Seneca and Burrus fought Nero with strong resistance. Burrus, with his practical military background, clashed with Nero as he became increasingly paranoid and superstitious. Not long after the death of

Simon Magus, Burrus died of poisoning, which was likely ordered by Nero.

Seneca did not last much longer. Shortly after the death of Burrus, Seneca was accused of playing a role in a plot to assassinate Nero, and was forced to commit suicide. Seneca's previous words had come back to haunt him at the very end. "I wanted to avoid the impression that all I could do for loyalty was die."

The stories of Seneca and Burrus taught me a valuable lesson. I did not want to play politics or align myself with power for my own personal benefit. Especially if it meant sacrificing what I believed in. Nero's advisors and Simon Magus were nothing but opportunists, leeching off the power of the emperor. In the end, they had neither power nor personal principle. Simon Peter and the Christians held on to their beliefs and principles, and so would I.

THE GREAT FIRE TORCHED the city of Rome in the month of Julius in 64 A.D. This event changed things for the worse for the Christians. The apocryphal story of Nero playing the fiddle while Rome burned is the diametrical opposite of the truth. I would not even mention it if it wasn't so universally believed to be true. In fact, Nero was furious and in a panic. After all, Nero lost more worldly possessions than anyone else because of the fire, and afterward he was eager to blame someone for the disaster. The Christians were among many named responsible. Historians have posited many theories, but very few credibly blame Nero or the Christians.

By the time I witnessed the fire it had already spread far across the city. Therefore, I cannot tell you firsthand who or what had caused it. At first, I smelled smoke and then I heard shouts of panic. Foolishly, rather than exit to the streets, I climbed to the roof of my insula and I saw the entire city ablaze. Luckily, I was able to exit my building and then leave my neighborhood before the smoke and fire overtook me. People screamed for help, stuck in the smoke, or unable to escape the fire that surrounded them. At one point, fearing for my life, I asked God—or anyone—to save me. Then I knew I had to save myself so I charged through the thick smoke and eventually found my way out of the city gates.

Allow me to bring Helena back into the fold, no pun intended, of the story. Helena finally released the Ennoia, as Simon Magus had foretold, exploding in the brightest and hottest light. This release of feminine spirit, held in for generations, transforming into the pure element of fire, was what set the city ablaze. This is what the Simonians believe happened, and I preferred to believe it as well.

I lost everything in the fire. I lost my apartment and all of the insulae that I had owned and rented. After I fled the city, I joined my Christian brethren that had survived in their makeshift gatherings in a camp near the Campus Martius where the fire had not spread. Jason had survived the blaze, and a kindhearted Christian family who lived nearby took us in and cared for us until he and I could get both our affairs in order. During that time, I visited Simon Peter's family. His wife had joined him. She brought two of his grown sons with her and they reunited as one happy family.

But, as I wrote, the fire was when the true suffering began for the Christians. Even though Simon Peter had impressed Nero, he had not appeased him, and Nero was eager to blame the Christians for the fire. The soldiers came after the Christians with a vengeance.

AFTER WORSHIP THE CHRISTIANS would gather outside of the church and socialize. The soldiers had been harassing us with increasing regularity recently, but it had not yet escalated to violence. Then one day we were attacked by Praetorian guards.

A guard charged at me, a shield on one arm, and his sword raised. I had no chance. As the guard swung his sword at my head, I instinctively held up my hands trying to defend myself. His sword struck my right hand and hammered through it, continuing downward to smash the top of my skull. In shock, I reached up with my uninjured hand, my fingers shaking as they felt the dent in my head. I became horrified, and blood started gushing out. My legs gave out as my body went further into shock, and I collapsed onto the ground that was already soaked with my own blood. I felt the sword slicing deep into my shoulder as the guard got another blow in. Mercifully, I was beyond pain. I looked at the ground in front of my face. I saw the blurred feet of soldiers and my own blood spilling onto the ground in front of me. After falling deeper into shock, I felt a sharp, stabbing sensation in my back.

And then, a darkness fell over me. Timelessness passed until there was no longer any now. And then, in literally no time, I found myself in a light, in the light. In heaven, with many of my fellow Christians. I was a martyr. My reader, you may recall that I was not baptized as a Christian. You may be asking, why was I not stuck in purgatory? This was not the case as I was sent straight to heaven. God's will be done.

As mortals, we're all afraid of death. That was the most horrifying and painful moment of my life, but it was also a short and merciful moment. In less time than you spent during your last trip to the post office, and I was already in heaven.

EPILOGUE

Following my death, and the martyrdom of Jason and twenty other Christians killed by soldiers that day, the Christians went through a severe period of persecution. They were routinely arrested and murdered. Hundreds of crucified Christians were set afire as markers on the roads that led to Rome. In 67 A.D., Simon Peter was crucified by the Romans. He chose to be nailed to the cross upside down, claiming that he was not worthy of the same death as Jesus Christ. Simon Peter's wife Tabitha died of old age in Rome and his children and grandchildren survived and prospered.

The next year Paul was beheaded by the Romans. Paul's letters to the Christian churches across the Roman Empire now comprise a critical portion of the New Testament. Lucas, known as Saint Luke, wrote one of the four canonical gospels, the Gospel of Luke. He died peacefully at the age of eighty-four.

After the fire, Nero set out to rebuild the city of Rome. But he also appropriated much of the ruined city for himself, using the land to build a new palace known as the Golden House. Nero continued to rule the empire until two legions and the Praetorian guards revolted and rose against him. Nero was forced to flee Rome. In 68 A.D., at the age of 30, he committed suicide. He was the last Caesar. His death left the empire in a state of dispute over his successor. Soon after the empire broke out in civil war.

In Jerusalem, the strife that James witnessed, escalated into revolt. In 70 A.D., the Temple was destroyed during the siege of Jerusalem. As my reader is surely aware, the conflict in Jerusalem did not end after that, and still does not cease. In my short life, I never visited the Holy City, and perhaps that is a blessing. I am still hoping for peace.

THE CLIMAX OF THIS tale, the magician's duel, is never taught in Sunday school, and was almost lost to obscurity. The future legacy of the two Simons is also disproportionate. Although Simon Peter, or Saint Peter, is famous across the world, Simon Magus was mostly lost to history. Simon Magus was written about briefly in the book of Acts in the New Testament, and scathingly by Saint Irenaeus. The gnostic beliefs that Gnipho and many of the Simonians held never became mainstream. In the 20th century, many gnostic texts were discovered in Hag Hammadi, Egypt. These "apocryphal" texts never made it into the Holy Bible. The early Christians had to decide what to believe in and what was the true faith. Christianity did not form overnight, as I witnessed first-hand. Instead the unification of the Christian faith took several centuries.

During the first few centuries after Christ, there were numerous Christian sects which were divided over Jewish traditions, widespread polytheism, the Holy Trinity, the divinity and resurrection of Christ, original sin, baptism, and even the basic purpose of Jesus Christ on earth. In 325 A.D., Emperor Constantine called for the Council of Nicaea which unified the Christian church and formed the Nicene Creed. The Nicene Creed, still recited by the faithful during worship, defined the Christian faith in one doctrine. The Gnostic Christians, such as Gnipho and, to a lesser extent, the Simonians, were henceforth called out as heretics.

But let us set aside Christian doctrine and dogma. How did the Christians transform from an oppressed minority to a major religion of the world? I have always credited the emperor Constantine for spreading Christianity far and wide. As the story goes, in 312 A.D. Constantine had a vision of a cross in the sky during the Battle of the Milvian Bridge. Afterward, he converted to Christianity which helped propagate the religion across the Roman Empire and eventually most of the western world. In another millennia, Spanish conquistadors would conquer much of the western hemisphere, and the Christian missionaries would convert the indigenous people that were conquered and survived the onslaught of European diseases.

Once again, I'm no historian or theologian. Although I give Constantine the credit, he was not the most devout Christian. Constantine had his son and his wife killed, and was only baptized on his deathbed. He was most likely an opportunists and politician, embracing a minority population of the burgeoning Christian faith. I hold more admiration for the brave evangelists of the first century. So many of the early Christians were willing to die for their faith. To this day, the Catholic Church thrives in the Vatican in

Rome, just across the river from the Campus Martius, not far from Simon Peter's church. Simon Peter, or Saint Peter, is considered the first Pope of the Roman Catholic Church. His remains are said to be interred underneath St Peter's Basilica in the Vatican.

SO, THIS WAS MY story. A first-hand account of the birth of Christianity in the first century A.D. Truman Capote, the author and journalist, once described the work of the beat authors as typing rather than writing. Perhaps that is all that I've accomplished as I've typed out my story from heaven. Since I've claimed no divinity, no skills in theology, I must add a claim to no formal writing skills. Although, since I finished typing out this account, I have accomplished exactly what I set out to do.

In closing, I impart some words of wisdom that have stuck with me for two thousand years. I recall my last visit with the atheist beggar before my death. The atheist beggar was in fact an agnostic beggar. He was not certain of a god, but he did not consider himself certain of anything. Those terms are not mutually exclusive. During that particular encounter, I indulged in a discussion with him about wisdom with an open mind and a generous serving of wine.

At one point he said, "Do you want to know what wisdom is? This is wisdom." And then he pointed to his head.

"You?" I laughed, not meaning to insult him.

"No, not me, man! I am pointing at my hair. Hair that has turned gray with old age."

"Ah, I see. Wisdom comes with age. I get it, you know more as you age," I said, following his meaning, I thought. As I said, there had been wine.

"Yes, and no. You are missing the point, man. Yes, many people become wiser with old age, but some do not. The older you get the wiser you should become . . . but then you should realize not how much you do know, but instead how much you do *not* know."

"Oh, I understand." If only I did.

"You are still missing the point. This is about the color of gray, not about aging," he explained.

"How do you mean?" I asked, my interest increased as my wine cup emptied.

"Gray means that most things are not black and white. Is there only good and bad? Don't good people do bad things, and bad people do good things? Are there not tradeoffs and middle grounds? Is there not moderation, a gray area, with pleasure, wealth, and selfishness?"

"Yea, I know what you mean!" I said.

"What if you gave up all worldly pleasure? Is there not some good, some beauty, in worldly pleasure? Should we not enjoy ourselves? Conversely, to entirely seek out only pleasure would be detrimental. It is more important to seek balance—not that I am a role model as such."

"Yes, I get it. For instance, should we not enjoy this wine? Did Jesus not turn water into wine? We should enjoy wine, but perhaps it is best enjoyed in moderation," I pontificated emphatically.

"Good, good, keep going," he encouraged me.

"Seneca believed that good men are totally good, and bad men are completely evil. Perhaps, there is a gray area where great men endeavor to do good, but also do terrible things, and visa versa."

"Yes, now you have it!" He exclaimed. "Now, take that

393

with you. The color of gray, and consider the tradeoffs from both sides. The people of the world want to simplify things and pick a side. Life is so much easier if you can just pick a good side and unite against a bad side. But I am just a worthless beggar with no worth, and yet I am also a wise man who has inspired you."

"Thank you, I will remember this conversation."

"I doubt it," the agnostic beggar said in earnest. But now we know he was wrong.

ACKNOWLEDGEMENTS

I'd like to thank my beta readers Amy Sussman and Zoey Pincelli for their valuable feedback during developmental editing phase. Special thanks to editor Matthew Kirkpatrick for his passion and creativity. And thanks again and especially to my editor Amy Sussman for pushing me to make a better book.

I found my first notes on Simon versus Simon in early 2011. I worked on these ideas in my head for many years. In 2017, I committed to writing a novel. I appreciate the feedback and support that my lovely wife Melissa gave me during this entire process. And I could always count on my pets to keep me company.

In memory of Ringo the parrot, 2002–2019.